ENCYCLOPEDIA OF LANGUAGE AND EDUCATION

Encyclopedia of Language and Education

VOLUME 3: ORAL DISCOURSE AND EDUCATION

The volume titles of this encyclopedia are listed at the end of this volume.

Encyclopedia of Language and Education

Volume 3

ORAL DISCOURSE AND EDUCATION

Edited by

BRONWYN DAVIES

James Cook University
Australia

and

DAVID CORSON

The Ontario Institute for Studies in Education
University of Toronto
Canada

KLUWER ACADEMIC PUBLISHERS

DORDRECHT / BOSTON / LONDON

Library of Congress Cataloging-in-Publication Data

```
Oral discourse and education / edited by Bronwyn Davies and David
Corson.
     p.   cm. -- (Encyclopedia of language and education ; v. 3)
  Includes bibliographical references and index.
  ISBN 0-7923-4639-4 (alk. paper). -- ISBN 0-7923-4596-7 (set : alk.
paper)
  1. Oral communication.  2. Language and education.   I. Davies,
Bronwyn, 1945-   . II. Corson, David.  III. Series.
  P95.O69  1997
  302.2'242--dc21                                      97-30202
```

ISBN 0-7923-4930-x (PB)   ISBN 0-7923-4639-4 (BH)
ISBN 0-7923-4936-9 (PB-SET)   ISBN 0-7923-4596-7 (HB-SET)

Published by Kluwer Academic Publishers,
P.O. Box 17, 3300 AA Dordrecht, The Netherlands

Sold and distributed in the U.S.A. and Canada
by Kluwer Academic Publishers,
101 Philip Drive, Norwell, MA 02061, U.S.A.

In all other countries, sold and distributed
by Kluwer Academic Publishers Group,
P.O. Box 322, 3300 AH Dordrecht, The Netherlands

Cover picture:*The Tower of Babylon,* Pieter Bruegel the Elder
Museum Boymans-van Beuningen, Rotterdam

Printed in the Netherlands (on acid-free paper)

TABLE OF CONTENTS

VOLUME 3: ORAL DISCOURSE AND EDUCATION

Section 3: Oral Language and the Curriculum

GENERAL EDITOR'S INTRODUCTION

ENCYCLOPEDIA OF LANGUAGE AND EDUCATION

This is one of eight volumes of the Encyclopedia of Language and Education published by Kluwer Academic. The publication of this work signals the maturity of the field of 'language and education' as an international and interdisciplinary field of significance and cohesion. These volumes confirm that 'language and education' is much more than the preserve of any single discipline. In designing these volumes, we have tried to recognise the diversity of the field in our selection of contributors and in our choice of topics. The contributors come from every continent and from more than 40 countries. Their reviews discuss language and education issues affecting every country in the world.

We have also tried to recognise the diverse interdisciplinary nature of 'language and education' in the selection of the editorial personnel themselves. The major academic interests of the volume editors confirm this. As principal volume editor for Volume 1, Ruth Wodak has interests in critical linguistics, sociology of language, and language policy. For Volume 2, Viv Edwards has interests in policy and practice in multilingual classrooms and the sociology of language. For Volume 3, Bronwyn Davies has interests in the social psychology of language, the sociology of language, and interdisciplinary studies. For Volume 4, Richard Tucker has interests in language theory, applied linguistics, and the implementation and evaluation of innovative language education programs. For Volume 5, Jim Cummins has interests in the psychology of language and in critical linguistics. For Volume 6, Leo van Lier has interests in applied linguistics and in language theory. For Volume 7, Caroline Clapham has interests in research into second language acquisition and language measurement. And for Volume 8, Nancy Hornberger has interests in anthropological linguistics and in language policy. Finally, as general editor, I have interests in the philosophy and sociology of language, language policy, critical linguistics, and interdisciplinary studies. But the thing that unites us all, including all the contributors to this work, is an interest in the practice and theory of education itself.

People working in the applied and theoretical areas of education and language are often asked questions like the following: 'what is the latest research on such and such a problem?' or 'what do we know about such

B. Davies and D. Corson (eds), Encyclopedia of Language and Education,
Volume 3: Oral Discourse and Education, vii–ix.
© *1997 Kluwer Academic Publishers. Printed in the Netherlands.*

and such an issue?' Questions like these are asked by many people: by policy makers and practitioners in education; by novice researchers; by publishers trying to relate to an issue; and above all by undergraduate and postgraduate students in the language disciplines. Each of the reviews that appears in this volume tries to anticipate and answer some of the more commonly asked questions about language and education. Taken together, the eight volumes of this Encyclopedia provide answers to more than 200 major questions of this type, and hundreds of subsidiary questions as well.

Each volume of the Encyclopedia of Language and Education deals with a single, substantial subject in the language and education field. The volume titles and their contents appear elsewhere in the pages of this work. Each book-length volume provides more than 20 state-of-the-art topical reviews of the literature. Taken together, these reviews attempt a complete coverage of the subject of the volume. Each review is written by one or more experts in the topic, or in a few cases by teams assembled by experts. As a collection, the Encyclopedia spans the range of subjects and topics normally falling within the scope of 'language and education'. Each volume, edited by an international expert in the subject of the volume, was designed and developed in close collaboration with the general editor of the Encyclopedia, who is a co-editor of each volume as well as general editor of the whole work.

The Encyclopedia has been planned as a necessary reference set for any university or college library that serves a faculty or school of education. Libraries serving academic departments in any of the language disciplines, especially applied linguistics, would also find this a valuable resource. It also seems very relevant to the needs of educational bureaucracies, policy agencies, and public libraries, particularly those serving multicultural or multilingual communities.

The Encyclopedia aims to speak to a prospective readership that is multinational, and to do so as unambiguously as possible. Because each book-size volume deals with a discrete and important subject in language and education, these state-of-the-art volumes also offer authoritative course textbooks in the areas suggested by their titles. This means that libraries will also catalogue these book-size individual volumes in relevant sections of their general collections. To meet this range of uses, the Encyclopedia is published in a hardback edition offering the durability needed for reference collections, and in a future student edition. The hardback edition is also available for single-volume purchase.

Each state-of-the-art review has about 3000 words of text and most follow a similar structure. A list of references to key works cited in each review supplements the information and authoritative opinion that the review contains. Many contributors survey early developments in their topic, major contributions, work in progress, problems and difficulties, and future directions for research and practice. The aim of the reviews, and of the Encyclopedia as a whole, is to give readers access to the international literature and research on each topic.

David Corson
General Editor Encyclopedia of Language and Education
Ontario Institute for Studies in Education of the University of Toronto
Canada

INTRODUCTION

Oral Discourse and Education, examines oral language as a field of study, looking at the various ways in which we can both theorise the place of talk in education, and examine the way talk is actually done in educational settings. Given the centrality of literacy based practices in schools, a volume focussing on talk brings quite different and important perspectives to the study of education. Talk is something that has all too often been devalued and taken for granted. What becomes evident throughout the papers included in this volume is that talk is of central importance in establishing identities and the cultures in which those identities are located. This is made difficult by the fact that we are unused to reflexively examining the way we talk. The associated lack of awareness makes possible a serious disjuncture between

a) what we believe talk should achieve, and

b) what can be seen to be achieved in actual talk in educational settings.

The papers in Section 1, Theorising Talk, elaborate different ways of theorising and thinking about oral discourse in educational settings.

The volume begins with a review by Olson of the relation between text and talk, between orality and literacy. He describes the heavy reliance on, and the authority granted to, written texts as a critical feature of education as we know it. He discusses the difficulty of focussing on talk as something to be analysed and spoken about which he sees as a central problem in researching oral discourse in educational settings.

In the second review Young elaborates a critical pragmatic theory of classroom talk where he argues that talk or dialogue is fundamental to democracy and thus to the processes of schooling in any democratic state. Drawing on Dewey's pragmatic theory and Habermas's critical theory he says "the essence of democracy is not the mechanisms involved, but the process of participation in ... self-forming dialogues – dialogues whose outcomes change human identities and relationships". Of central importance to classrooms, he argues, is the recognition that "democracy is never a finished state of affairs" and the capacity of citizens for social dialogue that is rational, and that can accommodate different and conflicting points of view, is fundamental to the evolutionary life of any community. Students must learn to engage in dialogue in which mutual respect and reciprocal valuing of each other is the basis for finding solutions to any problems which might inhibit the well being of the community.

In their review developing a sociocultural perspective on classroom

B. Davies and D. Corson (eds), Encyclopedia of Language and Education,
Volume 3: Oral Discourse and Education, xi–xviii.
© *1997 Kluwer Academic Publishers. Printed in the Netherlands.*

discourse, Measures, Quell and Wells also argue that language is "the principle means developed by human beings both for coordinating joint activity and for co-constructing knowledge about the world". Drawing on the theories of Vygotsky, Bakhtin and Halliday they elaborate a theory in which the responsibility of the teacher is to enable students to become "critical and creative actors and thinkers who also transform cultural practices and knowledge." Dialogue is thus seen as fundamental to education, both between teachers and students and amongst students.

Centring her theoretical analysis on the concept of communicative competence Grundy also elaborates the ideas of Habermas, but draws our attention to some serious flaws in the ideal of rational argument which lies at the heart of his philosophy. Starting with the premise that communicative classroom practices should privilege reasoned argument and challenge on the part of both teachers and students as they collaboratively construct the curriculum, Grundy then goes on to elaborate the way in which actual classroom practice falls short of these ideals. Teachers shape students' identities in ways which only become visible following close textual analysis of their talk. Student talk, too, from the earliest ages, can produce patterns of "communicative competence" which are oppressive and irrational and which serve to undermine the Habermasian ideal. While the ideals of Habermas's theory are liberatory in intent, his 'ideal speech situation' is one which arguably does nothing to counteract oppressive relations of power inherent in the culture. Grundy argues for the importance of participatory examinations of actual classroom talk on the part of the teachers and students which will generate "critical reflection by teachers, students and academic researchers upon the discursive practices which shape and through which they shape the world of learning in the classroom". She draws on some of the research informed by poststructuralist theory to show how this might be done.

Baker elaborates the ways in which ethnomethodological research has made the phenomenon of classroom talk observable and reportable. She reviews the methodological and conceptual tools developed by ethnomethodologists and used for examining actual talk in educational settings. Unlike the theoretical positions outlined in the earlier papers, ethnomethodology does not start with a set of cultural ideals against which actual classrooms might be evaluated and found wanting. Rather the focus of ethnomethodology is making the practices of the culture observable and reportable. Through detailed analysis of actual stretches of talk, ethnomethodology enables us to see how it is that the "members' methods", that is, of both teachers and students, construct those scenes which we recognise as "educational".

Alloway and Gilbert then elaborate the ways in which poststructuralist theory has also undertaken the examination of actual talk and as well, how it has worked to make visible the multiple and contradictory ways in

which the human subject is constructed, with all the tensions and contradictions between the discursive positionings made available or withheld.
The research reviewed here calls into question the certainties entailed in
Habermas's reliance on rational debate by showing the complex links
between discourse, subjectivity and desire. The authors conclude with
the observation that such "research offers the possibility of more sophisticated analyses that recognise the complex field of discursive play wherein
organising principles such as gender, race, ethnicity, class, age, and school-
based competence prove salient in determining the specificity of the subject
produced through classroom talk."

Section 2, Oral Language, Culture and Identity examines in detail the
ways in which culture and identity recreate themselves along gender, class
and ethnic lines. The reviews also explore the complex and intricate
interplay between being a person and being a member of a particular
group.

A.D. Edwards opens with a searching review of the literature theorising
the complex relations between language, culture and identity. Drawing in
particular on the work of Labov, Bourdieu and Bernstein he goes on to
elaborate research which shatters the illusion "that the discourse practices
of schools are culturally neutral and therefore fair". His review then
analyses the complex relations between spoken language practices, power
and status, with a particular focus on class relations.

Tannen, Kendall and Adger examine different conversational styles and
patterns across gender, class and ethnicity drawing on the ethnography of
communication, ethnomethodology and sociolinguistics. Teachers' attitudes to different narrative styles and different conversational styles are
shown to be intricately related to the patterns of privileging some groups
over others in classroom talk. In their discussion they provide the important insight that students' readings of what is appropriate (rather than their
assumed actual skills) are more important than we might have imagined.
Students' may not display the skills they have because they do not see
them as appropriate in the situation as they understand it. We can too
easily misread this as lack of those skills and work on skills (which they
already have) rather than work on different readings of what is appropriate
in multiple settings.

The problems of teachers' privileging the symbolic property of the
dominant classes is further developed in Heller's review. In particular she
addresses the treatment of non-standard varieties of dominant languages.
She points out that linguistic codes "represent institutional authority, or
challenge to that authority, and can be drawn on in ways which serve
principally to establish or resist the local, interactional order, and through
that order the larger institutional, and social, one." By examining the
discursive means by which privilege is established and maintained Heller
makes it clear that "educational language choices are never neutral".

V.K. Edwards also explores the difference in oral language styles amongst diverse cultural groups and makes the very interesting point that "discourse conventions cannot simply be described in terms of linguistic difference." "Rather", she says "they are inextricably linked with different cultural values . . . it is sometimes difficult to see how accommodation can be reached between groups which hold highly divergent views of education and society".

Gilbert goes some way to answering the problems raised by Edwards by developing the idea of critical oracy and its role in education for active citizenship. He points out that "the idea of active citizenship clearly implies that in promoting and challenging forms of power relations or social values, participants need a critical understanding of the consequences of arguments and actions, and their implications for the welfare of self and others." As well he argues the importance of incorporating poststructuralist understanding of the inscription of bodies and desire through discourse in developing forms of dialogue which genuinely facilitate critical oracy and critical citizenship.

The next three reviews focus primarily on gender and identity followed by two very different reviews on the development of social/communicative competencies.

In her review on play Davies shows how children's play and social structures and values are intricately connected. Research on play began with observations of what was taken to be natural and gradually focussed on the complex interplay between the social and the individual and the discourses through which each of these is constructed. The complex interplay between the real world and the fictional world is explored here and largely deconstructed. The lived bodily reality of the excitement and violence of virtual reality games for boys in video game arcades is a case in point. This review raises the problem of the recalcitrance of students' imagined selves and imagined (but real) lived patterns of desire in the face of new and 'politically correct' admonitions from adults.

Bjerrum Nielsen and Davies then elaborate in detail the complex relations between usual patterns of talk in classrooms and the formation of gendered-identities. The research reviewed indicates that the apparent success of strategies aimed at "gender neutrality" is illusory. The qualitative studies which established the failure of these early attempts have given way to "studies of cultural meanings, the shaping of individual desires and the discursive strategies through which embodiment of self as boy or girl, both in and out of school, becomes possible." Through such studies the "subtle interplay between the priorities and social orientations of girls and boys, the structure and content of classroom discourse and the response students receive from the teacher can be seen as almost inevitably maintaining and reinforcing the traditional gender order."

In her review on narrative and the shaping of identity Golden shows how the "shaping of identity is intimately tied to the storylines that a particular society makes available and desirable to its members . . . " Golden shows the multiple and contradictory ways identity is shaped through narrative, not least of which is the humanist storyline in which identity comes to be understood (and partially achieved) as essential to each person, and as unitary and non-contradictory.

In Green and Dixon's review this idea is pressed even further, with social competence being shown to be "not a unitary construct, but a situated one defined by particular disciplines, in particular ways, for particular purposes." What Green and Dixon argue is that the linguistic, social and contextual presuppositions that individuals bring to events "influence both the interpretation of the unfolding event and the choices a speaker makes in participating." As a result, "what people display to others through their interactions within an event reflects a complex set of interpretations and decisions as well as what was available in their communicative repertoires. . . . The group-individual dynamic" they argue "is central to understanding how social competencies are interactionally accomplished." Far from competencies being located in the person, an individual's repertoire for action "reflects the past and present opportunities talked into being within and across groups."

Pagliano's review, which follows, reveals how true Green and Dixon's analysis is, but adds a very interesting twist. Through an examination of students with speech and language impairment Pagliano shows just how devastating the effects of missing out on opportunities for talk can be. Whereas many papers in this volume found some difficulty in focussing specifically on oral language as opposed to language, this paper, in reviewing the issues involved in the absence of oral language, highlights as none other does, the centrality of oral language to identity and to membership within any cultural group. The failure of many educators to take sign language seriously because it is not written, highlights the valuing of written texts over oral texts in Western culture. The absolute centrality of oral language for the formation of identity and culture perhaps goes some way to explaining how it is that those who have achieved oral competence can find it so taken-for-granted that it is hard to actually make it an object of study. In contrast, Pagliano describes the extraordinary team efforts amongst child, family, teacher, specialist teacher, specialists such as speech pathologists and targeted community representatives who work together to achieve oral competence in those children who do not have it. He also reveals the mistakes that are made when it is assumed that absence of oral competence means absence of knowledge. Technologies which have been provided to make communication possible for those without oral language sometimes reveal a rich and complex set of knowledges.

Section 3, Oral Language and the Curriculum, focuses on oral language as it is made relevant in a number of school curricula. The first five reviews examine various aspects of talk in classrooms generally and the final four papers look at the specific classroom settings.

Pontecorvo begins this section by examining the ways in which teacher talk might be changed to lead to more effective learning situations. She shows ways in which the traditional IRE and IRF sequences can be modified and developed such that teachers can "scaffold" the development of students' thinking. Pontecorvo cites evidence that where students become confident users of exploratory talk, there are significant improvements in students' performance on joint reasoning tasks.

Mercer then takes up the issue of what effective teacher talk might be and shows how difficult it is to reach a satisfactory definition of effectiveness. He comments that "Few research methods for the analysis of the communicative process of teaching and learning are able to deal satisfactorily with the fact that in all talk, meanings depend on the continual regeneration of a context of shared understanding amongst speakers."

Westgate's paper focuses on student talk. He examines the difficulty teachers and students have in establishing effective small group talk amongst students. To avoid idle chat, where students simply talk superficially about process, some researchers have suggested ways of carefully regulating what happens in small group discussions. Westgate points out, however, that this then reduces the possibility of exploratory talk, the development of which is seen to be one of the most important outcomes from small group talk. It is suggested that if teachers want students to engage in dialogic collaborative talk they will have to find ways to make clear what it is that they want from students. Some development in "metadiscoursal awareness" and the encouragement of a reflexive approach, with carefully considered teacher intervention and support are probably necessary if we are to evolve more effective talk-contexts.

Lyle focuses specifically on collaborative talk, showing how on the one hand there has been a recognition of its value since the 1960s, and on the other, how classroom observation studies have shown a remarkable absence of it. Lyle reviews the literature which reveals what the key elements of successful collaborative and exploratory talk are. These include mutual respect, groupings based on friendships and the teachers' ability to suspend their role as "authorities on meaning" and instead "help the students clarify their understanding."

de Klerk takes up many of the issues in the earlier papers in Section 3 and brings them into a discussion of tertiary teaching. He discusses the lecture format, its history and its limitations, and looks at the increasing reliance on small group talk in university settings. Drawing attention to the increasingly multi-ethnic and multi-lingual nature of tertiary students he suggests that researchers study verbal interaction as it is linked to wider social processes and relationships. He suggests we should "explicate its role in confirming or consolidating or challenging and changing the organisations which shape it." He goes on: "Viewing oral discourse at tertiary level as a kind of social struggle which could result in change, both in the mode of discourse and of wider social and cultural domains will require increasing attention to be given to what these discourses are and how they operate. ... "

Scrimshaw's review of talk and computers shows how what we mean by talk is already going through interesting changes as a result of new technologies. The research reviewed shows that as students talk around computers, for example vying for access to the keyboard or mouse or collaborating on a task to be done, some cultural patterns (such as oppressive gender relations) may become more entrenched while at the same time, new skills may be being developed. Equally the substantive material found on computers may have the same features of simultaneously entrenching values and opening up new possibilities. "Talking" with others (even "virtual" others) via computer link-ups may well open up new discursive possibilities for students and is an area in urgent need of further research.

Pirie's review of the use of talk in maths opens another dimension of complexity in understanding the way talk works. The struggle to find everyday ways of talking about mathematical concepts creates its own set of difficulties. She says that while on the one hand, the "challenge for teachers is to reveal the intended power of mathematical language to be precise, unambiguous, brief and manipulable" they must do so "through the clumsy, imprecise, personal language of oral discourse." She also comments that technology will increasingly take over the routine aspects of mathematics and that the teacher's role will lie "in educating students in the processes of conjecturing, explaining and justifying their ideas, and classroom talk has a major part to play in such education."

Boulter's review focuses on the problems of science education beginning with the misconceptions science teachers have about what science is. Boulter cites the work of Lemke (1993) which views science, not as a mental accomplishment, but a "discursive performance in which signs and symbols including language are used to make and communicate meanings in the process of constructing the life of a community." She also cites the work of feminist researchers which reveals science as "culturally positioned in the white, male, middle class western world." She observes that in classrooms where theorising about the nature of the scientific process has become something both students and teachers engage in, "the reflective toss", where a student question is followed by an incorporation of his or her meaning into another question, has replaced the IRE format.

McGonigal concludes this volume with an analysis of the intricate relation between literacy studies and oral language. The production of major literacy texts in video form allows them to be studied as spoken text. As well, the linking up of students via the Internet allows them to "talk" to other students all over the world via the printed word. This has fundamentally blurred the difference between literacy and oracy. The majority of authors in this volume have struggled to extract oral language as a specific object to write about, and in part, that struggle is due to the taken-for-grantedness of orality in the process of communication and meaning-making. McGonigal's review suggests that some of the shifts in the study of literature may lead to a greater reflexive awareness of spoken language and thus a greater capacity to subject it to critique.

Bronwyn Davies

Section 1

Theorising Talk

DAVID R. OLSON

TALKING ABOUT TEXT AND THE CULTURE OF LITERACY

Although written texts have always found a favoured place in educational practice, the ways in which they have been regarded, consulted, interpreted and constructed have changed importantly in this century. Texts and text books were traditionally regarded as secular Scripture, the archived treasure of the culture's most valued knowledge. And education was defined more or less as expertise with those archival resources (Geisler, 1994). In more recent "Post-Modern" times, writing and written texts have come to be seen as merely one medium of communication among others, often in competition with television, film, computers and the internet. Correspondingly, the respect for written texts has waned along with an emphasis on competence in constructing and interpreting such texts, the skill we have traditionally defined and valued as literacy. This review is concerned with understanding what is gained and what is lost in the changing perceptions of the written word.

ORIGINS

In the 18th Century such language theorists as Vico and Condorcet developed the view that speech and writing were directly related. They took the properties of writing systems as direct indications of the speech competencies of their users. This permitted the inference that cultures without writing systems were primitive, those with writing systems based on words or on syllables, such as that employed in the Orient, as traditional, and those cultures with alphabets as modern. It was only in the 20th Century that the distinguished linguist Ferdinand de Saussure (1916/1983) emancipated speech from writing and was able to show that all human languages are, by and large, equivalent; there are no primitive languages. On the other hand, Saussure was largely to blame for the subsequent denial of the significance of writing altogether. For Saussure, writing was merely the transcription of speech. It was a means of distribution but not a distinctive mode of representation. This continues to be the most commonly held assumption about writing in linguistic theory and in anthropology both of which confine attention primarily to the spoken word. Literacy lost its primacy in linguistic, anthropological and psychological theory while it retained its importance on the educational and political agenda.

B. Davies and D. Corson (eds), Encyclopedia of Language and Education,
Volume 3: Oral Discourse and Education, 1–9.
© *1997 Kluwer Academic Publishers. Printed in the Netherlands.*

THE PRESENT

In the past three decades scholars have again become interested in the possibility that writing may impart a distinctive set of characteristics to language and mind. The work of Milman Parry (1971) on the oral tradition in what was then Yugoslavia, led him to speculate that in the absence of writing, knowledge tended to be formulated in orally memorable ways quite alien to those of modern literate traditions. The Homeric poems were seen as exemplary of such an oral tradition which was replaced in Classical Greek times by the literate Socrates, Plato and Aristotle. This was a theory greatly elaborated upon by such writers as McLuhan (1962), Goody & Watt (1968), Havelock (1982) and Ong (1982). Not only was it argued that the linguistic forms used to formulate and preserve knowledge had altered historically under the impact of writing but also the very idea of language, of correct "prescriptive" grammar, of dictionaries and logic were by-products of the long evolution of a written tradition.

An important problem with that theory was that of universalizability. It soon became clear that almost every known human culture has some set of graphic symbols for representing and preserving information whether in the form of grooves on bone, knots in strings, brands on animals or humans, totems, graphic signs such as that of the cross and so on. Even elaborate systems of writing have been developed which make no direct reference to the language spoken by the writers. Such "writing without words" was common in pre-conquest America (Boone & Mignolo, 1990). Furthermore, Chinese writing, once regarded as primitive relative to Western alphabets is no longer seen so – different but not inferior (Gaur, 1983). Finally, the supposed genius of the Greeks for their invention of the alphabet is now seen as the rather straightforward consequence of borrowing, of adopting a script suitable for a Semitic language to represent their own quite different language, Greek (Sampson, 1985; Harris, 1986; Olson, 1994). Hence, the uniqueness and cultural significance of the alphabet is again called into question.

Yet, as Derrida (1976, pp. 30–31) pointed out 'this factum of phonetic writing is massive: it commands our entire culture and our entire science, and it is certainly not just one fact among others.' Coming to grips with that phenomenon, our literacy, defines the new literacy agenda.

While many writers from Vygotsky (1962) to Ong (1982) have argued quite convincingly that writing increases consciousness, specific theories as to just how writing and literacy could play such a role have been absent until very recently.

MAJOR WORK

Over the past decade a number of scholars, some from the Piagetian school, others influenced by Vygotsky, Goody, Bruner and others have begun to formulate theories and conduct empirical tests of just how gaining competence with writing systems could have an impact on cognition. Emilia Ferreiro and her colleagues (Ferreiro & Teborosky, 1982) in a groundbreaking series of studies showed that when children were first confronted with written language they brought a series of assumptions about writing, none of which turned out to be true of the alphabet. First, they assumed that writing was directly related to the world, rather than to *language about the world*. Their own language was essentially unconscious to them and it appeared to be the case that they foresaw no role for language in their first visual marks. Even if they distinguished drawing from writing, they still assumed that written marks mapped objects and events rather than speech about those objects and events. Only with experience with written texts did they come to see that written symbols stood for pieces of speech, first words and later sounds within words.

In our own laboratory we have shown that pre-reading children treat written symbols as tokens for objects rather than as tokens for constituents of speech (Olson, 1994; Olson & Homer, 1996). In one telling example, pre-reading children were shown a card on which was written three words: THREE LITTLE PIGS. This small text was read to the children who then "read" the text back to the adult. However, following this, the experimenter covered up the third word and asked the children what the text now said. A common answer was "Two little pigs"; that is, the children assumed that each printed symbol stood for one of the objects. There was little understanding that the printed signs represented, not things, but words for things.

This early assumption can be shown another way. Children were asked to write: CAT. Children protest saying they don't know how to write. But if the experimenter persists, saying, just pretend you are writing, they will produce a scribble (or a short arbitrary letter string). When asked to write; TWO CATS, they produce two similar scribbles, claiming that it now reads "ONE CAT, TWO CATS." When asked if they could write: NO CAT, children claim that 'No, they can't write that' one child claiming 'There was no cat so I didn't write anything.' For these children writing does not represent a linguistic form but rather an object or a meaning.

There is a rich literature which makes a somewhat similar point in regard to children's awareness of the phonological form of spoken words. The now well-established finding is that although children have implicit knowledge of the phonological form of their language, they have no conscious awareness of the distinguishable phonemic sounds making up their speech

(Shankweiler & Liberman, 1972; Morais, Alegria & Content, 1987). Consequently, they cannot break a syllable into consonant and vowel pairs nor can they integrate separately presented consonants and vowels to produce a recognizable syllable (Vernon, submitted). All this changes when children learn to read. The visually presented alphabet provides a model, that is, a set of categories, in terms of which children learn to analyze their speech, detecting those sounds that correspond to the names or associated "sounds" of the letters (Olson, 1996).

There is a compelling symmetry between these findings with children and the history of the writing systems described above. Early writing systems attempted to represent information or "meanings" directly; only later, and after repeated borrowings, did graphic signs come to stand for words or the sounds of words. This is a story repeated by each child in learning to read an alphabet.

Such findings require a complete rethinking of the role of literacy in the formation and understanding of language and mind. It can no longer be assumed that writing is just a means of preserving speech, that learning to read and write calls on the processes that have already been exploited in learning to speak. Literacy in the form of concern to education is not analogous to or equivalent to speech; it provides an entirely different level of analysis. Writing is largely responsible for bringing our implicit knowledge of language into consciousness, for turning it into an object of reflection and anlysis. Learning to read and write is essentially a kind of a metalanguage for talking about the properties of speech!

FUTURE DIRECTIONS

Learning to read and write calls into play an important set of concepts for talking about language. Primary among these are such concepts as word, "the very words," meanings of words as opposed to meanings of speakers, sentences, paragraphs, essays, arguments, truth, validity, definitions and so on. In some cases the same lexical item is used as in pre-literate contexts but now with a new meaning. One such case is the concept "word." Oral discourse uses "word" to refer to sayings as in "I give you my word", whereas in literate discourse "word" refers to a lexical item. Only literate children and adults will grant that "of" or "or" or "not" is a word. Even the famous ten commandments were traditionally called the ten words, the *decalogue*.

But there are other concepts with a clear epistemological significance that come to be articulated in literate discourse, in particular for talking about text. The problem is this. In speech, one has direct access not only to the linguistic form of the utterance, but also to the so-called "illocutionary force" of an utterance. Tone, pitch, stress, prosody all give clues to listeners as to how an utterance is to be taken. Writing captures the words but loses the force intended by the speaker. Literate cultures have had to invent alternative lexical means for controlling how listeners take their texts. These linguistic devices centre on speech act and mental state terms such as imply, assert, claim, allege on one hand and infer, hypothesize, conclude, assume, interpret on the other. To illustrate, in speech one can signal that one insists on some statement or command by adopting an insistent tone of voice. In writing one loses that tone of voice and has to lexicalize that tone by means of a speech act verb such as "He insisted that." These are among the concepts that Corson (1995) has shown to constitute a "lexical bar" to students in their high school years who are less immersed in the culture of literacy, which largely means less practised in "talking about texts." Olson and Astington (1990) made an extensive analysis of these concepts and tested high school children on some of them. A typical item was the following:

It's Adam's birthday tomorrow. Barbara is just sneaking out of the house to buy a present for him when he sees her and asks her where she is going. Barbara says, 'We're out of milk. I'm going to the store.'
A. Barbara means that she is going to buy milk.
B. Barbara concedes that she is going to buy milk.
C. Barbara asserts that she is going to buy milk.
D. Barbara implies that she is going to buy milk.

Only about half of university undergraduates chose the correct verb "implies"; the majority chose "asserts." Perhaps only those "strictly brought up" as J. L. Austin (1965) once put it, would notice the difference. Yet it indicates the kinds of distinctions required for interpreting literate discourse. Literate expertise is largely a matter of managing such subtleties in the uses of language.

One additional finding was that Canadian children in General programs were much less competent with a battery of such concepts than those in more Academic programs, a finding quite compatible with Corson's argument.

The important point about such lexical concepts is that their use is not restricted to literary uses of language. Once acquired such concepts can find an important place in ordinary oral discourse. Classroom discourse, although often conducted orally, relies heavily on just those concepts elaborated in writing.

EDUCATION

Formal education is almost entirely a matter of literacy – of learning to read and write and to live mentally in a world defined in large part through books. Science education which is advertised as a form of "nature study" is less about birds and bees than about laws and equations, history education is less about happenings and events than it is about construals, records and documents; language study is not so much a matter of talk as of text and of talking about text.

But the "factum" of literacy has a sometimes detrimental effect on children's epistemological development. It is not a serious exaggeration to say that students and non-specialist are taught to think of knowledge as that body of truths deposited in that written archival tradition. Students are taught to study for coverage and recall, treating texts as authoritative and autonomous.

Children's assumptions about knowledge are greatly at variance with those held by experts in those fields. Experts have learned to read "through" a text to find the context, the intentions and the perspective of the writer of that text, that is, the rhetorical aspects of texts (Geisler, 1994; Wineburg, 1991; Haas & Flower, 1988).

Geisler (1994) points out that teachers and students focus on content, making learning and remembering the subject matter of a discipline the goal of their reading. Advanced students and professionals (experts), on the other hand, focus on the rhetorical forms of the texts they read, asking themselves such questions as "who is saying this?" "why are they saying this?" "what are they trying to get me, the reader, to think?" "do they have any warrant for saying that?" It is this rhetorical stance to a text that allows experts to criticize and, more importantly, to interpret texts – to bring them into the reader's own frame of reference. It is to assimilate a text rather than to accomodate to it, to advert to an older Piagetian distinction. Students and non-specialist seem to neglect this option.

We may see how this can work by appealing to Latour and Woolgar's (1979) analysis of the types of statements made by scientists as writers and as critical readers. As writers, scientists prefer simple factual claims shorn of their rhetorical form. Yet as readers these same scientists work on other people's texts to recover their rhetorical form asking themselves the questions mentioned above. Many writers have protested the fact that textbooks are unrelenting strings of apparently autonomous facts which give little or no indication of who is asserting them, with what degree of conviction, with what degree of warrant, with what intended effect, but to no avail. Perhaps, as Geisler has argued, textbooks are written to be learned not to be criticized or interpreted. The expert not the student is accorded the right to analyze and criticize. Bridging the gap becomes the central educational problem. She writes: 'In each area of specialization, then, students must actually be untaught the distrust of personal opinion and contextualized understanding that has been drummed into them through the period of general education' (1994, p. 93). Much of education makes good consumers if poor thinkers.

Just how to lead children to read, study, interrogate, summarize and criticize texts is an important research focus. Studies by Norris and Phillips (1987), Geisler (1994), Roth and Anderson (1988), and Wineburg (1991) have all indicated that while children are reasonably adept at summarizing and extracting information from written texts, they are extremely limited in their abilities to learn from texts – they continue to hold their pre-reading points of view – and they have difficulty in criticizing texts. Both of these difficulties may be related to the difficulty in seeing a text as the product of an actual author who is expressing a set of beliefs with which a reader may or may not agree. Children, like their 19th Century ancestors, tend to treat texts as secular Scripture. The agenda for the future must adress two concerns simultaneously. The first is to get children to take texts seriously and therefore to learn from them. Second, children must come to recognize that texts are compilations not of the "given" but of the more or less well defended views of their authors.

Writing is the favoured medium of expression because writing offers a unique opportunity to honor the goal of creating secure knowledge – statements which can be offered as true by anyone. Their critics criticize those statement by downgrading them to mere opinion. Modern epistemology is very much a matter of dispute over the force of statements – one person's fact is another person's conjecture. Statements which resist downgrading come to be treated as true and seen, inappropriately perhaps, as autonomous and above criticism. Experts read as they do because they recognize the fragility of knowledge claims and they write as they do because they hope to contribute to the world not merely their own beliefs but beliefs which they believe can and should be held by everybody. And that is what those textbooks are, compilations of those universalizable, if not eternal, beliefs.

While an important part of schooling, then, is that of learning to cope with these texts, an equally important part is that of turning texts back into oral form, into the words of some author or the words of oneself as one reads. Students learn to cite, to paraphrase, to extrapolate and to interpret, and in the end to turn ideas into new texts. In so doing they become part of a living tradition.

Ontario Institute for Studies in Education
University of Toronto, Canada

REFERENCES

Austin, J.L.: 1965, *How To Do Things With Words*, Oxford University Press, New York.
Boone, E. & Mignolo, W.D. (eds.): 1990, *Writing Without Words: Alternative Literacies in Mesoamerica and the Andes*, Duke University Press, Durham, NC.
Corson, D.: 1995, *Using English Words*, Kluwer, Dordrecht.
Derrida, J.: 1976, *Of Grammatology* (G. Spivak, trans.), Johns Hopkins University Press, Baltimore, MD.
Ferreiro, E. & Teborosky, A.: 1982, *Literacy Before Schooling (Los Sistemas de escritura en el Desarrollo del Nino)*, Heinemann (English translation), Exeter, NH (Original work published 1979, Siglo Veintiuno Editors, Mexico DF).
Gaur, A.: 1983, *A History of Writing*, The British Library, London.
Geisler, C.: 1994, *Academic Literacy and the Nature of Expertise: Reading, Writing and Knowing in Academic Philosophy*, Erlbaum, Hillsdale, NJ.
Goody, J. & Watt, I.: 1968, 'The consequences of literacy', in J. Goody (ed.), *Literacy in Traditional Societies*, Cambridge University Press, Cambridge, 27–68. (Originally published 1963 in *Contemporary Studies in Society and History* 5, 304–345.)
Haas, C. & Flower, L.: 1988, 'Rhetorical reading strategies and the construction of meaning', *College Composition and Communication* 39, 167–183.
Harris, R.: 1986, *The Origin of Writing*, Duckworth, London.
Havelock, E.: 1982, *The Literate Revolution in Greece and its Cultural Consequences*, Princeton University Press, Princeton NJ.
Latour, B. & Woolgar, S.: 1979, *Laboratory Life: The Social Construction of Scientific Facts*, Sage, London.
McLuhan, M.: 1962, *The Gutenberg Galaxy*, University of Toronto Press, Toronto.
Morais, J., Alegria, J. & Content, A.: 1987, 'The relationships between segmental analysis and alphabetic literacy: An interactive view', *Cahiers de Psychologie Cognitive* 7, 415–438.
Norris, S.P. & Phillips, L.M.: 1987, 'Explanations of reading comprehension: Schema theory and critical thinking theory', *Teachers College Record* 89, 281–306.
Olson, D.R.: 1994, *The World on Paper: Conceptual and Cognitive Implications of Writing and Reading*, Cambridge University Press, Cambridge.
Olson, D.R.: 1996, 'Towards a psychology of literacy: On the relations between speech and writing', *Cognition* 60, 83–104.
Olson, D.R. & Astington, J.: 1990, 'Talking about text: How literacy contributes to thought', *Journal of Pragmatics* 14(5), 557–573.
Olson, D.R. & Homer, B.: 1996, *Literacy and Children's Conceptions of Language*, International Congress of Psychology, August 21, 1996, Montreal.
Ong, W.: 1982, *Orality and Literacy: The Technologizing of the Word*, Methuen, London.
Parry, E. (ed.): 1971, *The Collected Papers of Milman Parry*, Oxford University Press, Oxford.
Roth, K. & Anderson, C.: 1988, 'Promoting conceptual change learning from science textbooks', in P. Ramsden (ed.), *Improving Learning: New Perspectives*, Kogan Page, London, 109–141.
Sampson, G.: 1985, *Writing Systems*, Stanford University Press, Stanford CA.
Saussure, F. de: 1983, *Course in General Linguistics*, Duckworth, London. (Original work published 1916.)
Shankweiler, D. & Liberman, I.: 1972, 'Misreading: A search for causes', in J. Kavanaugh & I. Mattingly (eds.), *Language by Ear and Language by Eye: The Relationships between Speech and Reading*, MIT Press, Cambridge MA, 293–317.
Vernon, S.: 1996, 'Types of segmentation in speech and writing in Spanish-speaking children', *Mimeo*. University of Quertero, Quertero, Mexico.

Vygotsky, L.: 1962, *Thought and Language*, MIT Press, Cambridge MA.
Wineberg, S.: 1991, 'On the reading of historical texts: Notes on the breach between school and academy', *American Educational Research Journal* 28, 495–519.

ROBERT YOUNG

A CRITICAL – PRAGMATIC THEORY OF CLASSROOM TALK

That which is called 'Critical Theory of Education' is actually a family of theories which are only loosely related. In the English-speaking world, the meaning of the term was dominated by attempts by American Marxists to define a broad-front strategy for Marxist theorising at a time, during the 'cold war', when the Marxist label was a disadvantage. In Germany, however, the term critical theory was more likely to be applied to the Frankfurt School and its descendants, a particular kind of Marx – influenced theory which saw itself as continuing the Marxist project but as disagreeing with many central aspects of Marxism as interpreted by Lenin. Habermas, a student of Adorno, is the chief contemporary descendant of this school of thought, although there are significant differences between Habermas' ideas and those of Adorno (see Held, 1980).

Habermas himself has changed his views over time due to critical engagement with other thinkers, and it is always appropriate in judging Habermas' ideas to recognise at least four different phases of his development: early sociological, epistemological, communicative, and post-metaphysical. These phases do not simply supersede each other, but involve shifts of methodology and viewpoint in which earlier work is incorporated in a reconstructed form.

Habermas writes uncompromisingly *into* particular, largely European, often German, debates, and makes no concessions in the way of explanation for the reader from other traditions. Accordingly, many English-speaking interpreters of Habermas have interpreted his work quite selectively, often in a manner which is at cross-purposes with any reasonable reconstruction of the original philosophical direction. There is a long history of such 'mis-interpretation' in British, and American social thought, some of it creative. And it is arguably the case that most claims concerning the significance or more often, recently, the insignificance of Habermas' ideas in English language discussion are poorly based, especially when married to a systematic distortion of recent French ideas.

It may come as a surprise to some that Habermas is best understood through a nexus between the pragmatism of the late Dewey, and anti-structuralist, phenomenologically-influenced linguistic sociology. John Dewey, is in some ways a more appropriate spiritual ancestor for Haber-

B. Davies and D. Corson (eds), Encyclopedia of Language and Education,
Volume 3: Oral Discourse and Education, 11–20.
© *1997 Kluwer Academic Publishers. Printed in the Netherlands.*

mas than Horkheimer or Adorno (see Biesta, 1995). While there is no
evidence that Habermas was directly influenced by his work, Habermas
has several times acknowledged a convergence. The pragmatism of the
late Dewey is a critical-pragmatism in which epistemological questions are
subordinated to the discourse of the community of inquiry. A more detailed
recognition of the culturally-ontogenetic, phenomenological dimension of
that discourse, derived from the phenomenologically influenced sociology of inquiry that developed after the 'linguistic turn' in social theory,
complements Dewey's account of the epistemic problematic of inquiry,
providing a synthesis in which epistemological questions, and associated
issues of the philosophy of consciousness are subordinated to a sociological, historical account of human communal culture-producing processes.
In his 1981/2 two-volume work, *The Theory of Communicative Action*,
which remains broadly definitive of his mature position, Habermas called
the move from an epistemology-centred approach to a concrete, cultural
history of inquiry, a 'paradigm shift', echoing Kuhn's famous characteri-
sation of the Copernican and Einsteinian shifts in physical-cosmological
thought.

This is a theory which places human learning capacity, especially
methodic, deliberate forms of inquiry, at the centre of modern and subsequent cultural-historical processes. In this view, it should be noted that
democratic forms of government are a part of the inquiry process as much
and even more than scientific institutes, and that however much various
obstacles to inquiry are removed, the process of learning retains some of
the qualities of a pragmatic, trial and error learning process. It is always
possible for such a process to fall into error and it is never possible to set
aside some assumptions as unquestionable or 'foundational'. Political and
normative learning, as well as aesthetic learning are as much a part of this
adaptive learning process as scientific and technological learning.

It is necessary to say something more about the concept of democracy
involved in Dewey and Habermas. Neither thinker is committed to particular forms of democracy. Both would probably agree, with Adorno, that
the forms of multi-party representative government with accompanying
interest groups, lobbyists, concentrations of media ownership and the like
that make up the governmental systems common to culturally European
societies, are at best 'half-democracies'. The essence of democracy is
not the mechanisms involved, but the process of *participation* in national
and increasingly international self-forming dialogues – dialogues whose
outcomes change human identities and relationships. Of necessity this
participation is not conceptualised solely in individualistic terms, but also
in terms of the participation of voices, of 'points of view', representative
of the classes of people identifiable with respect to any problematic. The
classes of individuals with respect to many economic problematics are
those individuals similarly placed with respect to control over three factors

of production – labour, capital, and resources. Similar classes or categories are picked out with respect to other issues such as the problematics of gender, race, political structures and so on. A democratic society is one in which decisions are made only after an untrammelled process of representation of views and upon the basis of seeking solutions to differences of interest which build on rationally-discernible common ground. Democracy itself is a path to be taken, never a finished state of affairs and no particular road to it is sacrosanct. It is also appropriate to point out that the concept of 'emancipation' or critique involved in critical theory is an evolutionary as well as a revolutionary concept of critique. Once a situation of at least half-democracy obtains, that is, a situation where at least a significant range of classes has an effective voice, whether this situation is of the contemporary European, or some other kind, it is possible to advance matters in an evolutionary way, through reason rather than revolutionary force (Habermas, 1991a). However, what is possible and what is appropriate is a culturally and historically contextual matter (see Young, 1992).

Critique, whether revolutionary or evolutionary, cannot stand outside history as a 'grand theory' which is foundational for value judgments. Nor can the history of democracy in one culture-area provide a pattern for all others. Critique must work from the background of a particular cultural and historical context, not in absoluteness or historical abstraction. Rather, critique is a fallible, fragile process of self-transcendence of communities, through systematic incorporation of voices of difference, mutual respect, and creative, but risky innovation and change (Habermas, 1974). In critique we humans learn in the normative sphere, in ethical and moral ways, in a process of inquiry, which is also an ontogenetic process of self-choosing and self-creating. Formal, specialised Educational processes, such as are found in school systems, universities and research institutes are a continuation of the wider, societal processes of self-formation through which a society constantly seeks to improve its whole way of life, technologically and economically, environmentally, socially, spiritually, culturally and politically.

The purpose of formal institutions of education is to prepare students for participation in wider spheres of social development and inquiry. Accordingly, curricula must be broad enough to provide for the full development of professionals and citizens and not narrowly technical. From an educators' point of view, critique is primarily the actual, concrete, immanent process of participation by former students in their spheres of professional actions and as citizens, in processes of social and cultural improvement or collective learning. Critical theory, though, is not critique. Critical theory is a general reconstruction of the capacity of participants for critique (Habermas, 1981; 1991a, Ch 2). Only participants can carry out critique (see Dews, 1986, p. 187) but critical theory or methodology of critique can be a useful guide to them in the same way as methodological discussion can be of use to scientists – it is not a substitute for scientific discovery, but can be an aid to it. Critical theory cannot be a substitute for the process of social dialogue within a community, for judgements in that dialogue about the risks a community is willing to take, or for the community's own creative development of culturally-appropriate forms of the public sphere of self-formative dialogue. The appropriate form that critical theory should take in the curriculum is broadly that of methodological reflection and the encouragement of critical agency through rational dialogue.

WHAT IS "CRITICAL AGENCY"?

What critical agency is *not* is the importation of ideas from another cultural context without due consideration for their appropriateness or their need for adaptation to local circumstances. It is not about the pursuit of pre-decided reform agendas or fashionable sets of 'politically-correct' issues. It is not about the politics of numbers, not even majority numbers. It is about the capacity for rational representation of one's own context and situation in a dialogue with others, differently situated, under the assumption of mutual respect and reciprocal valuing each of the other, in a mutual attempt at finding a joint solution to any problems which are getting in the way of a greater flourishing of the common way of life of all concerned. It is about the social institutionalisation of such dialogue and the formation of individuals fit to responsibly participate in it. It is a capacity to understand and represent one's own interests, but to do so while recognising others' attempts to do so too, with a view to reaching at least a compromise, if not a creatively new solution, to any problematic which mutually involves self and other. More specifically, it is a wide range of skills, awareness, and forms of wisdom with which we can deal with the fact that not all interlocutors understand their own interests or can represent them articulately, not all interlocutors respect each other and not all seek mutually acceptable problem solutions. It is also about a capacity to identify distortions and misrepresentations of communicative processes and the presence of pseudo-openness and pseudo-dialogue. It is about working to make others more respectful and more willing to accept that each person's or group's interests are also legitimate and to convince them that the condition for our common flourishing is a growth in our mutual recognition. Sometimes it is about the limits of dialogue (Young, 1996a).

Both critique and ideology are matters of degree and matters of skill, strategy and wisdom or lack of it. Resistance, critique and ideology are always present in each and every human communicative process, as Habermas' pragmatic theory of meaning (Habermas, 1982b; Young, 1996b) makes clear. Critical hermeneutics is the theory of meaning and interpretation in which the perennial presence of ideology, resistance to ideology and critique of ideology is recognised. Critical Agency is our capacity to be aware of this and to use our skill and courage to advance our social means of development.

CRITICAL HERMENEUTICS

Since the 'linguistic turn' in social theory, it has been recognised that much of that which differs between one human culture and another is akin to computer 'programming' rather than 'hardwiring'. While the computer analogy has its limits, and it is the common analogy of our age, it also has some value. Like computer programmers, human societies create their own cultures but cultures, in turn, having much greater 'inertia' than individuals, create the individuals socialised into them. The primary means of expression, transmission and change of culture is language and just as language is in tension with speech, which always in some sense stretches and changes language as it is uttered into ever changing interpretive environments, so too culture is in tension with social life, which always adapts and changes culture to meet new contingencies. Through living itself, language and culture are changed. While from an individual standpoint both the language and the culture of our birth appear as givens, from the standpoint of 'geological time', or history, these are always being reformed by the incremental erosions of change, and at times, by cataclysms. From a critical theory standpoint what is at issue is the study of the methodology through which we can understand and guide these processes of self-formation – the methodology whereby we can, collectively, write the programs, rather than merely seek to survive amid the detritus of the accidental fracturing of the past. Critical Theory does not provide guidance for the study of social 'hard-wiring'.

While critical hermeneutic and cultural analysis may be carried out at a variety of levels, it is best illustrated by analysis at the level of face to face talk, since that is the immanent concrete level at which all cultural processes are eventually realised. In Habermas' hermeneutics, the semantic theory is pragmatist, the first order semantics are truth-conditional (in a pragmatic sense) and the second order semantics are essentially existential and conditioned by a species-universal set of pragmatic assumptions of understanding (see Young, 1996b).

When communicators set out to understand each other, they anticipate, counterfactually, the presence of that for which they hope. As Davidson puts it, they apply the 'principle of charity' by assuming that the other respects their view, starts from valid assumptions, and reasons consistently. It is only when communication breaks down that a new kind of talk aimed at exploring the basis of the breakdown can (but need not) emerge. This is called 'discourse', in Habermas' special, narrow use of the term.

When an utterance is made, interlocutors not only orient themselves to its dictionary meanings (first order meanings) but to its place as a communicative action – the meaning it requires from having been uttered how and when it was uttered. Its first order and surface meaning may be a statement about some state of affairs in the world. Pragmatic tests will reveal whether or not that state of affairs is present or not and so, the first order truth is conditional and its meaning is truth-conditional. But the second-order meanings concern the meaning of uttering that statement *to* the persons present and the communication, which occurs by means of the utterance, influenced by their assumptions, or by non-verbal channels of the speaker's attitude. For instance, the uttering of a statement may be effectively a warning, and an act of unexpected friendship rather than a simple act of informing someone. It is in the total context that a 'passing theory' of the meaning event is constructed by the hearer, on the basis of all available information, memory, and habits of interpretation. This interpretation is fallible and in some sense provisional. It is a pragmatic basis for proceeding further.

When this passing theory is formed, it is either commensurate with the hearer's view of the world (and the speaker) or it is not. It is at this point that hearers can accept, reject or be uncertain about the pragmatic, holistic validity of the utterance – its fit with their cultural concrete, moral/ethical, and emotional world(s). It is at this moment that the ideological and critical processes are at work and either evoke resistance, possible critique, or acceptance. When that acceptance is accompanied by a suppression of existential unease – an unease evoked by lack of fit – one of the conditions for ideology is met. Ideology is one-sided ontogeny – one class of people creating a reality that expresses what they take to be their own interests but at the expense of other categories of individual. Ultimately this is realised only in actual speech situations – daily rituals of humiliation, patronisation, exploitation, designation, oppression and repression. However, ideology only becomes an historical problem if it is institutionalised rather than merely passing.

Resistance is always present, if repressed, because no human society is yet perfect. Resistance is the first stage of critique, so incipiently, critique is also always present, even if it is not always developed to a conscious, theoretic level. For critique to be developed, there often must be an education in articulateness – the development of a capacity to enter into productive, not merely negative, critical dialogue. Again, this critical agency must avoid utopianism and abstraction. It is a practical capacity and always works against a horizon of historical and cultural constraints. It is the art of the possible. Critics must always recognise that they cannot employ absolute standards, but must begin from an acceptance of the past and a recognition of its wisdom, in its time. Improvements will always be more or less incremental emancipations and the new situation will still be flawed, although hopefully less flawed, than the past. A certain 'principle of humility' must join the 'principle of charity' in construction of a critical passing theory which not only interprets the (cultural) world but also changes it. Benjamin (1969) called aspects of this humility 'anamnesis' – not forgetting.

THE CRITICAL-PRAGMATIC CURRICULUM

The critical-pragmatic curriculum has two interrelated dimensions: reconstructive science and critique proper. Reconstructive science is a general reconstruction of the critical process. It is a study of meaning, culture and cultural difference, democratic theory, morality and ethics, from a methodological standpoint. In this curriculum dimension, which cross-cuts all others, it is possible to rework and incorporate many traditional as well as quite recent curriculum movements. For instance, a capacity for teamwork, understanding of cultural difference, problem-solving, recognition of and taking the point of view of the other, communicative skills, and basic literacy and numeracy skills have been identified as Key Competencies in recent attempts to reform the school curriculum in western societies. Taken jointly, they articulate generic, across-the curriculum methodologies for flexibility and adaptability and for future learning in the workplace and lifelong. They were not identified by political reformers, however. In the Australian context, they were identified by a coalition of employers and trade unionists. Taken jointly, teamwork, handling cultural difference and problem-solving became generic competency for overcoming normative and practical social problems across differences of viewpoint and interest. In a sense all nations, communities and task-oriented groups within them, such as the people who gather in classrooms, are teams and all human flourishing involves working together with others. Cultural differences are among the most significant differences which humans must now face on a planetary scale. The first steps in problem-solving involve a recognition that social problematics are constituted by a variety of definitions of 'the problem', varying across differences of interest of categories or classes of people. Students only become adaptable and flexible problem-solvers if they become articulate and are able to reason well (using, as necessary, quantitative reasoning) and represent their own experience effectively. A general critical curriculum is simply a curriculum for effective self-representation in a context of mutual respect.

The second dimension is that of critique proper. This is the fallible application of reason, experience and social respect for differences of experience and interest, to specific forms of description and analysis – to history, geography, sociology, science etc. However, in the process of

learning how to criticise a student must also learn to respect the achievements of the past. Criticism can be precipitate, premature, and utopian as
well as appropriate, timely and realistic. To some extent, students cannot
criticise effectively until they have learned a great deal, but equally, they
will never criticise effectively if they must always wait on more learning
before critique begins. You must first learn a language before you can utter
articulate cultural criticism in it – or rather, to the extent that you have not
learned a language, your capacity for cultural criticism in it will be constrained. But there is a developmental path for learning to criticise as well
as for learning that which you criticise. The failure of educational systems
to develop critical capacity simultaneously with the learning of the subject
matter has been responsible for many sudden outbursts of irresponsible
(and ineffective) critique at relatively late stages of learning. The price,
though, of teaching students to criticise is that criticism – which is merely
the expression of a desire to learn and improve – will become universal.

Properly understood, the critical curriculum is a force for rapid but
responsible social learning. It certainly will not suit those who do not desire
change but equally it should suit those who want change with responsible
recognition of its price and the limitations of any society's capacity for
change. But the ultimate test of a critical curriculum is that it promotes
critical teaching and learning in the classroom.

CRITICAL TEACHING AND LEARNING IN THE CLASSROOM

The critical classroom is one in which classroom communication is guided
by teachers who exercise critical leadership in promoting and managing a
classroom community of responsible critical inquiry. From participation in
such classrooms, students can acquire the skills and dispositions necessary
for critical and responsible professional life and participation in the inquiry
of personal development, citizenship, industry and science.

The critical-pragmatic classroom is characterised by communicative
structures in which teachers guide students into practising the full range of
communicative forms found in mature inquiry participants in the sciences
and at the highest political levels. Children also need to learn questioning,
doubting, explaining, providing evidence, advancing arguments, drawing
upon experience, listening etc. This does not mean demanding that students
at whatever developmental level should display all these forms of communication at all times. Rather, these will be introduced in limited spheres
and will be supported and guided. However, at every developmental level,
within circumscribed areas of action, the fullest critique that students are
capable of should be encouraged (Habermas, 1991a, pp. 116–194).

Over time, the areas of critique should widen.

The common pattern of the classroom around the world has little of this character. Whether in China or Canada, New York, London, or Sydney, most classrooms are characterised by a closed communication structure the effect of which is indoctrinatory. Although many changes to classroom talk have occurred, and there is more student talk than in the past, there is no systematic evidence for significant changes in the structure of the traditional constitutive roles of teachers and learners. Such structures provide little training in inquiry and develop little capacity for adaptive and flexible lifelong learning.

When teachers and others, such as writers of textbooks, make validity claims by their utterances, students should be able in various organised ways to challenge those claims which do not reflect their own experience or interests.

Normal talk structures in the classroom do not have 'slots' for students to do this critical work. Normally, teachers ask all questions, lecture, explain and criticise student answers against some criterion of the correct answer. Instead, teachers should invite student questions, critique and explanation, thus providing a necessary, if not sufficient, structural basis for students to learn the skills of critique. One way of doing this is for the teacher to play the role of scaffolder of debate, summarising each student's view (So John, you are saying we need more evidence before we believe? Is that right?), and keeping track of the logic of the relationship of one student's view with another's (what you have just said, Jenny, seems to be in disagreement with what John said earlier. Is that right?). Notice that the teacher is not ruling that the summaries being made are definitive. The invitation to disconfirm or confirm the meanings reflected in the teacher's scaffolding function (Is that right? Have I understood you?) is an essential part of a process of keeping student views in their own 'ownership' and not making the talk structure yet another game of 'guess what teacher is thinking'. The teacher's authority in such teaching moves away from content authority to methodological authority, with teacher moves being aimed at eliciting clear reasons, adducing evidence, even if only anecdotal, and comparing and contrasting evidence and arguments, drawing out the logical, evidentiary and value structure of a problematic. In such a process, teachers must be careful not to be dismissive of the actual experience of students, which may be contrary to accepted views, especially of women students or students from cultural or political minorities (see Young, 1992).

In many countries where education has proceeded by traditional communication patterns there is now a desire, even an economic imperative, to move toward fostering the creativity and flexibility necessary to the 'information age'. This creativity and flexibility should not be feared if it is also disciplined by reference to evidence and argument. But it should also be recognised that once unleashed, this creativity cannot be confined to any narrow sphere of technical inventiveness. This broad capacity for learning will permeate all social learning and adaptation in a responsive and responsible movement towards managed change (see the review by Grundy in this volume).

The University of Sydney
Australia

REFERENCES

Benjamin, W.: 1969, 'The task of the translator', in H. Arendt (ed.), *Illuminations*, Schocken Books, New York.

Biesta, G.: 1995, 'Pragmatism as a pedagogy of communicative action', in J. Garrison (ed.), *The New Scholarship on Dewey*, Kluwer Academic, Dordrecht, 105–122.

Davidson, D.: 1984, *Inquiries into Truth and Interpretation*, The Clarendon Press, Oxford.

Dews, P. (ed.): 1986, *Autonomy and Solidarity; Interviews with Jurgen Habermas*, Verso, New York.

Habermas, J.: 1974, *Theory and Practice*, Heinemann, London.

Habermas, J.: 1981/2, *The Theory of Communicative Action*, Vol. 1, part 2, Heinemann, London.

Habermas, J.: 1982, 'Reply to my critics', in J. Thompson & D. Held (eds.), *Habermas: Critical Debates*, Macmillan, London.

Habermas, J.: 1991a, *Moral Consciousness and Communicative Action*, MIT Press, Cambridge, Ch. 2.

Habermas, J.: 1991b, *The Structural Transformation of the Public Sphere*, MIT Press, Cambridge (German 1961).

Held, D.: 1980, *Introduction to Critical Theory: Horkheimer to Habermas*, Hutchison, London.

Young, R.: 1992, *Critical Theory and Classroom Talk*, Multilingual Matters, Clevedon Avon.

Young, R.: 1996a, 'Decolonising education: The scope of educational thought', *Studies in Philosophy and Education* 15, 309–322.

Young, R.: 1996b, *Intercultural Communication: Pragmatics, Genealogy, Deconstruction*, Multilingual Matters, Clevedon Avon.

ELIZABETH MEASURES, CARSTEN QUELL
AND GORDON WELLS

A SOCIOCULTURAL PERSPECTIVE ON CLASSROOM DISCOURSE

In this review, we draw upon three strands of theory work that are currently being woven together in explorations of classroom discourse. The first strand concerns Vygotsky's theory of how social language serves to mediate the development of the individual's higher mental functions. The second is Bakhtin's work on heteroglossia and dialogism. And the third strand concerns Halliday's functional theory of language as social semiotic.

Central to all three strands is the recognition that language, in its different modes and genres, is the principle means developed by human beings both for coordinating joint activity and for co-constructing knowledge about the world. For this reason, all three place language at the heart of learning and teaching. By drawing learners into the discourses that direct, interpret and reflect upon the activities in which they engage together, teachers provide opportunities for learners to appropriate the culture's linguistic resources for meaning making and thereby to take over the 'theory' of experience that is encoded in the language; at the same time, by encouraging learners to take an active part in constructing new meanings, teachers can enable learners to become critical and creative actors and thinkers who also transform cultural practices and knowledge.

EARLY DEVELOPMENTS

Writing in the period following the Russian Revolution of 1917, Vygotsky set himself the task of reformulating psychology along Marxist lines. His aim was to create a discipline that would provide both a more adequate explanation of human behaviour and development and a basis for dealing with practical social and educational problems. Three interconnected themes run through his work: 1) the use of a genetic approach, i.e. one in which current behaviour is studied from the perspective of its historical development; 2) the social origin of individual intellectual abilities; 3) the role of tools, both material and semiotic, in mediating material and mental activity.

For Vygotsky, jointly undertaken goal-oriented activity was primary. At any time, a culture is constituted by the systems of social activity that have developed historically through the use and improvement of tools and practices to mediate humans' action and interaction in the world. Each individual enters the world with a biologically given potential; but the

B. Davies and D. Corson (eds), Encyclopedia of Language and Education,
Volume 3: Oral Discourse and Education, 21–29.
© *1997 Kluwer Academic Publishers. Printed in the Netherlands.*

development of a full human being is dependent on the 'appropriation', or taking over, of the tools and practices already in use in the culture. Within this general framework, Vygotsky focused specifically on the development of what he called the higher mental functions, such as voluntary memory and reasoning. These functions, he argued, are mediated by the use of semiotic tools, chief among which is language. Individual intellectual development is thus to be understood, in large part, in terms of the appropriation of the ways in which language is used in social interaction in the context of joint activity. This emphasis on social interaction as the basis for the development of the individual is captured in what he called 'the general genetic law of cultural development':

> Any function in the child's cultural development appears twice, or on two planes. First it appears on the social plane, and then on the psychological plane. First it appears between people as an interpsychological category, and then within the child as an intrapsychological category. ... Social relations or relations among people genetically underlie all higher functions and their relationships (Vygotsky, 1981, p. 203).

The importance of language in this framework becomes particularly clear in relation to what is probably Vygotsky's best-known claim, namely that instruction leads development (Vygotsky, 1978, 1987). Instruction relies heavily on linguistic interaction and, in order to be effective, it must focus, not on what the learner can already do, but on 'those functions that are in the process of maturing'. The defining limits for instruction to be productive are given by the zone of proximal development (zpd), that is to say, for any particular activity setting, the zone between what the learner can do unaided and the maximum that he or she can manage with assistance from a member of the culture more expert in the particular activity.

The emphasis on the social origins of the individual's language repertoire is further developed in the work of Bakhtin (1986). Like Vygotsky, he was influenced by Marxist ideas, although there is no evidence that they influenced each other's work. Language was represented by Bakhtin as a cluster of specific social practices which varies according to the group of people using the language and the functions for which they use it. This led Bakhtin to place the emphasis on situated discourse ('utterance') rather than on language as abstract system, and to argue that an utterance must be seen as both inherently dialogic and shaped in terms of a particular genre. Like other social practices, genres preexist the individual speaker, but they are first encountered by him or her in the concrete utterances of others. An individual's use of language, therefore, always involves 'heteroglossia':

> Our speech, that is, all our utterances (including creative works), is filled with others' words, varying degrees of otherness or varying degrees of "our-own-ness", varying degrees of awareness and detachment. These words of others carry with them their

own expression, their own evaluative tone, which we assimilate, rework, and re-accentuate (Bakhtin, 1986, p. 89).

The social nature of language is similarly emphasized in the work of Halliday (1978), as is the use of what Vygotsky called the genetic method. Taking a view somewhat similar to that of Bakhtin of the relationship between language system and language use (which he terms 'text'), Halliday has developed a theory of language which both provides a functional description of the language as system and, with the concept of register, relates the choices made from the system in particular texts to the semiotic characteristics of the situations and activities in which the texts are produced. All these features are very clearly evident in his work on language development and, in particular, in his proposal for a language-based theory of learning:

> When children learn language, they are not simply engaging in one kind of learning among many; rather, they are learning the foundations of learning itself. The distinctive characteristic of human learning is that it is a process of making meaning – a *semiotic* process; and the prototypical form of human semiotic is language. Hence the ontogenesis of language is at the same time the ontogenesis of learning (Halliday, 1993, p. 93).

RECENT AND CURRENT DEVELOPMENTS

As will be clear from the preceding summary, the theories originating with Vygotsky, Bakhtin and Halliday have much in common and, where they differ in emphasis, they can be argued to be complementary (Wells, 1994). However, as they originate in different disciplines, until recently it has tended to be one or other of the theories that has been developed in subsequent work rather than all three together.

As might be expected, considerable attention has been devoted to further specifying the relationship between the individual and the social, adumbrated in Vygotsky's general genetic law of cultural development. Here, the notion of a community of practice has gained considerable currency, with development being seen in terms of apprenticeship in the practices of the community. Lave and Wenger (1991) characterize learning as an integral aspect of 'legitimate peripheral participation' (LPP) in an ongoing community of practice; however, while they accept the need for novices to be provided with instruction, they place greater emphasis on opportunity to observe and to participate. A further feature of their work is the recognition of the wide range of social relations involved in any given practice as well as of the variety of contributions made by the individual participants to the collective activity. At the same time, LPP draws attention to the continuous spectrum of expertise, from newcomer to oldtimer, within a given community of practice, and to the tensions to which this inevitably gives rise. Indeed, for Engeström (1991), it is the attempt to resolve these and other tensions within a community of practice that provides the opportunity for cultural transformation.

The concept of participation is also central to Rogoff's (1990) account of early intellectual development, based on studies of child-rearing in different communities. Learning is here characterized as a 'cognitive apprenticeship', in which the incorporation of the individual into a community of practice is described in terms of the 'transformation of participation' that is reflected in the movement from peripheral to full participation. However, an important additional feature of this work is the demonstration that participation can take quite different forms in different communities. This latter theme has been explored by Gee (1992), but with a greater emphasis on the ideological bases and political consequences of different discourses and on the implications of these for the formation of individual identity.

Given this diversity in modes of participation, it must be assumed that a comparable diversity is to be expected in the ways in which learners may receive assistance in their zones of proximal development. To date, however, most work employing this concept has been carried out in Western cultures and has focused, in particular, on learning and teaching in classrooms. Tharp and Gallimore (1988), for example, use the notion of 'assisting performance in the zone of proximal development' to characterize responsive teaching, which they contrast with the time-honoured but, in their view, ineffective pre-formulated 'recitation script'. To replace the latter, they have developed a mode of pedagogical interaction that they call 'instructional conversation' and used the same concept of assisting performance to help teachers in a variety of non-mainstream communities to master this method of assisting children to become literate.

However, there are two aspects of their work that are of particular importance in extending thinking about the zpd. First, in highlighting the shift that takes place from other-control to self-control in the course of learning in the zpd, they draw attention to the active stance of the learner as she increasingly engages in 'self-regulation', and underline the importance of responsibility for the task being progressively transferred from the more competent 'other' to the learner. Second, in their work with teachers, they demonstrate that assisted performance is appropriate for adults as well as children, with the result that it is now generally accepted that the concept of the zpd can apply to learning at any age. Indeed, based on this assumption, a variety of collaborative action research projects are currently ongoing, in which teachers and researchers learn with and from each other as, together, they attempt to improve practice and increase their understanding of the underlying principles.

Closely related to Tharp and Gallimore's interpretation of the zpd as assisted performance is Bruner's concept of 'scaffolding' (Wood, Bruner & Ross, 1976), which has been used as the rationale for a number of educational interventions, most notably 'reciprocal teaching' (Palincsar & Brown, 1984). In fact, as Mercer (1995) argues, the concept of scaffolding can be relevant in a wide range of classroom activities in which the teacher's aim is not only to assist performance on the current task but to do so in such a way that, over time, the responsibility for the task is transferred to the students (see the review by Mercer in this volume).

Assistance does not always have to come from the teacher, however; as Vygotsky (1978) made clear, it can also be provided by peers. Indeed, as has become increasingly evident, collaborative activity in the classroom has the potential to provide for multiple zones of proximal development and, through group discussion, to create opportunities for the distribution of ideas and expertise within the group (Cazden, 1988; Forman & McPhail, 1993). This idea is taken one step further in current attempts to recast the classroom as a community of learners (Brown & Campione, 1994) or inquirers (Wells & Chang-Wells, 1992), in which the responsibility for the construction of knowledge is shared among all participants. Here, students assume an active role in formulating the topics and questions to be addressed and the teacher provides assistance by modeling and guiding specific forms of inquiry.

A similar broadening of the notion of the learning community underlies the work of Moll and colleagues (Moll & Greenberg, 1990) with working class Hispanic children and their families in Arizona. Starting with the premise that these children's homes have valuable forms of expertise of their own, that are learned and taught in the context of practical activities in the community, the researchers have worked with teachers to describe these 'funds of knowledge' so that they may become a resource that mediates learning in the classroom, by both children and adults. An important feature of this work is that, in integrating contexts of knowledge production that exist outside of schools with those of the classroom, they point up the value of differing kinds of expertise and emphasize their complementarity.

In all these extensions of Vygotsky's seminal ideas, several key themes stand out. First is a working out of the theoretical implications of the mutually constitutive, dialectical relationship between individual and society. A second common theme stems from the growing recognition of the interdependence of cognitive, affective and social factors in learning. Both lead to the practical emphasis on the centrality of community, on collaborative activity and on the valuing of diversity of participation. For productive joint activity is, simultaneously, the context for individual learning and identity formation, the source of multiple forms of guidance and assistance and, through the goal-directed interaction of diverse participants that is required, the arena in which existing practices and knowledge are critically evaluated and, as necessary, transformed.

EDUCATION AS DIALOGUE

If Vygotsky provides the general framework for this view of classroom as community, it is Bakhtin and Halliday who have provided the intellectual tools for the exploration of the discourses through which community is established and enacted. It is to them that we owe the conceptualization of education as dialogue (Brown & Campione, 1994; Wells & Chang-Wells, 1992).

Key concepts here are Bakhtin's (1986) emphasis on the speaker's response-orientation and his idea that each utterance is filled with echoes and reverberations of other utterances. As he convincingly argues, it is through the 'interanimation of voices' that new meanings are constructed. Equally important is the concept of genre as a socially situated communicative practice and therefore as a form of 'intermental' functioning (Wertsch & Toma, 1995). Together, these ideas do much to explain how cultural knowledge is created in joint activity and how, at the same time, it becomes differentially appropriated by the individual participants involved. Combined with a constructivist conceptualization of learning, Bakhtin's ideas have been influential in shaping current curricular reforms, particularly in the teaching of science and mathematics.

When it comes to the detailed investigation of classroom discourse, however, it is Halliday's contribution that is most evident, both directly in his work on social and functional variation in language use (Halliday & Hasan, 1989) and in the use that others have made of his linguistic theory of discourse. Basic to the latter is the premise that language provides for "the exchange of meanings" in specific interpersonal contexts (Halliday, 1978) and that, therefore, the appropriate unit of analysis is the exchange rather than the individual contribution.

In classrooms, the predominant spoken mode for the exchange of meanings – and, to date, the most intensively studied – is 'triadic dialogue' (Lemke 1990), which typically consists of three moves: initiation, response, and follow-up. As an exchange structure, the IRF can potentially perform a variety of functions, depending on the activity in which the participants are engaged and on the teacher's "philosophy" of education. Though criticized for the extent to which it frequently limits student participation (Lemke, 1990), the manner in which the moves involve demanding, giving and validating information can be argued to be central to the notion of teaching and learning as a reciprocal process (Newman, Griffin & Cole, 1989; Halliday, 1993). Moreover, when used dialogically, the F-move provides opportunities for the guided construction of knowledge, as the teacher evaluates, extends and contingently responds in ways which provide for the assisted performance of students (Wells, 1996).

FUTURE DIRECTIONS

Although, as argued in the introduction, the theories of Vygotsky, Bakhtin and Halliday are in many ways complementary, most of the work reviewed here has been based on one, or at most two, of these theories. Recently, however, there have been attempts to bring them together within the framework of activity theory (Leont'ev, 1981), which itself is derived from Vygotsky's theory of the primacy of joint activity. Emphasizing the tool-like mediating function of discourse in the operationalization of the activities and tasks through which the curriculum is enacted, this work draws on Hallidayan concepts of register and genre, as well as on Bakhtinian notions of heteropraxis and the heterogeneity of verbal thinking (Wertsch, 1991), in order to reconceptualize the relationship between context, activity and discourse (Orsolini & Pontecorvo, 1992; Wells, 1996). In this model, the 'text' jointly constructed on any occasion is seen as arising from the participants' selection from the language tool-kit of a discourse genre that is appropriate to the situational conditions and to the goal(s) of the activity. However, since goals and conditions are themselves influenced by the emerging text, the selection of genre must be seen, not as a fixed choice, but as an ongoing, dynamic process of negotiation.

While much research has centered on linguistic modes of meaning-making, Vygotsky's notion of psychological tools includes other semiotic systems. A developing area of interest is in the ways in which different semiotic systems interact in the mediation of joint activity in the classroom. Here Lemke's (1995) distinction between 'typological' and 'topological' forms of semiosis is likely to become increasingly important. On the same basis, the hegemony of written text seems likely to be increasingly challenged (Smagorinsky, 1995), as efforts are made to promote learning through the use of nonlinguistic sign systems (e.g. dance, art or design), so that students have more opportunities to express and develop their conceptual understanding.

To date, the theories discussed here have been most influential with respect to research and practice in the field of 'mainstream' education. However, this is changing as these theories are brought to bear on 'difference' of various kinds. A good example is to be seen in the changes that are taking place in research on second language acquisition, where reconceptualizations are taking place similar to those described in the opening paragraph of this review (Coughlan, 1995; Lantolf & Appel, 1994). Here, as in most of the areas reviewed, the influence is two-way: While the theories developed by Vygotsky, Bakhtin and Halliday continue to provide new and insightful ways of addressing issues of educational practice, the resulting field-based work, in turn, provides an opportunity to test and

develop the theoretical framework. But then, such a dialectical relationship between theory and practice is exactly what all three theorists would
advocate.

Ontario Institute for Studies in Education
University of Toronto, Canada

REFERENCES

Bakhtin, M.M.: 1986, *Speech Genres and Other Late Essays* (Trans. Y. McGee), University
of Texas Press, Austin TX.
Brown, A.L. & Campione, J.C.: 1994, 'Guided discovery in a community of learners', in
K. McGilly (ed.), *Classroom Lessons: Integrating Cognitive Theory and Classroom
Practice*, MIT Press/Bradford Books, Cambridge MA, 229–270.
Cazden, C.: 1988, *Classroom Discourse*, Heinemann, Portsmouth NH.
Coughlan, P.J.: 1995, 'Sociocultural theory, second language discourse, and teaching: An
interview with James Lantolf', *Issues in Applied Linguistics* 6(2), 137–145.
Engeström, Y.: 1991, '*Non scolae sed vitae discimus:* Toward overcoming the encapsula-
tion of school learning', *Learning and Instruction* 1, 243–259.
Forman, E.A. & McPhail, J.: 1993, 'Vygotskian perspectives on children's collaborative
problem-solving activities', in E.A. Forman, N. Minick & C.A. Stone (eds.), *Contexts
for Learning*: Oxford University Press, New York.
Gee, J.P.: 1992, *The Social Mind: Language, Ideology, and Social Practice*, Bergin &
Garvey, New York.
Halliday, M.A.K.: 1978, *Language as Social Semiotic: The social Interpretation of Lan-
guage and Meaning*, Arnold, London.
Halliday, M.A.K.: 1993, 'Towards a language-based theory of learning', *Linguistics and
Education* 5, 93–116.
Halliday, M.A.K. & Hasan, R.: 1989, *Language, Context and Text: A Social Semiotic
Perspective*, Oxford University Press, Oxford.
Lantolf, J. P. & Appel, G.: 1994, 'Theoretical framework: An introduction to Vygotskian
approaches to second language research', in J.P. Lantolf & G. Appel (eds.), *Vygotskian
Approaches to Second Language Research*, Ablex, Norwood NJ, 1–31.
Lave, J. & Wenger, E.: 1991, *Situated Learning: Legitimate Peripheral Participation*,
Cambridge University Press, New York.
Leont'ev, A.N.: 1981, 'The problem of activity in psychology', in J.V. Wertsch (ed.), *The
Concept of Activity in Soviet Psychology*, Sharpe, Armonk NY, 37–71.
Lemke, J.L.: 1990, *Talking Science; Language, Learning and Values*, Ablex, Norwood NJ.
Lemke, J.L.: 1995, *Textual Politics: Discourse and Social Dynamics*, Taylor & Francis,
Bristol PA.
Mercer, N.: 1995, *The Guided Construction of Knowledge*, Multilingual Matters, Clevedon,
UK.
Moll, L.C. & Greenberg, J.: 1990, 'Creating zones of possibilities: Combining social
contexts for instruction', in L.C. Moll (ed.), *Vygotsky and Education: Instructional
Implications and Applications of Sociohistorical Psychology*. Cambridge University
Press, New York, 319–348.
Newman, D., Griffin, P. & Cole, M.: 1989, *The Construction Zone: Working for Cognitive
Change in School*, Cambridge University Press, New York.
Orsolini, M. & Pontecorvo, C.: 1992, 'Children's talk in classroom discussions', *Cognition
and Instruction* 9(2), 113–136.
Palincsar, A.S. & Brown, A.L.: 1984, 'Reciprocal teaching of comprehension fostering
and comprehension monitoring', *Cognition and Instruction* 1(2), 117–175.

Rogoff, B.: 1990, *Apprenticeship in Thinking: Cognitive Development in Social Context*, Oxford University Press, New York.

Smagorinsky, P.: 1995, 'Constructing meaning in the disciplines: Reconceptualizing writing across the curriculum as composing across the curriculum', *American Journal of Education* 103, 160–184.

Tharp, R. & Gallimore, R.: 1988, *Rousing Minds to Life: Teaching and Learning in Social Contexts*, Cambridge University Press, New York.

Vygotsky, L.S.: 1978, *Mind in Society: The Development of Higher Psychological Processes* (M. Cole, V.J. Steiner, S. Scribner, & E. Souberman, eds.), Harvard University Press, Cambridge MA.

Vygotsky, L.S.: 1981, 'The genesis of higher mental functions', in J.V. Wertsch (ed.), *The Concept of Activity in Soviet Psychology*, Sharpe, Armonk NY, 144–188.

Vygotsky, L.S.: 1987, 'Thinking and speech', in R.W. Rieber & A.S. Carton (eds.), *The Collected Works of L.S. Vygotsky, Volume 1: Problems of General Psychology* (trans. N. Minick), Plenum, New York.

Wells, G.: 1994, 'The complementary contributions of Halliday and Vygotsky to a "Language-Based Theory of Learning" ', *Linguistics and Education* 6, 41–90.

Wells, G.: 1996, 'Using the tool-kit of discourse in the activity of learning and teaching', *Mind, Culture, and Activity* 3(2), 74–101.

Wells, G. & Chang-Wells, G.L.: 1992, *Constructing Knowledge Together: Classrooms as Centers of Inquiry and Literacy*, Heinemann, Portsmouth NH.

Wertsch, J.V.: 1991, *Voices of the Mind: A Sociocultural Approach to Mediated Action*, Harvard University Press, Cambridge MA.

Wertsch, J.V. & Toma, C.: 1995, 'Discourse and learning in the classroom: A sociocultural approach', in L.P. Steffe & J. Gale (eds.), *Constructivism in Education*, Lawrence Erlbaum, Hillsdale NJ, 159–174.

Wood, D., Bruner, J.S. & Ross, G.: 1976, 'The role of tutoring in problem solving', *Journal of Child Psychology and Psychiatry* 17, 89–100.

SHIRLEY GRUNDY

CHALLENGING AND CHANGING: COMMUNICATIVE COMPETENCE AND THE CLASSROOM

This review takes as its starting point the proposition that teachers and students together construct the curriculum of schools and classrooms. That is, the curriculum is not a 'product' imparted to students by teachers, it is a social practice, a dynamic event, which comes into existence as teachers and students interact in the activities associated with teaching and learning (Grundy, 1987). One of the implications of such a proposition is that when we think of curriculum change, we should not assume that students are merely the recipients of changes made by others. This dynamic view of curriculum construction implies that the curriculum can be formed, developed, and changed through the verbal interactions and exchanges of those engaged in the teaching/learning situation (students as well as teachers).

To claim that the curriculum is communicatively grounded, does not imply that it is simply the outcome of unrestricted classroom talk. Rather, the proposition explored is here that classroom talk through which an educative curriculum is constituted requires what Habermas (1984) calls "communicative competence". Essential to Habermas' (1984) notion of "communicative competence" is the requirement that communicative practices are grounded in rational argumentation based upon the demand for and provision of supporting evidence before claims are accepted. Moreover, "communicative competence" requires that the opportunity and capacity to demand supportive evidence and to challenge both assertions and evidence, should be equally distributed among communicating subjects. Communicative classroom practices which privilege reasoned argument and challenge by students as well as teachers are, therefore, important in the construction of the curriculum.

Clearly students and teachers have differential opportunities and abilities to mount challenges and support or defend arguments. Recent research which takes seriously the possibilities of opening up opportunities for students to challenge and thereby shape and change the curriculum is, therefore, explored. In doing so the review traces the threads of the tradition which has valued and advocated student voice in the construction of curriculum. This has been a substantial but diverse tradition which has sometimes been subject to severe and legitimate critique. This review, then, explores anew the positive possibilities of classroom talk as a form of curriculum construction.

B. Davies and D. Corson (eds), Encyclopedia of Language and Education,
Volume 3: Oral Discourse and Education, 31–41.
© *1997 Kluwer Academic Publishers. Printed in the Netherlands.*

EARLY DEVELOPMENTS

Classroom talk has long been recognised as the medium through which the 'hidden curriculum' (Jackson, 1968) is conveyed. The communicative practices of classrooms, such as the amount of talking by teachers as compared with students and the control of the talk by the teacher (directing who can talk and evaluating the spoken contributions), convey powerful messages to students about social power (Grundy, 1987). For instance, who is allowed to talk and who must listen in the classroom conveys messages about whose voices and, by implication, which persons, are of most and least worth. Early researchers (e.g. Sharp & Green, 1975) whose work was informed by Marxist insights, investigated the power dimensions of classroom talk in terms of social class. Many feminist theorists (e.g. Baker & Davies, 1987) have investigated ways in which gendered power relations are formed and reinforced through the patterns as well as the substance of classroom talk.

The focus of such research has been teacher/student talk, specifically the ways in which the teacher controls classroom talk, thereby conveying to students messages about their proper place and role in society. This is, for instance, the approach taken in Grundy's (1994) paper in which it is argued that the patterns of language used by the teacher, particularly the use of the personal pronoun and various other linguistic devices, signal inclusion/exclusion or approval/disapproval. These patterns of speech, it is argued, form a discernible sub-text about appropriate identity formation within what is ostensibly a history lesson.

Some strands of the research in the area of classroom talk have developed a focus specifically upon student talk. Curriculum theorists, such as Rudduck (1991) have investigated ways in which students may actively impede innovation, through digression or resistance talk. Researchers in the area of science education as well as learning theorists working from within the epistemological position of "constructivism" have explored the way in which talk in classrooms supports students as active constructors of knowledge, not simply passive receivers (see, for instance, Mercer, 1995, and his review in this volume). Moreover, some feminist writers have acknowledged that it is not only teachers who are engaged in the construction of the gendered curriculum. Davies' (1989) study of pre-school students' interaction patterns uncovered some of the ways in which students at a very young age act to produce gender relations through words and actions.

Studies such as these have highlighted some of the ways by which teachers and students exercise control over the talk of the classroom, and hence communicatively shape the curriculum. The implication of many such studies, however, is that the shape of the resulting curriculum which is constructed through classroom talk is a matter more for regret than celebration. While such research may contain valuable insights into what teachers might do to facilitate the construction of more positive curriculum events or to ameliorate the more detrimental effects of student resistance, suggestions of ways forward are largely made on the basis of offering counter practices to those which form the focus for the research.

It is argued below, however, that there are other possibilities for the active participation of students in the construction of the curriculum of the classroom. It is also argued that such active engagement by students as co-participants in the construction and control of talk is not simply an option for classrooms, it ought to be the foundation of classroom learning. The sort of classroom talk that is envisaged by such a claim is that which is implicit in Habermas' (1984) theory of "communicative competence".

MAJOR CONTRIBUTIONS

A considerable amount of useful theoretical work has been undertaken on the application of Habermasian critical theory to education and specifically the practice of teaching (Carr & Kemmis, 1983; Carr, 1995; Grundy, 1987). With the exception of some important work which will be explored later in this review (e.g. Young, 1989, 1992; Miedema, 1994) the application of the theory of communicative competence to student/teacher talk in classrooms is largely speculative.

As a critical theorist Habermas has constantly struggled with the propensity of modern technical reason to reduce all of human thought and action to the controllable and the predictable through the privileging of 'positivistic science' (Carr, 1995). The tradition of critical theory, particularly through Habermas' work has been

> to articulate a form of science in which the practical role of critical self-reflection and conscious human agency could be properly acknowledged and for which the rational empowerment of individuals could be a central aim (Carr, 1995, p. 113).

While Carr makes reference here to "individuals", critical rationality is not a matter of individual reason alone. Young (1992) notes that 'critical reason' is social not individual. 'Action cannot be truly critical, and thus rational, if it is rational for only one individual or one nation' (Young, 1992, p. 7). It would, of course, be possible to regard positivist reason as essentially collective in as much as scientific 'truths' must be generalisable to populations, not merely referent to single cases (individuals). This is not, however, the form of reason privileged by critical theory. Habermas is interested in a form of rationality which is communicatively based. Indeed, it is a form of rationality which derives its critical edge from the communicative demands of possible consensus and challenge. This is a form of communicative rationality grounded in community as well as communication. Young (1992, p. 7) contrasts individualistic with communicative forms of rationality:

> In the Western world [we] ... have been asking our questions [about knowledge] ... in the wrong order. We have been asking, as individual subjective consciousnesses: "How can I know that something ... is true?" ... Habermas takes the view that the question we should start with is: "How can members of a community come to an agreement that something is true?"

For critical theory, then, rationality is a matter of agreement among people; but not forced agreement. It must be agreement (or consensus) grounded in communicative practices and 'argumentative processes in which reasons are advanced, debated, and evaluated' (Benhabib, 1986, p. 241). The argumentative processes to which Benhabib refers are grounded in requirements that speakers defend the validity of their utterances:

> Acts of linguistic communication, Habermas argues, presuppose four validity-claims: that what we say is comprehensible, that it is true, that it is right ... and that it is a sincere ... expression of the speaker's feelings (Outhwaite, 1994, p. 40).

The demand that the 'force of the better argument alone' should be the rational basis of argument is not a demand for objective, cognitive persuasion. Rather, consensus is to be grounded in the obligations of speaking subjects to engage in speech acts which are susceptible of empirical verification, are comprehensible to the listening subjects, are appropriate within the context, according to agreed social norms, and are sincerely uttered. Consensus is not simply a matter of the obligations of the speaker to meet the validity criteria. Listening subjects have both the right and the obligation to challenge speakers to provide evidence in support of the claims they make. Thus it is that critical reason privileges challenge. Communicative competence is evidenced by speech situations in which speakers have increasingly equal chances to demand and to supply evidence to support the validity claims in all of the domains of critical reason (comprehensibility, truth, appropriateness and authenticity).

Much of the literature dealing with the implications for education of the theory of communicative competence explores the role of the teacher as an active agent in curriculum construction rather than merely the technician who transfers objective knowledge to passive recipients. However, if school education is to foster democratic values and provide personally and socially worthwhile learning experiences, then classroom pedagogy needs to be grounded in communicative principles and practices which foster open inquiry and challenge among students and between students and teachers.

THE CRITICAL PEDAGOGY TRADITION

As indicated above, there is not a substantial body of English language research specifically addressing or informed by the Habermasian theory of communicative competence as reflected in classroom discourse. There is, however, a critical pedagogy tradition which is concerned to advocate and to explore the possibilities of 'liberatory' discourses in schools and classrooms. These liberatory discourses are grounded in communicative practices which open up the possibilities of challenge by students. The work of educators and researchers within this tradition has been informed by an ethic which respects, indeed privileges, the rights to speak, especially of those whose voices are often silenced by authority (Aronowitz & Giroux, 1991). As noted previously, some of these researchers are critical curriculum constructivists and others are feminist theoreticians and practitioners. Mention needs to be made of this work, for it is within this strand of research that it is possible to discern some possibilities for the communicative competence principles to be enacted in classrooms.

In the early seventies Stenhouse headed a team responsible for the development and introduction of the Humanities Curriculum Project (HCP). Central to the HCP was the idea of the 'impartial chairperson' who facilitated discussion and debate of contentious social issues, requiring that dialogue be grounded in the provision and interpretation of evidence (Stenhouse, 1975). In a recent reflective re-visiting of the work undertaken as part of the HCP, Rudduck (1991) related an excerpt of classroom talk in which a student overtly critiqued the role the teacher was playing in the discussion. The student claimed that she had abandoned the neutral chairing role and had become a participant in the conversation. Addressing his fellow students 'Jim' challenged them to redistribute communicative power among themselves, rather than handing it over to the 'chair':

> Jim: Oi, you lot, instead of talking to Miss, talk between us lot. Everything you say, you say to Miss. Why not talk between us lot? (Rudduck, 1991, p. 64).

Rudduck notes 'from that point we made progress' for only then did students begin to shape and control the curriculum.

The HCP did not make overt connections to critical theory and certainly was not an attempt to 'implement' Habermas' theory of communicative competence. However, it is possible to discern some of the central principles of communicative pedagogy within the conceptualisation and realisation of the HCP. Communication, for instance, was privileged as the medium of learning. This was not instructive talk from teacher to students but communication among all participants with the teacher increasingly divesting herself of power to control the talk. The criteria for the judgement of the validity of an argument in the HCP related to the presentation, interpretation and challenging of evidence. Arguments needed to be supported and could be challenged on the basis of evidence. These communicative requirements connect with the Habermasian emphasis upon the 'force of the better argument alone' and privilege 'challenge' in the construction of knowledge and of the curriculum. The HCP, therefore, provides an early example of students having the opportunity to 'challenge and change' the curriculum.

The tradition of 'radical pedagogy' or 'liberating education' has continued to value the active participation of students in the construction of the curriculum and schooling (see, for instance, McLaren, 1989; Freire & Shor, 1987). Within this tradition the idea of student 'voice' has been crucial. 'A student's voice', McLaren (1989, p. 230) wrote, 'is not a reflection of the world as much as it is a constitutive force that both mediates and shapes reality within historically constructed practices and relationships of power'.

This tradition, then, which broadly identifies itself with critical theory (although not necessarily overtly with Habermas' work), recognises the power of the communicative practices of the school and the classroom to shape the curriculum. Within this tradition, however, although the possibilities for student voice to 'mediate and shape reality' are recognised, it is also conceded that often the only challenges that students are able to mount within schools, and hence, the only way that the communicative practice of challenge is able to shape the curriculum is through the challenge of resistance. This is what Freire and Shor (1987) described as the 'culture of sabotage'.

Recently, however, a number of educational writers have explored the positive possibilities of Habermas' theory of communicative competence for schooling. This is work that takes seriously the potential for students to be active constructors of the curriculum through a restructuring of the power dynamics of classroom talk, but also explores the limitations of these possibilities. Young's (1989, 1992) work is of particular significance here. In his 1992 work, Young explicitly focuses upon the implications of the theory of communicative competence for the classroom. Building upon Millar's (1986) work, which identifies the capacity of children to enter into moral argument, demanding and supplying justificatory utterances at an early age, Young (1992, p. 25) argues that

> children ... come as active co-creators of the communicative
> context which is itself the inferential basis for understanding or
> misunderstanding the teacher's utterances.

Utilising the well developed methodology of analysis of transcribed classroom talk, Young demonstrates how some teachers are able to enter into classroom dialogue in ways that privilege collaboration among teacher and students in the evaluation and analysis of statements in which students as well as teachers are invited to evaluate responses and to ask probing or clarifying questions. Young (1992, p. 118) notes:

There is still talk asymmetry in this classroom, but it is a different asymmetry from that in the dominant classroom type. This asymmetry is complementary, since the rights of pupils as rational interlocutors are preserved, while the teacher's superior knowledge and rational skills are still able to be employed on the pupils' behalf in the fostering of the inquiry of the class. Complementary asymmetry of this kind is educational teaching.

The asymmetry of the educational relationship between teacher and pupil remains a problem for the application of Habermas' theory of communicative competence to classroom talk. For Miedema (1994), the problem revolves around a gap in Habermas' (1984) analysis of forms of action. Miedema claims that, as well as the other forms of human action which Habermas discusses (Grundy, 1987), we also need to recognise a form of human action which he calls 'pedagogical action'. While such action is asymmetrical because of the different ways the potential to mount and defend arguments is available to students and teachers, Miedema claims that 'pedagogical action ... anticipate[s] the situation in which the child will become an adult' and communicative action becomes more of a possibility.

Pedagogical action, in Miedema's terms is not simply a process of training in communicative action. It is itself an authentic set of communicative practices which take seriously the power dimensions of communicative situations in classrooms and respect the demands for all participants in the speech act to meet the validity criteria of truth, appropriateness and authenticity. It is the teacher's responsibility, however, to recognise both the structural and social asymmetry of classroom talk, make the process of communicative action explicit to students and open up spaces where challenge becomes a generative process of curriculum formation within the class. Although not explicitly grounded in the Habermasian theory of communicative competence, the communicative practices which Chas engaged in as she attempted to explore alternative discursive possibilities with students (Davies, 1993) are similar to the 'pedagogical action' which Miedema describes.

PROBLEMS AND DIFFICULTIES

This tradition of critical curriculum theorizing and analysis as well as the possibilities for classrooms to be places in which students have genuine opportunities to speak and be heard, has come under severe and appropriate critique from a number of feminist scholars. A useful collection of these critiques is to be found in Luke and Gore (1992). The chapters by Orner (1992) and Ellsworth (1992) are particularly pertinent. Lather (1991b) and Fraser (1989) present similarly cogent critiques of the critical pedagogy tradition and its assumptions. The feminist critiques, often informed by poststructuralist perspectives, point to the largely male authorship of the critical theory and critical pedagogy traditions, to the way in which gendered silences and power relations are often glossed in the analysis of classroom talk and to the masculinist foundations of the rationality demands of Habermas' 'ideal speech situation'.

These criticisms are well founded. There are obvious silences around the issue of gender in the analysis of classroom talk within these traditions. The power dimensions of the analysis are often those of the teacher/student, where 'teacher' is the 'ungendered' exerciser of speech/power and 'student' the similarly 'ungendered' oppressed or resisting subject. Within critical and liberatory pedagogy traditions the gendered dynamics of classroom talk is often ignored. Treating 'teachers' and 'students' as structural categories ignores the insight that speech and silence, resistance and compliance are sometimes as strongly determined by gender as by status. (See, for instance Jess' analysis of the gendered talk of students engaged in free play in her kindergarten class, in Davies, 1996.)

Feminist critics, such as Ellsworth (1992), have voiced suspicion of the form of rationality which underpins the communicative ideals of the critical theorists. She claims:

> Rational argument has operated in ways that set up as its opposite an irrational Other, which has been understood historically as the province of women and other [sic] exotic Others. In schools, rational deliberation, reflection, and consideration of all viewpoints has become a vehicle for regulating conflict and power to speak (Ellsworth, 1992, p. 94).

While one response to such pertinent and persuasive critiques may be to give up on communicative rationality, another lies in the exploration of possibilities for moving beyond the regulatory effects of communicative practices in classrooms. Communicative practices devoid of challenge and unmediated by the validity obligations of comprehensibility, truth, appropriateness and authenticity will be constitutive of a compliant student body and an authoritative curriculum. The question that arises, therefore, is whether it is possible to create forms of classroom practice which recognise the capacity of students to be active constructors of the curriculum, but of a curriculum which genuinely empowers students to be active participants in and shapers of their own learning *as well as* that of others.

FUTURE DIRECTIONS

It is clearly important that ethnographic and deconstructive work (Lather, 1991a) around the issue of the discursive power patterns of classroom talk continues. It is the argument of this review, however, that it is also important that the democratic and emancipatory potential of talk in classrooms also continues to be an area for research and action.

It is increasingly being recognised that classroom talk cannot be separated from the organisational and structural talk of the school. Corson (1996), for instance, explores 'emancipatory discursive practices' in schools, providing what he sees as 'a dire, disturbing, and uncomfortable description' of the essentially oppressive way that the discourses of management and administration operate, both in schools and in classrooms. Corson argues that what is needed is a form of participatory research which will be generative of critical reflection by teachers, students and academic researchers upon the discursive practices which shape and through which they shape the world of learning in the classroom.

Clearly we need to understand the ways in which classroom discourses (those of students and teachers as structurally positioned, but also as located within class, gender, ethnic, racial and sexual histories) and school discourses (the discourses of institutionalised power) operate to reproduce the dominant power relations of society and schooling (See Davies, 1996). However, experiments in emanacipatory discourses are also needed. As noted above, Miedema (1994) advocates the development of a form of pedagogical action which is grounded in communicative practices susceptible of critique on the basis of the four validity claims (truth, comprehensibility, appropriateness and authenticity). Such a form of pedagogy has much in common with the approach to 'creating spaces for reconstructing knowledge [through] feminist pedagogy', advocated by Thompson and Gitlin (1995). The feminist pedagogy advocated by Thompson and Gitlin is also grounded in communicative practices ("conversation as method"). These communicative practices privilege mutuality and collaboration ("we" relations). They involve the notion of challenge by advocating 'experimental shifts in the relationships'. These experimental shifts open up possibilities for restructuring knowledge since the way to understand reality is to change it (p. 138). Their approach shares with the theory of communicative competence also the emphasis upon appropriateness. Within the feminist pedagogy advocated, however, appropriateness is problematised. Thus, the conversational method criteria of Thompson and Gitlin blend well with the communicative competence validity criteria of Habermas, except for the insistence of the latter upon the consensually determined criteria of 'truth'.

These forms of feminist and communicative pedagogy will open up possibilities for classroom discourse that may enable teachers and students to move beyond the fundamentally rationalist approach of the Humanities Curriculum Project (with its emphasis upon evidence-based argument). This recent work suggests that the questions that need to be explored in greater depth are as follows:

What happens to the curriculum of a classroom:

- when relations of power among speakers begin to alter so that the relationships of the speaking subjects themselves become the subject of investigation?

- where the appropriateness of what is said by and to whom as well as the sincerity of the speaking subject become matters for critical attention?

- when the comprehensibility of utterances to all participants in the situation becomes a matter of concern to all participants in relation to their own utterances, to their own understanding of the utterances of others, and also to the possibilities of understanding by others of the utterances of others?

- when speakers can be challenged on the grounds of the authenticity and sincerity of their utterances?

- when students have greater access to information (for example, via the Internet) so that the teacher's role as provider of evidence to support claims to truth about curriculum content can be challenged?

While we can speculate upon the way that the curriculum of classrooms could be enriched through the adoption of such communicative practices, it is clear that the 'ideal speech situation', which is implicit in the vision of the classroom provoked by the above questions, is not entirely realizable because of the asymmetrical power relations between teachers and students. What is possible, however, is to understand the classroom as a site of developing communicative competence; a site in which increasingly students can engage in the process of curriculum construction and curriculum change as they learn and experience the possibilities and the lived realities of challenge.

Murdoch University
Australia

REFERENCES

Aronowitz, S. & Giroux, H.: 1991, *Postmodern Education: Politics, Culture, and Social Criticism*, University of Minnesota Press, Minneapolis.

Baker, C. & Davies, B.: 1987, 'A lesson in sex roles', *Gender and Education* 1(1), 59–76.

Benhabib, S.: 1986, *Critique, Norm, and Utopia: A Study of the Foundations of Critical Theory*, Columbia University Press, New York.

Carr, W.: 1995, *For Education: Towards Critical Educational Inquiry*, Open University Press, Buckingham.

Carr, W. & Kemmis, S.: 1983, *Becoming Critical: Knowing through Action Research*, Falmer Press, London.

Corson, D.: 1996, 'Emancipatory discursive practices', in K. Leithwood, P. Hallinger, J. Chapman & D. Corson (eds.), *International Handbook for Educational Leadership and Administration*, Kluwer, Dordrecht.

Davies, B.: 1989, *Frogs and Snails and Feminist Tales: Preschool Children and Gender*, Allen and Unwin, Sydney.

Davies, B.: 1993, *Shards of Glass: Children Reading & Writing Beyond Gendered Identities*, Allen and Unwin, Sydney.

Davies, B.: 1996, *Power/Knowledge/Desire. Changing School Organisation and Management Practices*, Department of Employment, Education, Training and Youth Affairs, Canberra.

Ellsworth, E.: 1992, 'Why Doesn't this Feel Empowering? Working Through the Repressive Myths of Critical Pedagogy', in C. Luke & J. Gore (eds.), *Feminisms and Critical Pedagogy*, Routledge, New York.

Fraser, N.: 1989, *Unruly Practices: Power, Discourse and Gender in Contemporary Social Theory*, University of Minnesota Press, Minneapolis.

Freire, P. & Shor, I.: 1987, *A Pedagogy for Liberation: Dialogues on Transforming Education*, Macmillan, London.

Grundy, S.: 1987, *Curriculum: Product of Praxis?* Falmer Press, London.

Grundy, S.: 1994, 'Being and becoming an Australian: Classroom discourse and the construction of identity', *Discourse: The Australian Journal of Educational Studies* 15(1), 16–31.

Habermas, J.: 1984, *The Theory of Communicative Action*, Beacon Press, Boston.

Jackson, P.: 1968, *Life in Classrooms*, Holt, Rinehart and Winston, New York.

Lather, P.: 1991a, 'Deconstructing/deconstructive inquiry: The politics of knowing and being known', *Educational Theory* 41(2), 153–173.

Lather, P.: 1991b, *Getting Smart: Feminist Research and Pedagogy with/in the Postmodern*, Routledge, New York.

Luke, C. & Gore, J. (ed.): 1992, *Feminisms and Critical Pedagogy*, Routledge, New York.

McLaren, P.: 1989, *Life in Schools: An Introduction to Critical Pedagogy in the Foundations of Education*, Longman, New York.

Mercer, N.: 1995, *The Guided Construction of Knowledge: Talk amongst teachers and learners*, Multilingual Matters Ltd, Clevedon.

Miedema, S.: 1994, 'The Relevance for pedagogy of Habermas' theory of communicative competence', *Interchange* 25(2), 195–206.

Millar, M.: 1986, 'Leaning how to contradict and still pursue a common end – the ontogenesis of moral argumentation', in J. Cool-Gumperz et al. (eds.), *Children's Worlds and Children's Language*, Mouton de Gruyter, Berlin.

Orner, M.: 1992, 'Interrupting the calls for student voice in 'Liberatory' education: A feminist poststructuralist perspective', in C. Luke & J. Gore (eds.), *Feminisms and Critical Pedagogy*, Routledge, New York.

Outhwaite, W.: 1994, *Habermas: A Critical Introduction*, Polity Press, Cambridge.

Rudduck, J.: 1991, *Innovation and Change*, Open University Press, Milton Keynes.

Sharp, R. & Green, A.: 1975, *Education and Social Control: A Study in Progressive Primary Education*, Routledge and Kegan Paul, London.

Stenhouse, L.: 1975, *An Introduction to Curriculum Research and Development*, Heinemann, London.

Thompson, A. & Gitlin, A.: 1995, 'Creating spaces for reconstructing knowledge in feminist pedagogy', *Educational Theory* 45(2), 125–150.

Young, R.: 1989, *A Critical Theory of Education: Habermas and our Children's Future*, Harvester Wheatsheaf, London.

Young, R.: 1992, *Critical Theory and Classroom Talk*, Multilingual Matters, Clevedon Avon.

CAROLYN BAKER

ETHNOMETHODOLOGICAL STUDIES OF TALK IN EDUCATIONAL SETTINGS

Ethnomethodological studies of talk in educational settings are concerned with the explication of the 'routine grounds of everyday life' (Garfinkel, 1967) in classrooms, staff meetings, diagnostic and testing sessions, parent-teacher interviews, and other settings in which the practical work of school-ing goes on. These studies are concerned to show, through careful and detailed analyses of actual interactive events, how members in these set-tings use talk and other resources to accomplish the phenomena and objects that are otherwise treated as givens in social science and education. Eth-nomethodological studies examine how members in educational studies achieve as orderly, recognisable and accountable such matters as lessons, the institutional categories of "teachers" and "students", what counts as reading, classroom order or disorder, teacher authority, power, formality, student ability, and a host of other presences in school life.

EARLY DEVELOPMENTS

The range of works that comprise the current field of ethnomethodology in education draw primarily on Garfinkel's (1967) studies of practical reason-ing and practical action, and Sacks' 1968–1974 lectures on conversation (Sacks, 1992) in which we find the beginnings of what are now known as conversation analysis and membership categorisation analysis.

The title of one of Sacks' earliest published pieces, "An Initial Inves-tigation of the Usability of Conversational Data for Doing Sociology" (1972) marks quite clearly the difference between ethnomethodological approaches to talk and those arising from other disciplines such as ling-uistics or communication or critical theory. The study of talk, and more specifically, and always, talk-in-interaction (Schegloff, 1988), and even more precisely, the study of the *organisation* of talk-in-interaction, is a specialised means of studying social action and social order.

From ethnomethodology comes a distinct set of interests in how mem-bers of settings assemble those settings and the objects and people in them to be just what we ordinarily take them to be. Talk is a primary resource for doing this work. Conversation analysis, created and developed using con-versational materials as data, provides a set of precision tools for showing how talk-in-interaction is organised, how it is carried out.

B. Davies and D. Corson (eds), Encyclopedia of Language and Education,
Volume 3: Oral Discourse and Education, 43–52.
© *1997 Kluwer Academic Publishers. Printed in the Netherlands.*

These approaches to the study of talk (meaning throughout this review, the organisation of talk-in-interaction) and social life have had extensive application in education. Before proceeding to a review of early and more recent work relevant to language and education, I set out below some of the distinctive features of ethnomethodological and conversation-analytic work:

1. Ethnomethodological analyses begin by studying actual instances of talk-in-interaction rather than beginning with a theory or theoretical position on education or learning into which "talk" is fitted.

2. The detailed transcripts that are made from recordings are aids to analysis of the recorded materials. Analytic claims are referred continuously to the details of the recorded talk.

3. Ethnomethodological analyses are concerned to reveal the methods people use to organise their talk such that it is orderly and accountable. The point of ethnomethodological analysis is explication, not explanation. Analyses are undertaken to saturate questions of "how" particular kinds of work gets done in the organisation of talk; analysts may then wish to proceed to answer the "why" questions (Silverman & Gubrium, 1994).

4. Ethnomethodological analyses are not motivated by a belief in some particular theory of education or communication. Nor is the concern to posit or achieve an ideal or better form of practice. Although ethnomethodological analyses can inform consideration of many educational matters, the point of the analysis is not prescriptive.

5. Ethnomethodological analyses treat talk as social activity, not as "language use". The concern is with what people do with words, how and when in an ongoing course of interaction, not with what words they use. While people necessarily use language in order to talk, what they take themselves to be doing is talking about something or trying to accomplish something. Constructions such as "language users" are linguists' and educators' categories, not members' categories. Members for the most part take themselves to be doing social-interactional things with words, such as questioning or answering, complaining, agreeing, proposing and so on; and on another level of abstraction, to be teaching or learning or communicating.

6. Talk is understood to be systematically organised by speakers and hearers in a setting. Talk is done by speakers with reference to some system of rules for turn-taking (Sacks, Schegloff & Jefferson, 1974) which varies from informal, conversational encounters to different kinds of institutional encounters (Heritage, 1984). The "systematics" of talk are both context-free and context-dependent: speakers' methods for gaining the floor or doing disagreement look similar across settings, while speakers design their turns with sensitivity to the local circumstances of hearer(s), prior turns, task(s) and setting. Ethnomethodological and conversation analytic studies are therefore able to find the "institutionality" in talk. This is an

absolutely consequential matter in view of many proposals within educational discourse to change patterns of talk. Talk and social organisation are intimately related.

7. In ethnomethodological studies, speakers and hearers (including children) are treated as competent analysts of ongoing talk *as social activity*. The sequential analysis of turns at talk shows how speakers orient to prior turns and how they foreshadow subsequent turns, and by extension courses of conversation.

8. Ethnomethodological analyses of talk recognise that talk is part of, and reflexively constitutive of, the setting itself. From within ethnomethodological analyses of talk, "context" is therefore understood to be produced by the talk as much as the talk is designed for the "context". In addition, who we are talking as, situationally speaking, and what we are up to, speaking that way, can change within the course of talk in formal and informal settings (Zimmerman, 1992).

MAJOR CONTRIBUTIONS

Early work applying principles of ethnomethodology to language in educational settings includes the volume *Language Use and School Performance* (Cicourel et al., 1974) which contains a series of studies of the practical accomplishment of such educational matters as testing, placement practices and classroom lessons. The central question addressed was how school personnel formulate children's abilities and progress in the course of the routine activities of schooling. Hester (1992) studied the 'social construction of educational subnormality' in professional talk. McDermott's (1976, 1977) work on group reading sessions, Heap's (1979) work on the organisation of preference in a reading lesson and Mehan's (1979) detailed analysis of a corpus of teacher-led lessons were influential early works on classroom talk. Mehan showed that student competence in lessons consisted of both form and content, specifically, fitting their talk into the teacher-led Initiation-Reply-Evaluation sequence. McHoul (1978) drew on Sacks, Schegloff & Jefferson (1974) to study how the "sense of formality" of classroom talk was attributable to specific differences from informal conversation in terms of gaps, pauses, and the organisation of speakership. Payne (1976) showed how through the concerted work of teacher and students a lesson is "made to happen" as a lesson. Work by MacKay (1974) and Speier (1976) opened the field of child-adult talk and children's play talk to ethnomethodological analysis.

In addition to these particular studies, possibilities and applications of ethnomethodology as a means of investigating differently a wide range of topics within education were addressed in works by Payne & Cuff (1982), Hester (1985), Heyman (1986), and Heap (1985). To a large extent these descriptions of ethnomethodology offered grounds for changing the questions that could be asked about educational settings, objects and phenomena.

From the beginning, ethnomethodological studies presented challenges to the naturalisms and normalisations with which the work of teaching, testing, assessment and decision-making in schools is routinely done and described. From a "commonsense" (largely psychological) perspective on schooling, there are a number of a priori assumptions that ground and govern educational thought and practice. Among these are a priori assumptions about abilities and their distribution, about children and learning and their essential qualities, and about how these can/should be used to make decisions about students, grades, grading procedures, and how these can be found to be rational and logical procedures.

There has been considerable further work in four areas of the ethnomethodology of education that exemplify the interest taken in the organisation of talk. These areas are: studies of classroom talk; studies of classroom knowledge production, studies of classroom literacy; and studies of administrative and meeting talk (see the review by Heap in Volume 8).

Studies of classroom talk and interaction

A large and growing corpus of ethnomethodological work has provided close sequential analysis of classroom talk and interaction, to show the fine detail of how members organise their classrooms, recognise their features, and account for their own work as classroom members. A considerable number of these studies have examined the organisation of formal classroom talk, particularly lesson talk organised around questions and answers. This includes a series of studies by French & MacLure (1979, 1981) and MacLure & French (1980) on questioning and answering in infants classrooms, showing how right and wrong answers get produced. McHoul & Watson (1984), using the resources of membership categorisation analysis, have studied classroom talk in geography lessons, showing that reference to and reasoning between formal and informal knowledge categories is part of the challenge of teaching and learning geography. How people reason with categories appears to be central to anyone's grasp of the sense of a course of talk-in-interaction.

Studies such as these have recognised the vagueness and indexicality of much instructional talk, as well as its rituals. Indexicality means that words and activities are not self-defining, and that their situated, occasioned meaning has to be determined by others on each occasion of their use; hence we are continuously involved in interpretive work to decide the here-and-now sense of indexical items. Classroom talk is no different. Questioning and answering, in classroom talk as in tests, become topics for analysis, and not merely unexplicated resources for doing the work of teaching or being taught. These studies have been informative about the analytical work that students must do to access school knowledge and teachers to recognise that work, thus posing differently the problem of academic "competence". In this they serve as a strong challenge to cognitivist views of education, intelligence, and achievement.

These studies, examining the organisation of questioning and answering, have application to familiar and longstanding educational topics such as classroom relationships, power and authority relations and teacher-student relations, all of which are shown to be locally produced in the course of classroom talk and interaction. Baker & Perrott (1988) studied "morning news" events in primary schools using an ethnomethodological approach, showing how the teachers' questioning regimes were reproduced by students and how students "news" did or did not come to count as valuable school knowledge. With these approaches, the topic and problems of classroom relationships can be recast as the topic and problems of what classroom members do to produce that which other research "finds" unproblematically in looking at institutional life.

Studies by Payne & Hustler (1980) on "the practical management of a cohort", by Hustler & Payne (1982) describing an ethnomethodological view of classroom power, and by MacBeth (1990) on 'classroom order as practical action' undertake close sequential analyses of audiotapes and videotapes of classroom events to provide a new perspective on "order" and "management". The ethnomethodological study of classroom talk and interaction can be read as a micro-politics of the classroom and provides for this without importing much that is extraneous to the talk and interaction itself. Studies of classroom "control", studies of classroom "management" and studies of classroom "order" as framed within most educational theory posits these activities and processes to be something other than and in addition to the work of teaching and being taught.

Many studies within the ethnomethodology of education are concerned with how institutional relations and practices are put together. The "institutionality" of a course of talk or interaction can be explored particularly using the resources of conversational analysis. The value of ethnomethodological studies in this regard provides an account of why it is so difficult to change classroom talk: the institutionality and the social relations are built into, and organised by, the texture of the talk.

Studies of classroom knowledge production

In much educational literature, activities such as "learning" and "teaching" are treated as singular and essential processes, and the categories of "teacher" and "students" are similarly seen as pre-assembled entities. Ethnomethodological analysis can be used to explicate how "what counts as knowledge" is assembled interactionally on the classroom floor and to describe institutionally-specific knowledge-production practices that are consequential for the production of relativities of success and failure in schools.

The study of classroom knowledge production has been addressed in work by Heap (1985, 1991) on what counts as classroom knowledge; and by Heyman (1986) on 'formulating topic' in instructional talk. Working from analyses of activity structures in reading lesson talk, Heap (1985, p. 267) provides "a basis for attending to the questions of how different kinds of knowledge are accomplished, i.e. transmitted, produced or displayed, through discourse formats". Different discourse formats can accomplish different kinds of classroom knowledges and skills, a view that usefully refuses to adjudicate on whether some form of talk is good or effective or not, since the value of the talk is in relation to the point of the lesson. Heyman studies the work of announcing and recalling lesson topics through formulations, which are utterances that characterise what we have done/said, are talking about now, will do next). In order to follow lessons, students need to hear the teacher's formulations and thereby orient to the work of the lesson as traced through such formulations. Heyman shows how topic formulations both make the ongoing course of lesson talk orderly, and how they can alternatively serve as trouble sources for students' understandings of what is going on or what they are supposed to talk about. Such studies of knowledge-production and topic formulation go right to the core of the practice of teaching and learning through talk.

Such analyses invite readers to trace in the recorded talk and interaction, as it unfolds, how it is that speakers make sense of each other and of the work they are accomplishing. By crediting classroom speakers – including students – with conversational-analytical skills, it is not possible to define the researcher alone as the analyst of the scenes being studied. MacKay (1974, p. 190) pointed out the "paradoxical" character of teachers' work with children: "On the one hand, the teacher relies on the child's interpretive competencies to understand the lesson but, on the other, treats him (sic) throughout as incompetent (i.e. she creates or gives the 'correct' answers.)" From an ethnomethodological position, no one is treated as a "cultural dope" and this has considerable ramifications for how the work of students and the construction of social order in classrooms can be studied (see the review by Norton in Volume 8).

Studies of classroom reading events

Recent ethnomethodological work on reading has proposed a radical shift in how "reading" and reading instruction can be theorised and studied. What has been applied in this work to the case of school reading can apply to studies of other conventional topics sharing family resemblances with these, for example "writing", "learning", "teaching". Heap (1991) and McHoul (1991) have argued that reading cannot be understood as a

singular, objective, mental process (as understood within the psychological notion of "the reading process"). They have shown the necessity
for examining how "reading/s" are practised and locally accomplished
in classrooms. From this situated perspective we also have a means to
resist viewing classrooms as social containers in which invisible mental
processes ("learning" is similar to "reading" in this respect) are the researcher's ultimate topic. Instead this work has examined how teachers
and students use activity structures in classroom talk to produce what
"counts" as reading in classrooms, how specific literacy practices are constructed in classroom talk, and how the organisation of teacher-student talk
about texts assembles relations between students ("children"), teachers and
texts (Baker & Freebody, 1989).

Studies of professional meetings and parent-teacher talk

The work of institutions goes on in a variety of spaces and places where
consequential talk is done. Talk is, to a very large extent, the "work" of
education (cf. Boden, 1994). Anywhere that people are talking educationally, the work of schooling is going on. In addition to studies of classroom
talk, ethnomethodological studies have addressed talk in other professional
arenas. Gronn (1983, 1984) studied "talk as the work" of school administration, particularly how staff meeting talk was accomplished (for more on
the analysis of administrator discourse, see the review by Waite in Volume
1). Mehan (1983, 1991) studied talk in special education placement com-
mittees to show how students were found by speakers to belong to one or
another educational category, which is related to how such decisions were
arrived at in the course of talk involving "lay" and "expert" people. Hester
(1992) and Hester & Eglin (1997), using the powerful device of membership categorisation analysis, have studied referral meetings between
teachers and educational psychologists, showing how moral meaning is at-
tached to students and their activities. Baker and Keogh (1995) studied the
organisation of talk in parent-teacher interviews undertaken in a secondary
school, showing the ways in which parent and teacher responsibilities are
negotiated in the talk, and the delicate work that both parties do in accounting for the standard of achievement or behaviour of the child/student
about whom they are meeting.

FUTURE DIRECTIONS: STUDYING 'TALK AS THE WORK' OF EDUCATION

Ethnomethodological studies of language in education have contributed
alternative formulations of what "the problem" is, where it might be
located, and how to look at it. The unique contribution and challenge
of ethnomethodologically informed studies is to find and elevate to a po-

sition of high analytical interest the details of the everyday work of class-room and other school participants. We can find there how it is that this work of members is a consequential part of the production of institutional categories and relations, and reflexively, social structure.

It is only when talk is seen and studied as *social* activity that any coherent or compelling links can be made between talk and *social* structure. This sociological claim is important to educational research, especially research that sets out to "make things better" by changing language practices, for example. It is not language practices *per se* that assemble the social and moral order. It is social practices such as specific ways of talking (reading, writing, describing, accounting, and so on) that do this. Only by investigating how educational institutions are put together routinely, commonsensically, locally in specific sites of educational talk-as-work, can we find places where that work might be done differently.

Everywhere that educational institutions are "talked into being" (Heritage, 1984, p. 283) is a site for further ethnomethodological study. Ethnomethodology also provides an escape from concurrence with the pervasive, standard educational categories inherited from other social sciences that have been accepted unproblematically as pre-given entities or processes. Instead, ethomethodological studies have investigated how those categories of person and of activity are used to do conventional educational work. Far from being a conservative enterprise, ethnomethodology questions the taken-for-grantedness, the essentialisms, and the naturalisations that are deeply embedded in educational theories and practices.

The University of Queensland
Australia

REFERENCES

Baker, C. & Freebody, P.: 1989, 'Talk around text: constructions of textual and teacher authority in classroom discourse', in S. De Castell, A. Luke & C. Luke (eds.), *Language, Authority and Criticism: Readings on the School Textbook*, Falmer, London, 263–283.

Baker, C. & Perrott, C.: 1988, 'The news session in infants and primary school classrooms', *British Journal of Sociology of Education* 9(1), 19–38.

Baker, C. & Keogh, J.: 1995, 'Accounting for achievement in parent-teacher interviews', *Human Studies* 18(2–3), 263–300.

Boden, D.: 1994, *The Business of Talk: Organisations in Action*, Polity, Cambridge.

Cicourel, A.V., Jennings, K.H., Jennings, S.H.M., Leiter, K.C.W., Mackay, R., Mehan, H. & Roth, D.R.: 1974, *Language Use and School Performance*, Academic Press, New York.

French, P. & MacLure, M.: 1979, 'Getting the right answer and getting the answer right', *Research in Education* 22, 2–23.

French, P. & MacLure, M.: 1981, 'Teachers' questions, pupils' Answers: An investigation of questions and answers in the infant classroom', *First Language* ii, 31–45.

Garfinkel, H.: 1967, *Studies in Ethnomethodology*, Prentice-Hall, Englewood Cliffs, NJ.

Gronn, P.: 1983, 'Talk as the work: The accomplishment of school administration', *Administrative Science Quarterly* 28, 1–21.

Gronn, P.: 1984, '"I have a solution ...": Administrative power in a school meeting', *Educational Administration Quarterly* 20(2), 65–92.

Heap, J.L.: 1979, 'Rumplestiltskin: The organisation of preference in a reading lesson', *Analytic Sociology* 2(2), card 1.

Heap, J.L.: 1985, 'Discourse in the production of classroom knowledge: Reading lessons', *Curriculum Inquiry* 15, 245–279.

Heap, J.L.: 1991, 'A situated perspective on what counts as reading', in C.D. Baker & A. Luke (eds.), *Towards a Critical Sociology of Reading Pedagogy*, John Benjamins, Amsterdam and Philadelphia, 103–139.

Heritage, J.: 1984, *Garfinkel & Ethnomethodology*, Polity Press, Cambridge, UK.

Hester, S.: 1985, 'Ethnomethodology and the study of deviance in schools', in R. Burgess (ed.), *Strategies of educational research*, Falmer, London, 243–264.

Hester, S.: 1992, 'Recognising references to deviance in referral talk', in G. Watson & R.M. Seiler (eds.), *Text in Context: Contributions to Ethnomethodology*, Sage, Newbury Park, 156–174.

Hester, S. & Eglin, P.: 1997, 'The reflexive constitution of category, predicate and context in two settings', in S. Hester & P. Eglin (eds.), *Culture in Action: Studies in Membership Categorization Analysis*. University Press of America, 25–48.

Heyman, R.: 1986, 'Formulating topic in the classroom', *Discourse Processes* 9, 37–55.

Hustler, D.E. & Payne, G.C.F.: 1982, 'Power in the classroom', *Research in Education* 28, 49–64.

MacBeth, D.H.: 1990, 'Classroom order as practical action: The making and un-making of a quiet reproach', *British Journal of Sociology of Education*, 11(2), 189–214.

MacKay, R.W.: 1974, 'Conceptions of children and models of socialization', in R. Turner (ed.), *Ethnomethodology*, Penguin, Harmondsworth, 180–193.

MacLure, M. & French, P.: 1980, 'Routes to right answers: On pupils' strategies for answering teachers' questions', in P. Woods (ed.), *Pupil Strategies*, Croom Helm, London, 74–93.

McDermott, R.P.: 1976, Kids Make Sense: An Ethnographic Account of the Interactional Management of Success and Failure in One First-Grade Classroom, Unpublished doctoral dissertation, Stanford University.

McDermott, R.P.: 1977, 'Social relations as contexts for learning in school', *Harvard Educational Review*, 47(2), 198–213.

McHoul, A.W.: 1978, 'The organisation of turns at formal talk in the classroom', *Language in Society* 7, 183–213.

McHoul, A.W. & Watson, D.R.: 1984, 'Two axes for the analysis of "commonsense" and "formal" geographical knowledge in classroom talk', *British Journal of Sociology of Education* 5, 281–302.

McHoul, A.W.: 1991, 'Reading S', in C.D. Baker & A. Luke (eds.), *Towards a Critical Sociology of Reading Pedagogy*, John Benjamins, Amsterdam and Philadelphia, 191–201.

Mehan, H.: 1979, *Learning Lessons: Social Organization in the Classroom*, Harvard University Press, Cambridge, MA.

Mehan, H.: 1983, 'The role of language and the language of role in institutional decision-making', *Language in Society* 12, 187–211.

Mehan, H.: 1991, 'The school's work of sorting students', in D. Boden & D. Zimmerman (eds.), *Talk & Social Structure: Studies in Ethnomethodology and Conversation Analysis*, Polity, Cambridge, 71–90.

Payne, G.C.F & Cuff, E.C. (eds.): 1982, *Doing Teaching: The Practical Management of Classrooms*, Batsford, London.

Payne, G.: 1976, 'Making a lesson happen: An ethnomethodological analysis', in M.

Hammersley & P. Woods (eds.), *The Process of Schooling*, Routledge and Kegan Paul, London, 33–40.

Payne, G. & Hustler, D.: 1980, 'Teaching the class: The practical management of a cohort', *British Journal of Sociology of Education* 1(1), 49–66.

Sacks, H.: 1972, 'An initial investigation of the usability of conversational data for doing sociology', in D. Sudnow (ed.), *Studies in Social Interaction*, The Free Press, New York, 31–74.

Sacks, H.: 1992, *Lectures on Conversation, Vols I and II*. Edited by G. Jefferson. Blackwell, Oxford.

Sacks, H., Schegloff, E.A. & Jefferson, G.: 1974, 'A simplest systematics for the organization of turn-taking in conversation', *Language* 50, 696–735.

Schegloff, E.A.: 1988, 'Description in the social sciences I: talk-in-interaction', *IpRA Papers in Pragmatics* 2(1–2), 1–24.

Silverman, D. & Gubrium, J.F.: 1994, 'Competing strategies for analysing the contexts of social interaction', *Sociological Inquiry* 642, 179–198.

Speier, M.: 1976, 'The child as conversationalist: Some culture contact features of conversational interactions between adults and children', in M. Hammersley & P. Woods (eds.), *The Process of Schooling*, Routledge and Kegan Paul, London, 98–103.

Zimmerman, D.: 1992, 'Achieving context: Openings in emergency calls', in G. Watson & R.M. Seiler (eds.), *Text in Context: Contributions to Ethnomethodology*, Sage, Newbury Park, 35–51.

NOLA ALLOWAY AND PAM GILBERT

POSTSTRUCTURALIST THEORY AND CLASSROOM TALK

Poststructuralist theories, with their focus on subjectivity, discourse and the plurality of textual meaning, have had much to offer in research on classroom talk. The possibility that poststructuralism offers, of understanding meaning as produced *within* language rather than reflected *by* it, has moved language study and language research into a social and political domain. Questions of authority, of power relations, and of the discursive construction and control of knowledge, become legitimate fields of inquiry within a poststructuralist paradigm, and, for research on classroom talk, this has been an important and significant shift.

Poststructuralist discourses, for instance, allow for the possibility of reading the complexity of the multiply positioned and constructed human subject; the silences, contradictions and contestations in talk and text; and the possible plurality of meaning contained in any language event. Consequently poststructuralist research paradigms offer a critique of traditional empirical and structuralist paradigms. In classroom talk, for instance, it is the plurality of meaning that is possible in any speech event, and the multiple positioning of speaker and listener within different and often competing discourses, that become of interest and concern.

However there is no single or unified set of theories outlining the poststructuralist "method". As Solsken and Bloome suggest, poststructuralism might best be viewed as 'a set of perspectives broadly outlining stances toward knowledge, power and society' (1992, p. 121), and it is not surprising that researchers from a range of educational research paradigms and domains have appropriated various aspects of poststructuralism in their work on classroom talk. In addition, poststructuralist discourses have been described as "liberating" for researchers. As Davies notes:

> One liberating aspect of poststructuralist thought is that it allows me to recognise the multiple discourses in which I participate and to see myself differently constituted through each of them. It allows me to imagine a discourse in which I can position myself as neither male nor female, but human. It also allows me to see fully . . . the extent of my entrapment in known discourses (1989, p. 139).

The versions of poststructuralism that have been most commonly taken up within educational research discourses, however, have been versions that incorporate aspects of Marxism, psychoanalysis and various feminisms

B. Davies and D. Corson (eds), Encyclopedia of Language and Education,
Volume 3: Oral Discourse and Education, 53–62.
© 1997 Kluwer Academic Publishers. Printed in the Netherlands.

(Weedon, 1987), although it is feminist poststructuralism that appears to have become the most common form of poststructuralist application to educational research (Davies, 1989; Weiner, 1994). This grounding of poststructuralist assumptions about language, discourse and subjectivity within a political framework such as feminism, has also meant that poststructuralist research in education (unlike poststructuralist or deconstructive work in literary theory) has usually avoided the danger of being regarded as a-political and a-historical.

EARLY DEVELOPMENTS

The most significant contribution to the early development of poststructuralist theory for classroom work came through the publication of *Changing the Subject: Psychology, Social Regulation and Subjectivity* in 1984. This text, co-written by Henriques, Hollway, Urwin, Venn and Walkerdine represents a watershed in understandings of 'subjectivity' and the discursive construction of knowledge and power. The text provides a critique of the individual-society dualism and its effects on theory and practices; an analysis of psychological practices of social regulation and the construction of the 'individual' as a product of discourses developed through these practices; and a retheorisation of subjectivity. Most of the major poststructuralist theorising in educational research has drawn from the theories of subjectivity that were formulated through this text.

Henriques et al. (1984) take up the poststructuralist concept of the human subject multiply positioned within a number of different discourses, but theorise about how it is that the human subject experiences "identity". By drawing selectively upon psychoanalytic discourses and power-knowledge relations, the text describes 'the motivational dynamics through which individuals are positioned in discourses' (p. 205), and then opens the possibility that 'those processes which position us are also those which produce the desires for which we strive' (p. 205). It is this linking of discourse, subjectivity and desire which has become particularly powerful in illuminating educational research contexts.

MAJOR CONTRIBUTIONS

Some of the most significant work in applying a poststructuralist approach to classroom talk has come from Davies (1989, 1993, 1994). In her major study of the oral readings pre-school children made of non-sexist children's stories (1989), Davies used poststructuralist discourse, arguing that it 'provides a radical framework for understanding the relation between persons and their social world and for conceptualising social change' (1989, p. xi).

Davies shows how poststructuralist theory, unlike socialisation theory, moves beyond concepts of roles and stereotypes in explaining identity formation. In her study, she argues that a basic tenet of poststructuralism is that 'the self' is experienced as multiply positioned and multiply located, as opposed to the liberal humanist conceptualisation of the unitary, consistent and essentialist self underpinned by socialisation theory. Her study concludes however, that, within the discursive practices made available to children, 'the only comprehensible identity available to them is as "boy" or "girl", "male" or "female"' (p. 141). Davies' research argues that this gendered dualism can be shifted, if children are given access to poststructuralist discourse: to understandings of how discursive practice constitutes them differently.

Walkerdine's (1990) work on the cultural production of the school girl similarly focuses on the poststructuralist shift to multiplicity. Using examples from classroom talk and practice wherein teachers' and girls' experiences are understood to be contextually contingent and discursively produced, Walkerdine suggests that:

> ... both female teachers and small girls are not unitary subjects uniquely positioned, but are produced as a nexus of subjectivities, in relations of power which are constantly shifting, rendering them at one moment powerful and at another powerless (1990, p. 3).

Walkerdine uses children's talk at nursery school to argue that:

> ... the contradictions, the struggles for power, the shifting relations of power all testify to the necessity for an understanding of subjectivi*ties*, not a unique subjectivity (Walkerdine, 1990, p. 14).

The ways in which girls in particular are multiply positioned and regulated through classroom talk is illustrated in Bird's research in New Zealand primary classrooms. Bird observes that while girls are often 'positioned alongside teachers as holders of knowledge and school rules' (1992, p. 149) they are simultaneously positioned as targets of boys' harassment. As deputised teachers/mothers, girls may be authoritatively positioned to subordinate boys' interests and will. As targets of harassment, girls, in turn, may be subordinated as boys resist female authority and exert male-identified authority through physical coercion and intimidation. Given the poststructuralist lens used to interpret discursive interactions in these classrooms, neither girls' nor boys' experiences of themselves are recognised as consistent or unitary. Rather, unevenness, contradiction, complexity and multiplicity are understood to characterise the process of subjectification.

While poststructuralist theory introduces the notion of multiple subjectivities and multiple speaking positions, it is clear that subject and speaking positions are not limitless or infinitely available. Reflecting on the ways that girls were positioned in Bird's classrooms, Jones (1993) contends that

> ... while the subject positions available to girls in the primary
> classroom (and elsewhere) are multiple, they are still inevitably
> inflected with wider gendered power relations as girls take
> on the "available" subject position of mother/teacher/nurturer.
> ... There is no "pure" (or non-gendered, or non-patriarchal)
> space within which girls develop, and become powerful (Jones,
> 1993, p. 161).

The same conclusion could be drawn for the boys in this study, in that they too take up their subjectivities within the discursively produced, patriarchal spaces available to them.

How teachers position students in relation to gender is further elaborated through a number of studies that have drawn on poststructuralist theory in interpreting teacher-student talk. Baker and Davies (1989), for example, analyse a situation in a seventh grade classroom, where a teacher wanted to teach a liberating lesson on sex roles. The researchers claim that, because the teacher was only able to draw upon the usual patterns of student-teacher talk, the lesson failed in its purpose. The paper argues that, for the lesson to have been more liberatory, the teacher and students in this classroom needed access to a 'different type of discourse for articulating what they know and what they want to convey, for constructing more respectful and less oppressive theories and social relationships' (Baker & Davies, 1989, p. 75).

A similar argument is made through the work of Kamler (1997/forthcoming) and of Wright (1989), both of whom embrace theories of subjectivity and of discourse-power relations in their linguistic analyses of teacher talk. Kamler's reading of an early childhood teacher's implicit maintenance of gendered classroom speaking positions reinforces the work of Baker and Davies (1989). Similarly, Wright's analysis of the differences between female and male physical education teachers' "talk" to students, provides evidence of the potential usefulness of a discourse for teachers (and students) which makes the conventions of such "talk" visible.

While the studies discussed so far show how gender is made relevant through classroom talk, Luke et al (1995) demonstrate how race is also made relevant through teachers' regulation of classroom discourse. The researchers in this study expose the unintended, but nonetheless cultural imperialist stance involved in teachers' focussing on monocultural representations in texts and talk. The researchers argue that the universalisation of white middle class knowledge and culture, the exclusionary talk and silence related to those not so constituted, can be read as "supremacist practices", as acts of "symbolic violence" (p. 230). The researchers draw on aspects of poststructuralist theory to argue that in this case, the production of cultural hegemony through teacher-directed classroom talk was particularly relevant to the Aboriginal and Torres Strait Islander children represented in significant numbers in the classrooms observed. According to the authors, what teachers allow to be spoken, omitted or silenced can be understood as:

> ...a part of the complex and at times contradictory politics of representation through which identity is shaped and formed. When this is the case, the educational problem is not with 'racism' per se, in any conventional or common sense definition of the word. Rather the problem rests with an apparent lack of discursive resources for talking about race and culture (Luke et al., 1995, pp. 230–231).

As teachers discursively position children, so too can children position their teachers through classroom discourse. Through a poststructuralist analysis of a dialogic episode between a teacher and two nursery school boys, Walkerdine (1990) shows how subjects can be produced within a variety of discursive practices. While one of the two boys triggers the verbal exchange with the teacher by referring to a nursery school girl as a 'cunt', both boys engage in a litany of derogatory and sexual references to the teacher, Miss Baxter, which are demeaning and sexist. While Miss Baxter dismisses the boys as 'being very silly', Walkerdine 'reads' them as struggling to dominate the female teacher by positioning her as powerless object within sexist discourse. As Walkerdine explains, these boys do not experience themselves *just* as little boys. By refusing the discourse of the nursery classroom that renders them powerless in the face of adult authority, they potentially re-position Miss Baxter as powerless within the misogynist discourse that they are able to draw on as males. Walkerdine (1990) argues that Miss Baxter

> ...has not in a sense ceased to be a teacher, but what is important is that she has ceased to *signify* as one: she has been made to signify as the powerless object of male sexual discourse (p. 5).

As well as focussing on the ways that teachers position children, or that children position their teachers, poststructuralist studies of classroom talk also theorise the ways that teachers and children *together* produce classroom practice. In achieving this level of insight, Jones (1989) contrasts the discursive practices that evolve between teachers and their working class Polynesian students with those that evolve with their middle class Pakeha (European) students in an all-girls' secondary school in New Zealand. Jones uses instances of classroom talk to illustrate how:

> Both the teachers *and* the students actively construct 'what goes on' in the classroom. Indeed as they seek to make sense of and cope with the classroom situation, the students interact with their teachers quite selectively, determining to a large extent what actually happens in the classroom (Jones, 1989, p. 23).

As students from the two groups participated with teachers in the production of what counted as valuable teaching and learning experiences, their discursive histories and the speaking positions available to them became salient features in the cultural production of classroom practice. Teacher and student talk operated as a classroom dialectic that resulted in differential academic and life opportunity outcomes for identifiable groups of students. In this respect, students and teachers together can be read as co-authors of students' experiences in the classroom and of their academic destinies.

To this point, the research reviewed has indicated how children can be discursively positioned in relations of privilege by teachers, how teachers can be positioned by children, and how teachers and children together can produce classroom discourse and practice. However, there are occasions when children in classrooms work and play, independent of direct teacher influence. Some research studies go beyond notions of what schools and teachers do to children to glimpse at how children discursively produce and maintain relations with one another.

In a study of preschoolers' talk around a computer Alloway (1995) highlights the ways that girls and boys position one another in asymmetrical relations of power. Without direct teacher intervention, girls and boys regulated one another's access to the computer activity in a system of relations that, for the most part, privileged boys' use of the technology. In a female-identified activity like 'home-corner', the situation was reversed wherein girls were likely to be more powerfully positioned to subordinate boys' interests in their play.

The ways that students regulate one another is also taken up by Nilan's research. Her studies focus on talk that generates between students as they work in dyads on a cooperative writing activity. Drawing on aspects of neo-Marxist, feminist and poststructuralist theory, Nilan (1995a, 1995b, 1996) shows how discourses of gender and social class are equally relevant in determining the speaking positions available to both girls and boys. Nilan (1995a) argues that 'The distinction between working-class girls and boys and ruling-class girls and boys is a profound, not a superficial, distinction' (1995a, p. 28). During a collaborative writing activity in a co-educational secondary classroom, Nilan (1996) shows how the different discursive positions available to the children were mediated though a complex interplay of gender, socio-cultural privilege and academic status/prowess. Gender alone was insufficient in interpreting the discursive patterning of dominance and deference that emerged amongst students as they negotiated the activity.

A similar argument has been advanced by Gilbert and Gilbert (1995) in their study of teenage girls at risk of educational failure. Gilbert and Gilbert analysed the discourses that teenage girls drew upon to describe their lives at home, at school and with their peers. The focus was on the way in which various forms of educational disadvantage and risk were experienced by girls, and compounded or modified in the discourses of femininity / masculinity which defined important aspects of family, school and other social relations. The study's argument was that:

> ... processes of disadvantage need to be seen in the way adolescent girls are positioned by the discourses of what it is to be a woman, a schoolgirl, and a member of specific cultural groups, classes and geographical locations. It is the interplay of these discourses and how they contradict or accentuate each other that explains how disadvantage is constructed, interpreted and experienced in particular sites (Gilbert & Gilbert, 1995, p. 22).

PROBLEMS AND DIFFICULTIES

In its focus on multiplicity and plurality of readings and meanings, its abandonment of the notion that 'Truth' necessarily exists independently of the knower, and its anti-objectivist and anti-foundationalist stance, poststructuralism runs the risk of promoting value equivalence and relativism. Where one reading is understood to be as valid as another, the question arises as to whether any position or any political platform can be sustained or privileged. Poststructuralism's non-essentialist stance necessarily fragments categories such as gender and race, the disintegration of which may weaken emancipatory endeavours where plurality and heterogeneity are endlessly invoked. In summarising the work of others (see especially Hartsock 1990; Bordo, 1990) Nicholson (1990) claims that 'theorising needs some stopping points and that for feminists an important theoretical stopping point is gender. To invoke the ideal of endless difference is for feminism either to self-destruct or to finally accept an ontology of abstract individualism' (p. 8). The main difficulty for poststructuralist theorising lies, perhaps, in this direction.

While there is richness in a discourse which makes visible the multiply positioned human subject, and the infinite plurality of the text, there is also a potential ineffectiveness if multiplicity and plurality lead towards infinite regress to the individual who is seen to exist only by virtue of each specific socio-cultural and historical context and moment. Within educational contexts, as this review has indicated, most researchers who choose to work with poststructuralist discourse have not ignored these socio-cultural and historical contexts. Poststructuralist discourse is used more as a conceptual tool for releasing a text from a singular 'truth', and for making visible the complex textual positioning of its speaker and listener. This release has often been assisted by structuralist linguistic analyses (as in Kamler and Wright), or feminist critique (as in Davies and Alloway), or critical social readings of class or race (as in Jones, Nilan and Luke et al.).

Poststructuralist research within educational contexts has thus usually avoided the danger of producing multiple readings of textual interactions where none is more privileged than another. Instead, poststructuralist research has usually been used, as Davies (1989) claims, to "make sense" of data, and "formulate answers" to research questions.

FUTURE DIRECTIONS

For the field of Education, poststructuralist research opens out the possibility of continued interrogation of knowledge and 'truth' as socio-cultural and historical productions. Researchers, teachers and students alike are invited to adopt a less dogmatic, more tentative approach to their own, as well as to one another's truth claims – to see how knowledge is constructed within particular discursive sites and at particular historical moments, rather than existing independently of the knower. As Davies (1994) claims:

> The poststructuralist shift involves both students and teachers positioning themselves differently in relation to authority and to discourse. The teacher's authority can no longer rest on an assumed access to "Truth". Rather, teacher and students together make visible their locatedness in multiple discourses (p. 63).

The task for educators is to identify the theoretical 'stopping points', to avoid a slide into radical relativism, and to understand the power of a 'fractured foundationalism' (See Stanley & Wise, 1990) whereby universalising claims to truth and knowledge are constantly contested. For students and teachers, the position is potentially a powerfully transformative one as they 'see the commonality between themselves and others constituted through similar discourses and understand the political and emotional disjunctures that arise from different discourses, different positionings and different sites or contexts' (Davies, 1994, p. 63).

Early research studies on poststructuralist theory and classroom talk predominantly focussed on singular identity categories such as gender, but increasingly, the move has been towards multiplicity as researchers focus on dimensions such as gender and socio-cultural identification that are made relevant through classroom talk. Future research offers the possibility of more sophisticated analyses that recognise the complex field of discursive play wherein organising principles such as gender, race, ethnicity, class, age, and school-based competence prove salient in determining the specificity of the subject as produced through classroom talk. The sacrifice will be in the direction of substitution of the economy of categories for richer understandings of how subject positions are negotiated within discursive systems of relations and meanings. The ultimate challenge will be to recognise the tensions that lie between macro- and micro-level political analyses, to take account of multiplicity, heterogeneity and difference while leaving intact the coalitions that are indispensable in moving beyond a reductive politics of individualism.

James Cook University
Australia

REFERENCES

Alloway, N.: 1995, *Foundation Stones: The Construction of Gender in Early Childhood*, Curriculum Corporation, Carlton, Melbourne.

Baker, C. & Davies, B.: 1989, 'A lesson on sex roles', *Gender and Education* 1(1), 59–76.

Bird, L.: 1992, 'Girls taking positions of authority at primary school', in S. Middleton & A. Jones (eds.), *Women and Education in Aotearoa. Vol 2*, Bridget Williams Books, Wellington, 149–168.

Bordo, S.: 1990, 'Feminism, postmodernism, and gender-scepticism', in L. Nicholson (ed.), *Feminism/Postmodernism*, Routledge, New York, 133–156.

Davies, B.: 1989, *Frogs and Snails and Feminist Tales: Preschool Children and Gender*, Allen and Unwin, Sydney.

Davies, B.: 1993, *Shards of Glass: Children Reading and Writing Beyond Gendered Identities*, Allen and Unwin, Sydney.

Davies, B.: 1994, *Poststructuralist Theory and Classroom Practice*, Deakin University, Geelong, Victoria.

Gilbert, P. & Gilbert, R.: 1995, *What's Going On? Girls' Experiences of Educational Disadvantage*, J.S. McMillan Publishing Group/DEETYA, Canberra.

Hartsock, N.: 1990, 'Foucault on power: A theory for women?', in L. Nicholson (ed.), *Feminism/Postmodernism*, Routledge, New York, 157–175.

Henriques, J., Hollway, W., Urwin, C., Venn, C. & Walkerdine, V.: 1984, *Changing the Subject: Psychology, Social Regulation and Subjectivity*, Methuen, London.

Jones, A.: 1989, 'The cultural production of classroom practice', *British Journal of Sociology of Education* 10(1), 19–31.

Jones, A.: 1993, 'Becoming a "Girl": Post-structuralist suggestions for educational research', *Gender and Education* 5(2), 157–166.

Kamler, B.: 1997, forthcoming, '"This Doll Who's Come To School": Morning Talk As Gendered Language Practice', in B. Kamler (ed.), *Constructing Gender and Difference: Critical Research Perspectives On Early Childhood*, Hampton Press, Creskill, NJ.

Luke, A., Kale, J., Garbutcheon Singh, with Hill, T. & Daliri, F.: 1995, 'Talking difference: Discourses on aboriginal identity in grade one classrooms', in D. Corson (ed.), *Discourse and Power in Educational Organizations*, Hampton Press, NJ, 211–231.

Nicholson, L.: 1990, 'Introduction', in L. Nicholson (ed.), *Feminism/Postmodernism*, Routledge, New York, 1–16.

Nilan, P.: 1995a, 'Negotiating gendered identity in classroom disputes and collaboration', *Discourse and Society* 6(1), 27–47.

Nilan, P.: 1995b, 'Making up men', *Gender and Education* 7(2), 175–187.

Nilan, P.: 1996, 'Looking for gender differences in a co-educational paired writing activity', *Australian Educational Researcher* 23, 101–129.

Solsken, J. & Bloome, D.: 1992, 'Beyond poststructuralism: Story and narrative in the study of the everyday world', *Paper presented at the annual meeting of the American Educational Research Association (AERA)*, San Francisco, California, April.

Stanley, L. & Wise, S.: 1990, 'Method, methodology and epistemology in feminist research processes', in L. Stanley (ed.), *Feminist Praxis: Research, Theory and Epistemology in Feminist Sociology*, Routledge, London, 20–49.

Walkerdine, V.: 1990, *School Girl Fictions*, Verso, London.
Weedon, C.: 1987, *Feminist Practice and Poststructuralist Theory*, Basil Blackwell, Oxford.
Weiner, G.: 1994, *Feminisms in Education: An Introduction*, Open University Press, Buckingham.
Wright, J.: 1989, 'The construction of gender through tenor choices in physical education lessons', *Australian Review of Applied Linguistics* 12(1), 83–101.

Section 2

Oral Language, Culture and Identity

A.D. EDWARDS

ORAL LANGUAGE, CULTURE AND CLASS

The dominant tradition in linguistics in the 1960s required rigorous con-
centration on structure abstracted from use. From that perspective, speech
communities were homogeneous and 'surface' differences between speakers were irrelevant to the task of describing their language. This chapter
reviews research undertaken in various 'socially realistic' traditions, most
of it intended to explore social class differences in linguistic usage or in
what language is predominantly used to do. Other contributions to this
volume focus directly on the educational consequences of such diversity,
but much of the research outlined here has also identified discontinuities
between the languages or discourses of home and school or, more broadly,
between the local and the wider community. Although this review begins
with Labov's (1966) demonstration of the 'highly systematic structure of
social and stylistic stratification' evident in differences previously dismissed as 'free variation', its main concern is with what speech reveals of
the speakers – their social backgrounds, sense of identity, and perceptions
of a social world which their use of language both reflects and shapes.

EARLY DEVELOPMENTS

Labov's demonstration of 'structured heterogeneity' in the speech community of Lower East Side New York marked a new 'sociological dialect-
ology' (Trudgill, 1974). Phonological differences which linguistic research had treated as free variation were now shown to be 'patterned
and predictable' when analysed in relation to the interaction of speaker,
addressee and setting. Although 'lower class' speakers tended to move
towards prestige forms in more formal situations, differences in how consistently and confidently these were used provided members of that speech
community with a powerful resource for placing themselves and others
in their social world (Labov, 1966). To complicate this account of social
and stylistic stratification still further, there was also evidence that conflict
between the norms of the wider society and those of the local community
produced a heightening of working-class features to express solidarity or
resistance to mainstream culture.

A second major research strand had strong roots in Bernstein's early
explorations in the 'sociology of language', which were prompted by
dissatisfaction with sociology's reliance on notions of socialization while

B. Davies and D. Corson (eds), Encyclopedia of Language and Education,
Volume 3: Oral Discourse and Education, 65–73.
© *1997 Kluwer Academic Publishers. Printed in the Netherlands.*

failing to explain how that process worked. An ambitious theory moved from the class structure through the structuring of social relationships to social class differences in modes of communication which then reproduced the conditions of their own existence. It prompted a programme of research into social class differences in the conversations of parents and children, especially in the 'critical contexts' of instruction and control (Bernstein, 1973). At about the same time, Bourdieu's (1973) concept of 'habitus' as a 'system of dispositions' mediating between social structure and cultural practices drew attention to how the dominant languages of schooling and other public domains served to preserve the advantages of those middle-class speakers best able to employ its forms and de-code its meanings. The rapid growth in these socio-linguistic and sociological lines of enquiry into social class differences is outlined and illustrated in Edwards (1976).

MAJOR CONTRIBUTIONS

Research into social dialects has demonstrated how linguistic differences both reflect and construct social reality. If speech is stratified by social class in ways partly beyond the speaker's awareness and control, it also provides a rich resource for displaying adherence to the norms of the vernacular culture (Romaine, 1982). Thus socio-linguistic variables indicate not only present status and affiliation, but also aspirations to belong elsewhere. For example, lower-middle class speakers appeared especially hostile to stigmatized features and tended to over-correct their speech in more formal situations, thereby providing linguistic evidence of social ambition and insecurity. Labov's combining of social class and stylistic stratification has had profound influence on research into social dialects (for example Trudgill, 1974: Macaulay, 1977; Romaine, 1982; Horvath, 1985). The sharpness of dialect boundaries, and the extent of homogeneous usage within them, are likely to be proportionate to the frequency of social interaction between dialect speakers across them and how far that interaction is confined to formalized (superior-subordinate) relationships of the workplace. In a Belfast study influential both for its findings and for the methods used to obtain them, Milroy (1980) related pressures to 'conform to localised vernacular norms' to the strength of social networks. Networks were strongest where they were both 'dense' and 'multiplex' – that is, where most members knew all the others and interacted with them in a variety of roles (friend, neighbour, fellow worker). Such networks are more likely in working-class communities of the 'traditional' kind, and they may create powerful counter-pressures against breaking vernacular norms to get on in the world outside that particular community. Indeed, it was 'quite rare in these working-class groups for a person to prefer status to solidarity' (Milroy & Milroy, 1985, p. 58).

Much of the impetus for studying social dialects came from determination to counter theories of linguistic deficit by demonstrating that non-standard speech was no less systematically structured than the standard forms from which it diverged (Milroy & Milroy, 1985). That evidence was offered as a warning against judging the ability of speakers by how they sounded. Yet a socially realistic approach to language differences had to recognise that while any variety is structurally capable of communicating whatever its community of speakers require, varieties may differ widely in functional range – that is, in what their habitual users are enabled 'legitimately' and 'credibly' to do. They may for example be effectively excluded from the 'serious business' of the wider society. Thus research into social class differences focused both on adherence to the vernacular as an expression of solidarity and on the consequences of 'sounding disadvantaged' (Giles & Powesland, 1975; Edwards, 1989). Non-standard speakers might be heard as friendly and sincere (as 'honest clods or good-natured peasants', to quote a vivid statement of the risks) but were unlikely to be heard as credible or authoritative purveyors of information or taken seriously as applicants for positions of 'responsibility' or when challenging representatives of the official world. In highly theorized form, Bourdieu (1973) showed how socially privileged styles of communication serve to demonstrate the 'natural' superiority of those possessing the relevant facility with words, and how the dominated become accomplices in their own domination by accepting that superiority. Put more simply, uncertainty about what to say and how to say it has powerful silencing effects.

The other main research strand has been about social class differences in the uses of language. Language is as it is because of what it is organised to do (Halliday, 1978). That dominant theme in Halliday's work explains its relevance to Bernstein's exploration of how social class differences in language use both reflect and reproduce different conditions of life (Bernstein, 1996, p. 149). In progressively more formalised exposition, Bernstein has argued that the class structure determines the 'principles' by which social relationships are structured and texts produced, and so shapes consciousness. As he has insisted repeatedly, his theory is not about differences of dialect but about differences in 'semantic orientation'. His interest in choice of words is as 'realisations' of the underlying semantic. In relation to social class differences in how children are socialized through the ways in which language is used to structure the social world, he has described working-class culture (at least in its 'traditional' forms) as having more strongly classified age, gender and work roles. In those conditions there is more transmitting and reinforcing of what 'everyone knows', and less ambiguity and negotiation in the organising of what are relatively more 'positional' and less 'personal' relationships. His use of 'restricted codes' to refer to the predominant modes of communication in such conditions did not refer to limitations of vocabulary or grammar, but to meanings which are fully accessible only to those who share enough of the speaker's cultural knowledge and experience to be able to fill in what is meant but not said.

WORK IN PROGRESS

Implicit in the research already reviewed and explicit in much of it are concepts of continuity and discontinuity between the languages (or discourses) of home and school. Socio-linguistic explanations for social class differences in educational achievement are explored more fully in other contributions to this volume. In relation to high rates of working-class failure, they are less prominent now than in the 1960s and 1970s. This is partly because 'class analysis has been disappearing in research in education as the focus has shifted to race, gender, region, and indigenous groups' (Bernstein, 1996, p. 13).

The cross-cutting influences of gender and class were observed by Labov (1966) in the tendency of women's speech to diverge less than that of men from prestige forms. That finding has been replicated in subsequent research and interpreted (for example by Trudgill, 1974) as reflecting a greater concern for appearances among those less likely to be firmly located by occupation in their social world. It also appears that some stigmatised features are strongly associated with male working-class speech, so that certain kinds of 'rough' usage have strong connotations of masculinity and the covert prestige (for men but not for women) which these create (Fasold, 1990, pp. 99–103). Some of the most interesting research into cultural differences in modes of communication has focused on minorities, but has relevance to studies of social class because of its concern with how distance from the mainstream culture is maintained, extended or diminished (Labov, 1972). Thus Heller (1995) provides a powerful portrayal of how choice of language or within a language operates to exert, mitigate, collude with or resist power (see her review in this volume).

Direct interest in the structuring of communication by social class and the consequent reproduction of class-based inequalities has continued to shape research into how 'appropriate' meanings are recognised and realised (Holland, 1981; Hasan & Cloran, 1990; Moraes, Fontinhas & Neves, 1992). The examples indicate the multi-national contexts of that research, and Bernstein (1996, pp. 91–133) provides a review of studies shaped by his concept of socio-linguistic codes. Their conclusions are not about social class differences in what children can do with language, but in what they are disposed to do. For example, working-class children and adults appear less (or less readily) oriented towards the communication of propositional messages and relatively more oriented to organising and maintaining social relationships. To the extent that middle-class children are likelier to shift away from 'everyday' categorizations of objects and events and towards the recontextualising they associate with school tasks, it is because 'class cultures act to transform micro-differences into macro-inequalities' and so constitute 'a major regulator of the distribution of students to privileging discourses and institutions' (Bernstein 1996, p. 11).

Research in the ethnographic tradition exemplified by Hymes (1993) and Cazden (1995) has provided rich evidence of sub-cultural diversity in children's experience of being read to, instructed, questioned, and encouraged to ask about the world. An impressive example is Heath's (1983) study of two working-class communities in South Carolina. It documents striking differences between black and white working-class communities in the kinds of story-telling to which children listened and which they themselves practised. Stories told by the white children tended to be factual, linear, and intended to inform. Those told by black children tended to be non-linear, decorated with artful exaggerations, and intended to entertain. The first mode was much more closely aligned with non-fictive uses of language in classrooms. But while the second mode might seem to provide opportunities to shine in such classroom events as 'story-time', it too risked being rejected as inappropriate to the serious business of schooling (see the review by Auerbach in Volume 2). Cazden (1995) reviews and continues work in this tradition.

Such research raises questions about the consequences of social class differences in the value placed on oral traditions for schooling based heavily on what Gee (1990) calls 'text-based literacy'. Thus the effect of standardization is to legitimate the norms of formal registers rather than those of everyday language. Since working-class people have less experience of those formal registers, there is a greater distance between their language and that normally thought appropriate for schooling. They are then disadvantaged by a tendency to denigrate varieties of spoken language which depart markedly from the standard dialect even when these present few difficulties of mutual comprehensibility across social boundaries (Milroy & Milroy, 1985). While research into social class language differences has also been informed by studies of the richness of oral cultures in societies less dominated by the written word and by those forms of speech most approximating to it (Edwards & Sienkewicz, 1990), it has also had to take into account the inconveniences created for a modernising state by an array of languages or varieties and the consequent pressures towards standardization (Corfield, 1991, in particular Washington's account of the languages of colonial India). As Gee (1990) describes the change, old divisions between literate elites and illiterate 'masses' have been replaced by 'highly stratified access' to different literacies.

Such research is part of a broad area of enquiry which has broken the illusion that the discourse practices of schools are culturally neutral and therefore fair. Bourdieu's concept of 'scholarly' (or 'magisterial') language is used to show how educational success is distributed according to students' preparedness and disposition to use it themselves and to de-code its meanings. Corson's (1995) concept of a 'lexical bar' refers more specifically to the progressively higher proportion of words of Graeco-Roman origin in the language of schooling, and to the cultural obstacles inhibiting working-class students from using them with comfort or regarding what they convey as knowledge relevant to the world they know.

PROBLEMS AND DIFFICULTIES

That Labov's findings have been 'so readily duplicated' by subsequent studies is 'a testament to the robust nature of class stratification' despite large differences in how social class is conceptualised and measured (Fasold, 1990, p. 225). Indeed, the patterning of choice evident among even small numbers of speakers seemed to provide social scientists with precise indicators of social class membership. But there are also strong grounds for questioning the solidity of that evidence.

Objections to reducing class to occupational status are illustrated by Bernstein's (1996, p. 149) rather dismissive description of Labov's work as 'social diagnostics'. Combining occupation with income and education to provide a more culturally sensitive variable presents the difficulty that the three components are 'implicationally related' (Hasan & Cloran, 1990, p. 68). Nor does it even alleviate the problem of locating the 'social class' position of women who are not currently employed, or whose working careers have been disrupted or impeded by family responsibilities. Horvath (1985) 'solved' the problem by not assigning unemployed women to any class at all. That solution is rejected by Hasan and Cloran (1990) because the life chances of women and children are so strongly affected by the occupation of the main 'breadwinner'. Their interest in social class differences in semantic orientation led them to divide their sample into 'lower autonomy' and 'higher autonomy' categories according to the degree of power and control exercised in working life, and to discover more personal modes of communication in 'white collar working-class' families.

Research into social class differences in communication, especially when intended to demonstrate how pervasively differences are turned into disadvantages, has been criticized for seeming to offer superficial cultural solutions to problems which are essentially about the distribution of power and resources. It is therefore perenially difficult to find a balance between revealing the dire effects of linguistic discrimination and mistaking the symptoms for the case. Thus a main theme in Bourdieu's work has been the power of words to order and command the world while concealing the material interests of those dominant groups whose forms of spoken and written language have been made to count (Bourdieu, 1991). Yet while penetrating that cover of 'natural' superiority is important, 'robbing the wolf of sheep's clothing does not make the teeth less dangerous', nor does it enable the sheep to parley on equal terms (Lemke, 1995, p. 15). In short, socially sensitive language policies may alleviate some effects of socio-linguistic disadvantage while leaving social and economic inequalities intact.

Much of the research cited in this review has nevertheless been prompted by the problems created for non-mainstream groups by the existence of essentially monocultural schooling in multi-cultural societies. The obvious sites for such research are multi-lingual communities of the kind described by Heller (1995). But if modes of communication more common in working-class families are largely excluded, devalued or misinterpreted in mainstream schools, then similar questions arise about whether 'vernacular education' would be fairer. They arise despite a lack of evidence of its effectiveness, and considerable evidence that students and parents alike may resist it as a denial of opportunity. Bourdieu regarded the failure of schools to provide working-class students with the skills which schools demanded, as perpetuating inequality. But would it be feasible, Lemke asks, to teach them to speak and write 'the genres of power' when those genres are marked by 'very strict and often rather subtle rules', and when the self-interest of dominant groups is likely to produce new ways of rewarding hidden attributes of 'style' and so maintaining 'distinctions' (Lemke, 1995, p. 144)?

FUTURE DIRECTIONS

The existence of systematic social class differences both in the patterning of speech and in what speech is used to do has been thoroughly documented, as has the very uneven distribution of those modes of communication which seem strategic for educational success. While it is clear that facility in the discourses of schooling and other domains of 'public' life is not a matter of culturally neutral competences, it remains unclear what is gained intellectually from extending speech repertoires beyond those acquired and reinforced in the local communities – whether it makes possible less 'naive' and more 'critical' forms of consciousness and so a greater capacity to perceive possibilities of social change (Freire & Macedo, 1987). That question is likely to shape a great deal of future research, as is the 'testing' of that bleak proposition (exemplified by Bourdieu and Gee) that those not apprenticed to the dominant discourses of their society by their upbringing can rarely be 'schooled' to use them with confidence and so carry conviction.

University of Newcastle upon Tyne
England

REFERENCES

Bernstein, B. (ed.): 1973, *Class, Codes and Control: Volume 2: Applied Studies towards a Sociology of Language*, Routledge & Kegan Paul, London.

Bernstein, B.: 1996, *Pedagogy, Symbolic Control and Identity: Theory, Research, Critique*, Taylor & Francis, London & Bristol, Penn. USA.

Bourdieu, P.: 1973, 'Cultural reproduction and social reproduction', in R. Brown (ed.), *Knowledge, Education and Cultural Change*, Tavistock Press, London, 71–112.

Bourdieu, P.: 1991, *Language and Symbolic Power*, Polity Press, Cambridge.

Cazden, C.: 1995, 'Visible and invisible pedagogies in literacy education', in P. Atkinson, B. Davies & S. Delamont (eds.), *Discourse and Reproduction*, Hampton Press, Cresskill New Jersey, 159–172.

Corfield, P.J. (ed.): 1991, *Language, History and Class*, Blackwell, Oxford England and Cambridge USA.

Corson, D.J.: 1995, *Using English Words*, Dordrecht, Kluwer.

Edwards, A.D.: 1976, *Language in Culture and Class*, Heinemann, London.

Edwards, J.R.: 1989, *Language and Disadvantage* (second edition), Edward Arnold, London.

Edwards, V. & Sienkewicz, T.J.: 1990, *Oral Cultures Past and Present*, Basil Blackwell, Oxford.

Fasold, R.: 1990, *Sociolinguistics of Language*, Blackwell, Oxford UK and Cambridge USA.

Freire, P. & Macedo, D.: 1987, *Literacy: Reading the Word and the World*, Routledge, London.

Gee, J.: 1990, *Social Linguistics and Literacies: Ideology in discourses*, Falmer Press, London.

Giles, H. & Powesland, P.: 1975, *Speech Style and Social Evaluation*, Academic Press, London.

Halliday, M.: 1978, *Language as Social Semiotic*, Edwards Arnold, London.

Hasan, R. & Cloran, C.: 1990, 'A socio-linguistic interpretation of everyday talk between mothers and children', in M. Halliday, J. Gibbons & M. Nicholas (eds.), *Learning, Keeping and Using Language*, John Benjamins, Amsterdam/Philadelphia 67–100.

Heath, S.: 1983, *Ways with Words: Life and Work in Communities and Classrooms*, Cambridge University Press, London.

Heller, M.:1995, 'Language choice, social institutions and symbolic domination', *Language in Society* 24, 373–405.

Holland, J.: 1981, 'Social class and changes in orientation to meaning', *Sociology* 15, 1–18.

Horvath, S.: 1985, *Variation in Australian English: The Sociolects of Sydney*, Cambridge University Press, Cambridge.

Hymes, D.: 1993, 'Inequality of language: Taking for granted', in J.E. Alatis (ed.), *Language, Communication and Meaning*, Georgetown University Press, Georgetown USA, 2–40.

Labov, W.: 1966, *The Social Stratification of English in New York City*, Centre for Applied Linguistics, Washington DC.

Labov, W.: 1972, *Language in the Inner-City*, Basil Blackwell, Oxford.

Lemke, J.: 1995, *Textual Politics: Discourse and Social Dynamics*, Taylor & Francis, London and Bristol, Pennsylvania.

Macaulay, R.K.: 1977, *Language, Social Class and Education: A Glasgow Study*, Edinburgh University Press, Edinburgh.

Milroy, L.: 1980, *Language and Social Networks*, Basil Blackwell, Oxford.

Milroy, J. & Milroy, L.: 1985, *Authority in Language: Investigating Language Prescription and Standardization*, Routledge & Kegan Paul, London.

Moraes, A., Fontinhas, F. & Neves, I.: 1992, 'Recognition and realisation Rules in acquiring

school science: The contribution of pedagogy and the social background of students',
British Journal of Sociology of Education 13, 247–270.

Romaine, S. (ed.): 1982, *Sociolinguistic Variation in Speech Communities*, Edward Arnold,
London.

Trudgill, P.: 1974, *The Social Differentiation of English in Norwich*, Cambridge University
Press, London.

DEBORAH TANNEN, SHARI KENDALL
AND CAROLYN TEMPLE ADGER

CONVERSATIONAL PATTERNS ACROSS GENDER, CLASS, AND ETHNICITY: IMPLICATIONS FOR CLASSROOM DISCOURSE

Tannen (1984) introduces the term "conversational style" to refer to the unique collection of communicative habits that individuals develop – all the ways they say what they mean – influenced by regional and cultural background, ethnicity, class, age, and gender, as well as numerous other influences such as sexual orientation, profession, and personality. According to Tannen, when individuals' systems for signaling meaning and framing interaction are relatively similar, meaning is likely to be understood more or less as intended. When they are relatively different, speakers' meaning, interactional intentions, and abilities may be misjudged.

In schools that draw their student bodies from multiple speech communities, classroom interaction is susceptible to breakdowns in communication including misunderstandings and misjudgments attributable to conversational style differences; such breakdowns can profoundly affect the school's accomplishment of its mission. This review summarises research into the nature of stylistic differences that are associated with gender, social class, and ethnicity, and their impact on classroom discourse – and on students' educational experiences.

EARLY RESEARCH

Investigation of conversational style patterns across class, gender and ethnicity has its roots in the study of classroom language within the ethnography of communication, ethnomethodology, and sociolinguistics. Early research identified cultural differences in communicative styles between teachers and their students as a major factor in low achievement, since teachers tend to evaluate students' participation based on their own sociolinguistic expectations. Cazden's history of research from 1966 to 1986 on 'actual classroom talk' (1986, p. 433) notes that the focus on communicative style grew out of a new awareness that speech behavior is sensitive to context and that the classroom context is not wholly of the participants' making.

Other early research, mainly from psychology, sociology, communications, and education, explored differences in gender-related communicative styles as a factor in girls' lower performance, focusing on girls' and boys' differential interaction with the teacher in whole-class formats.

B. Davies and D. Corson (eds), Encyclopedia of Language and Education,
Volume 3: Oral Discourse and Education, 75–85.
© 1997 Kluwer Academic Publishers. Printed in the Netherlands.

Overviews of work during the 1970s and 1980s identify the pattern that has been investigated by subsequent work: Boys tend to talk more in the classroom across the educational spectrum (Coates, 1993; Sadker & Sadker, 1994; Swann, 1992; Treichler & Kramarae, 1983).

MAJOR CONTRIBUTIONS

Major work on ethnic and social class differences in conversational style includes Philips' (1983) ethnography of children's school and community behavior (based on research conducted in the early 1970s) on the Warm Springs Indian Reservation. Philips demonstrated that patterns of students' participation that were negatively evaluated in school were positively valued in the community. Native American students participated in official classroom interaction less than their teachers expected them to, responding less often and less fully to teachers' questions, seldom initiating or interrupting to get the floor. Such patterns were illuminated by norms in the community, where children who asserted themselves were viewed as pretentious and bold, and where children were expected to participate in collective rather than solo performances. Significantly, Philips showed that the discontinuity between community and school norms could result in Indian children behaving more rambunctiously than their Anglo peers – not as a reflection of behavior tolerated in the Indian community but because the level of physical activity accepted by the White teachers was so much greater than that accepted by Indians that the Indian children mistakenly concluded, in effect, that there were no holds barred in the White classroom.

Other cultural groups show a disinclination to take the floor in mainstream classes. Malcolm (1979, 1982) reports that indigenous (Aboriginal Australian) students may decline to reply to a teacher's elicitation, or may do so belatedly or in concert with another speaker. Pacific Island students at a New Zealand girls school withdraw from academic interaction that would spotlight the individual, a culturally inappropriate role for them (Jones, 1987). Corson (1993) points out the role of teachers in maintaining interactional conditions that cast culturally based conversational style as a problem.

Heath (1983) not only compared community and school norms of interaction but also shed light on the interaction of race and class. Based on long-term ethnographic work in two rural working-class communities, one Black and one White, Heath found that the children from the working-class communities did not learn the social interactional rules for school literacy events that are more similar to the community interactional patterns of the mainstream middle class townspeople, both Black and White. For example, children from the Black working class community had difficulty when teachers called for 'a strict recounting of facts based on a lesson' because

'The request for a story which simply recounts facts accurately has no parallel in their community' (Heath, 1983, p. 296). Children from the working class White community were able to do this, but were not able to fulfill teachers' requests to ' "make up" a story or to put themselves "in the shoes of a character" in a story from their reading book,' because in their community such 'fanciful, creative, and imaginative accounts . . . would bring punishment or a charge of lying' (p. 296).

At the Kamehameha Early Education Project in Hawaii, anthropological insights on such conflicting school/community norms contributed to design of a culturally appropriate literacy program for non-middle class Native Hawaiian children who were having trouble learning to read (Au & Jordan, 1981). Reading lessons incorporated aspects of a Hawaiian speech event, "talk story", characterized by co-narration among multiple speakers (Watson-Gegeo & Boggs, 1977), and teachers learned to participate as interested adults and co-narrators rather than as dispensers of turns at talk. The researchers emphasize that the reading program includes other elements as well, but the successful incorporation of children's culturally-based cognitive and interactive abilities into school literacy tasks has provided an important exemplar for research-based intervention.

The micro-ethnographic work of Frederick Erickson and his students, begun in the 1970s, also contributed to understanding the processes and consequences of mismatched interactive styles between home and school, particularly with regard to rhythmic synchrony, turntaking, and listener behavior. Focusing on the co-occurrence of stylistic elements and participant identity, Erickson and his students devised methods for tracking elements of 'participation structures' such as turn-taking patterns and rights to the conversational floor (Erickson & Shultz, 1981). Comparing participation structures in structurally similar events – meal time in Italian American children's homes and classroom lessons – Florio and Shultz (1979) found that an Italian-American child would be chastised at school for talking "out of turn" when he participated in a way that was accepted and expected at home.

Current research continues to reflect many of the concerns that are the focus of this classic work: attention to literacy events, the fine-grained analysis of structurally complex interaction, and investigation of the educational consequences of culturally-associated style differences. Many subsequent and current studies reflect the direct or indirect influence of the theoretical framework of contextualization cues developed by Gumperz (1982) and the focus on literacy practices in home and school developed by Cook-Gumperz (1986).

One such research program has evolved from Michaels' (1981) study of "sharing time" in a racially integrated first grade classroom. Michaels identified two culturally-based narrative styles used by students when called upon to address the class: a topic-centered style, preferred by the

White teacher and generally followed by White students, mentioned a narrow topic and produced related details sequentially. In contrast, a topic-associating, episodic style, often used by Black students, established a general topic and then took up other topics suggested by it. The styles differ both in possible topics for a narrative and in how topics are developed. Children whose narrative style differed from that of the teacher were penalized for telling stories that seemed pointless.

Subsequent research on teachers' responses to children's use of these two narrative styles involved playing recordings of episodic and topic-centered stories told in standard English for students at the Harvard Graduate School of Education. As anticipated, Whites preferred the topic-centered stories: They found the episodic stories hard to follow and attributed them to low-achieving students with language problems or even family or emotional problems (Cazden, 1988). Black graduate students appreciated the topic-centered stories, but also praised the use of detail and description in the episodic stories.

Related work by Gee (1989) identifies contrasting narrative devices in a story told to peers by an 11-year-old working class Black girl and one told by a White middle class girl of the same age to an adult. The Black girl conveyed meaning by patterns of rhythm, sound play, repetition, syntactic and semantic parallelism, and changes in tempo, pitch and loudness; the White girl relied primarily on content strategies, such as topic/comment and background/foreground.

Another important contribution to understanding the influence of ethnicity on narrative style is Scollon and Scollon (1984), showing how the discourse structure of Athabaskan narratives and the negotiated nature of Athabaskan conceptions of story meaning contrast with the essayist tradition preferred at school – to the detriment of Athabaskan children in Anglo-influenced classrooms.

Collins (1988) shows that teachers' instructional practices can be influenced by students' community-influenced verbal style. In examining elementary school reading groups, Collins observed that children who used discourse styles and dialect features associated with Black English Vernacular (BEV) when reading aloud frequently received instruction that centered on decoding – sound-word drill – whereas children who read aloud in standard English received instruction that centered on comprehension: Correction of their errors focused on the meaning of the passage they were reading.

In considering the connection between community-influenced style and school success, Corson (1993) argues that the poor school achievement of children from working class, low-income, or minority social group backgrounds is due not entirely to discontinuities between the home and the school, but also to the family's orientation to the dominant style. Some non-mainstream parents work to replicate a school-like interactional setting at home. This echoes McDermott and Gospodinoff's (1981) contention that stylistic contrasts 'are secondary to the political relations between members of the different groups both in the classroom and in the larger community' (p. 212), and that such political relations explain why stylistic differences are not ameliorated over time. Gee (1990) argues too that the differences in style must be seen as ideological – aspects of the broad Discourses that sort students for school success or failure. These issues are relevant for gender-related conversational styles as well.

Early work on gender and language led researchers to investigate the nature of classroom talk in which girls tend to participate less than boys. Based on two decades of observing and analyzing classroom interaction, Sadker and Sadker (1994) identified some of the strategies used by boys, girls, and teachers that result in boys speaking more in the classroom: Boys tend to call out more often, volunteer to speak more often, and disrupt more than girls. Teachers collude in making boys' voices heard by responding to boys' comments regardless of content, waiting longer for them to answer, fixing their gaze on the boys' section of the classroom when formulating questions, and by giving boys more helpful feedback (for example, by asking boys more difficult questions and more follow-up questions, while girls are often rewarded for contributions with a compliment).

A number of researchers argue that the discrepancy in how often girls and boys participate results, in part, from educational practices that institutionalize styles more typically used by boys and men (Corson, 1993; Sadker & Sadker, 1994; Tannen, 1991; Treichler & Kramarae, 1983). Maltz and Borker (1982), summarizing research by numerous others, explain that girls and boys learn to use different strategies in same-sex peer groups. Girls' groups tend to have an egalitarian ethos, so girls learn to use strategies that maintain an appearance of equality. Boys' groups tend to be organized hierarchically, so boys learn to use strategies that raise their status such as attempting to seize center stage by exhibiting skill, displaying knowledge, and challenging and resisting challenges.

Tannen (1991) outlines ways in which college classrooms are more congenial to young men's language experiences than to young women's: First, classroom discussions entail putting oneself forward in front of a large group of people and being judged based on verbal display. Second, students may have different ethics of participation. Many men who speak freely in class assume that it is their job to think of contributions and to try to get the floor to express them, whereas many women monitor their participation not only to get the floor but also to avoid getting it too often, so as not to appear aggressive or overbearing. Those who speak freely may assume that less talkative students have nothing to say, and those who rein themselves in may assume that the talkative students are taking more than their share of class time. Third, our educational system is based on the assumption that learning occurs best in a public debate format by which individuals express ideas in the most absolute form possible, followed by argument and challenge. Ong (1981) demonstrates that this ritual opposition is more reflective of male culture, experience, and training than of female (see reviews by V. Edwards; A.D. Edwards; and Heller in this volume, and by Freeman; Baugh; and Norton in Volume 8).

WORK IN PROGRESS

Most of the work on conversational style and classroom discourse has shown that styles influenced by ethnicity, class, and gender can result in a conflict of norms that contributes to some students' marginalization and failure. But several studies in classrooms where the social identities of teachers and students are more similar have found participants following shared norms that contrast with general patterns of school talk. Foster (1995) examined an African American professor's strategic use of grammatical forms and interactional strategies associated with African American English (AAE). While the professor generally used standard English in accomplishing classroom control, her discourse about the curriculum was peppered with AAE forms, repetition, variations in pitch and tempo, and call and response that invites student participation.

Adger's (1998) study of talk in elementary classrooms where students and teacher are Black focuses on dialect choice as conversational style. Students shift away from African American Vernacular English forms, their usual dialect for instructional talk, toward standard English when literacy tasks invite them to take up the authoritative footing usually reserved for teachers. The popular view that only standard English is appropriate for classroom talk is disputed by these empirical studies that connect dialect and activity types.

Investigation of classroom talk has begun to focus on student/student interaction among language minority students in group work where students construct their own learning and establish a shared, school-centered community (Gutierrez, 1995). Lerner (1995) finds that such groups provide the interactional resources for young bilingual students to develop the literate discourse style that schools value. He observed young students using the incomplete question format with rising intonation typical of teacher talk to guide their group work. Investigating ways in which bilingual third graders framed group activity, Duran and Szymanski (1995) found that without the teacher's presence, students carried out language and literacy development activities such as producing extended academic talk, correcting pronunciation, and collaboratively producing text.

Recent research on gender-related styles has also begun to focus on peer interactions in small groups in order to determine whether girls and boys participate more equally in that format. A number of studies identify parameters that may influence the nature and quantity of participation. Group composition may influence a student's talk because, as Tannen observes, 'Conversational styles are not absolute; everyone's style changes in response to the context and others' styles so that the same person who can be "oppressed" into silence in one context can become the talkative "oppressor" in another' (1991, p. B3).

Reay (1991) considers how girls' and boys' talk in small groups is affected by gender composition. In a house-building activity, an all-girls group organized collaboratively, made decisions by consensus, framed ideas as suggestions and as proposals for joint action, appealed to 'fairness', and gave each other positive feedback. In contrast, a mixed-sex group was organized hierarchically. The boys in the group used explicit commands and marginalized one of the girls.

Holden's (1993) study of 30 small groups in a primary school suggests that both curriculum area and proportion of girls to boys affect the nature of talk and its distribution. In language tasks, girls talked more than boys, unless there were more boys than girls in the group. In the latter situation, talk was distributed the least unequally, though boys still talked more than girls. In addition, this configuration increased boys' use of abstract language to reason, hypothesize and sometimes come to a conclusion, but it substantially decreased girls' use of this type of talk. Conversely, in mathematics/technology tasks, talk was distributed the least unequally when there were more girls than boys.

Sommers and Lawrence's (1992) study of eight mixed-sex peer response groups in college-level writing classes suggests once again the significance of participant structure. The authors found that girls and boys participated equally in 'teacher-directed' groups in which the teacher instructed students to take the floor in turn. This contrasted with 'student-directed' groups which were allowed (or required) to devise their own participant structures – with the result that men spoke more often and took more turns, while women tended to acquiesce more and initiate less. In both types of groups, women and men tended to contribute in different ways: Women tended to mitigate their suggestions, phrasing them as questions or possibilities, or as what they thought or felt. Men tended to make suggestions as definitive statements.

Further evidence that small group structure may in some instances bene- fit boys and disadvantage girls is provided by Cheshire and Jenkins (1991) who analyze the interactions of three mixed-sex groups taking the oral General Certificate of Secondary Education English exam. They found that girls tended to use supportive strategies: backchanneling, overlap- ping, asking questions, and building on others' topics. However, some of the judges attributed these behaviors to the entire group, incorrectly extending them to the boys. In addition, some judges assessed supportive talk in gender-stereotypical ways, penalizing girls for not playing a sustaining role, but rewarding boys who made relatively limited attempts to support others.

PROBLEMS AND DIFFICULTIES

Unfortunately, research on the educational consequences of conversational style differences has had limited impact on the problem of differential school performance. The classic studies are read in teacher education courses, and many of the researchers who contribute to the study of conversational style across gender, class, and ethnicity also work closely with teachers. Yet traditional instructional methods rooted in conversational norms characteristic of the dominant group continue to predominate. Assumptions that privilege those norms and cast others as incorrect and irrelevant to adult success continue to be broadly accepted. Some teachers resist the idea of differentiating among students. As Tannen explains,

> Ignoring such issues as gender and ethnicity becomes a source of pride: 'I treat everyone the same.' But treating people the same is not equal treatment if they are not the same.
> The classroom is a different environment for those who feel comfortable putting themselves forward in a group than it is for those who find the prospect of doing so chastening, or even terrifying. ... Telling them to feel free to jump in will not make them feel free; one's sense of timing, of one's rights and obligations in a classroom, are automatic, learned over years of interaction (1991, p. B3).

Researchers and educators are challenged not only to find ways to bring this body of research to bear on schools but also to influence more generally social attitudes toward ways of speaking. (See Volume 6 on "Knowledge About Language" and the many reviews that address the need for greater language awareness among teachers.)

FUTURE DIRECTIONS

School, classroom, and community-based research on patterns of conversational style has the potential to help schools accommodate the increasingly diverse population of students. Researcher/practitioner teams need to examine local school processes and outcomes and respond to their findings in ways that benefit students. Erickson (1997) and Heath (1994) provide models for how teachers can engage students in investigating language and style in their own communities and incorporating this learning into school practices.

An assumption underlying much of the work on gender-related conversational styles is that increased talk in the classroom is beneficial. Research is needed to determine whether increased talk is in fact beneficial to all students or whether for some students observation and listening are more important. Placing value on equal individual participation in itself reflects culturally-mediated norms.

Potential questions for inquiry include how schools can balance the need to respect students' linguistic, conversational and interactional styles with the possible need for students to learn the styles that are valued in school and in the world of work they are expected to enter. With respect to gender, for example, numerous studies support the finding that boys' interaction tends to be more competitive, girls' more egalitarian, at least on the surface. The style used by many boys and men is more closely aligned with educational practices and values than the style used by many girls and women. But what are the implications of these patterns? Should girls be taught to be more competitive? Should boys be taught to be less so? Should schools attempt to accommodate both styles? Rich and DeVitis (1992) identify competitiveness in – to name only a few areas – testing, grading, promotion, class ranking, scholastic awards, and students' striving against others for teachers' limited attention and favorable treatment. Educators must determine how best to accommodate or attempt to modify student behavior within a system that actively values competition and individual achievement. Moreover, at the same time that children's individual futures are being shaped by their school experience, educators must consider what values children are acquiring and how these values will shape the society of which the children will become members.

Georgetown University, USA
and
Center for Applied Linguistics, USA

REFERENCES

Adger, C.T.: 1998, 'Register shifting with dialect resources in instructional discourse', in S. Hoyle & C.T. Adger (eds.), *Kids Talk: Strategic Language Use in Later Childhood*, Oxford University Press, Oxford and New York.
Au, K. & Jordan, C.: 1981, 'Teaching reading to Hawaiian children: Finding a culturally appropriate solution', in H. Trueba, G.P. Guthrie & K.H. Au (eds.), *Culture and the Bilingual Classroom: Studies in Classroom Ethnography*, Newbury, Rowley, MA, 139–152.
Cazden, C.,: 1986, 'Classroom discourse', in M.E. Wittrock (ed.), *Handbook of Research on Teaching*, Macmillan, New York, 432–463.
Cazden, C.: 1988, *Classroom Discourse: The Language of Teaching and Learning*, Heinemann, Portsmouth, NH.
Cheshire, J. & Jenkins, N.: 1991, 'Gender differences in the GCSE oral English examination: Part 2', *Language and Education* 5, 19–40.
Coates, J.: 1993, *Women, Men, and Language: A Sociolinguistic Account of Gender Differences in Language*, Longman, London & New York.
Collins, J.: 1988, 'Language and class in minority education', *Anthropology and Education Quarterly* 19, 299–326.

Cook-Gumperz, J.: 1986, 'Literacy and schooling: An unchanging equation?', in J. Cook-Gumperz (ed.), *The Social Construction of Literacy*, Cambridge University Press, Cambridge.

Corson, D.J.: 1993, 'Language, gender and education: A critical review linking social justice and power', *Gender and Education* 4, 229–254.

Duran, R.P. & Szymanski, M.H.: 1995, 'Cooperative learning interaction and construction of activity', *Discourse Processes* 19, 149–164.

Erickson, F.: 1997, 'Culture in society and in educational practices', in J.A. Banks & C.A. McGee Banks (eds.), *Multicultural Education: Issues and Perspectives*, 3rd edition, Allyn and Bacon, Boston.

Erickson, F. & Shultz, J.: 1981, 'When is a context? Some issues and methods in the analysis of social competence', in J. Green & C. Wallat (eds.), *Ethnography and Language in Educational Settings*, Ablex, Norwood, NJ, 147–160.

Florio, S. & Shultz, J.: 1979, 'Social competence at home and at school', *Theory into Practice* 18, 234–243.

Foster, M.: 1995, 'Talking that talk: The language of control, curriculum, and critique,' *Linguistics and Education* 7, 129–151.

Gee, J.P.: 1989, 'Two styles of narrative construction and their linguistic and educational implications', *Discourse Processes* 12, 287–307.

Gee, J.P.: 1990, *Social Linguistics and Literacies: Ideology in Discourses*, Falmer, Hampshire, UK.

Gumperz, J.J.: 1982, *Discourse Strategies*, Cambridge University Press, Cambridge.

Gutierrez, K.D. & Meyer, B.: 1995, 'Creating communities of effective practice: Building literacy for language minority children', in J. Oakes & K.H. Quartz (eds.), *Creating New Educational Communities: Ninety-fourth Yearbook of the National Society for the Study of Education*, University of Chicago Press, Chicago, 32–52.

Heath, S.B.: 1983, *Ways with Words: Language, Life, and Work in Communities and Classrooms*, Cambridge University Press, Cambridge.

Heath, S.B.: 1994, 'Stories as ways of acting together', in A.H. Dyson & C. Genishi (eds.), *The Need for Story: Cultural Diversity in Classroom and Community*, NCTE, Urbana, IL.

Holden, C.: 1993, 'Giving girls a chance: Patterns of talk in co-operative group work', *Gender and Education* 5, 179–189.

Jones, A.: 1987, 'Which girls are "learning to lose"?', in S. Middleton (ed.), *Women and Education in Aotearoa*, Allen and Unwin, Wellington, 143–152.

Lerner, G: 1995, 'Turn design and the organization of participation in instructional activities', *Discourse Processes* 19, 111–131.

Malcolm, I.: 1979, 'The west Australian aboriginal child and classroom interaction: A sociolinguistic approach,' *Journal of Pragmatics* 3, 305–320.

Malcolm, I.: 1982, 'Speech events of the aboriginal classroom', *International Journal of the Sociology of Language* 36, 115–134.

Maltz, D.N. & Borker, R.A.: 1982, 'A cultural approach to male-female miscommunication', in J.J. Gumperz (ed.), *Language and Social Identity*, Cambridge University Press, Cambridge, 196–216.

McDermott, R. & Gospodinoff, K.: 1981, 'Social contexts for ethnic borders and school failure', in H. Trueba, G.P. Guthrie, & K.H. Au (eds.), *Culture and the Bilingual Classroom: Studies in Classroom Ethnography*, Newbury, Rowley, MA, 212–233.

Michaels, S.: 1981, ' "Sharing time": Children's narrative styles and differential access to literacy', *Language in Society* 10, 423–442.

Ong, W.J.: 1981, *Fighting for Life: Contest, Sexuality, and Consciousness*, The University of Massachusetts Press, Amherst.

Philips, S.U.: 1983. *The Invisible Culture: Communication in Classroom and Community on the Warm Springs Indian Reservation*, Longman, New York.

Reay, D.: 1991, 'Intersections of gender, race and class in the primary school', *British Journal of Sociology of Education* 12(2), 163–182.

Rich, J.M. & DeVitis, J.L.: 1992, *Competition in Education*, Charles C. Thomas, Springfield IL.

Sadker, M. & Sadker, D.: 1994, *Failing at Fairness: How Americas' Schools Cheat Girls*, Touchstone, New York.

Scollon, R. & Scollon, S.: 1984. 'Cooking it up and boiling it down: Abstracts in Athabaskan children's story retellings', in D. Tannen (ed.), *Coherence in Spoken and Written Discourse*, Ablex, Norwood, NJ, 173–197.

Sommers, E. & Lawrence, S.: 1992, 'Women's ways of talking in teacher-directed and student-directed peer response groups', *Linguistics and Education* 4(1), 1–35.

Swann, J.: 1992, *Girls, Boys, and Language*, Blackwell, Oxford & Cambridge MA.

Tannen, D.: 1984, *Conversational Style: Analyzing Talk Among Friends*, Ablex, Norwood, NJ.

Tannen, D.: 1991, 'Teachers' classroom strategies should recognize that men and women use language differently', *The Chronicle of Higher Education* 37(40), B2–3.

Treichler, P. & Kramarae, C.: 1983, 'Women's talk in the Ivory Tower', *Communication Quarterly* 31(2), 118–132.

Watson-Gegeo, K. & Boggs, S.T.: 1977, 'From verbal play to talk story: The role of routines', in S. Ervin-Tripp & C. Mitchell-Kernan (eds.), *Child Discourse*, Academic, New York, 67–90.

MONICA HELLER

LANGUAGE CHOICE AND SYMBOLIC DOMINATION

Research on language choice and symbolic domination in schooling can be seen as one approach to one of the major sociological questions regarding education, namely the role of education in social and cultural reproduction. Sociologists and anthropologists of education have long argued that, while schooling often is supposed to be a major means of meritocratic, and hence democratic, access to social success, in fact its evaluation procedures favour the already successful. In other words, schooling simply reproduces existing social hierarchies, whether based on class, ethnicity, race, religion or gender.

Most of this research was based on examination of patterns of school achievement, that is on the statistically skewed outcomes of the educational process. Bourdieu and Passeron's (1970) pioneering work on this subject focussed attention on the process of social selection through education. Central to their argument is the notion that schools contribute to social and cultural reproduction because the knowledge they value is not, as they claim, universal, but rather is the privileged property of the dominant classes. As a result, students who come to school already possessing that knowledge have a better chance of doing well at school than those who do not. However, in order to fulfill this function effectively, it is crucial that it be masked; that is, all participants must accept the basic, albeit false, assumption, that schools really are meritocratic. Bourdieu and Passeron term symbolic domination the ability of the dominant classes to convince themselves and others that the existing social hierarchy is thus justified on the basis of inherent properties of people or knowledge (this might include personality characteristics such as talent or drive, or properties of knowledge, such as the relative purity or clarity of languages).

For Bourdieu and Passeron, language is central to the exercise of symbolic domination, for it is through language that reality is socially constructed. Clearly, this implies that there are many ways in which linguistic variation, as it is tied to social differentiation and stratification, is relevant to social and cultural reproduction. However, for the purposes of this review I will limit myself to two of the more evident ways in which language contributes to this process, that is, through preferences for the acquisition and display of knowledge through certain languages (or language varieties) rather than others, or for the acquisition and display of knowledge of certain languages themselves.

B. Davies and D. Corson (eds), Encyclopedia of Language and Education,
Volume 3: Oral Discourse and Education, 87–94.
© *1997 Kluwer Academic Publishers. Printed in the Netherlands.*

In the rest of this review, I will show how Bourdieu and Passeron's notions have met up with an Anglo-American tradition of sociolinguistic interest in linguistic and social difference and school success, and how the resulting cross-fertilization is currently permitting an analysis of the local and global conditions influencing social selection through language choice in multilingual educational settings. This type of analysis opens the door to explorations not only of social reproduction (the only scenario Bourdieu and Passeron discussed), but also of challenges to existing forms of symbolic domination. In the final section, I will consider some implications of these current areas of research for future trends in research, policy and practice.

DEFICIT, DIFFERENCE AND DOMINANCE: SOCIOLINGUISTIC APPROACHES TO SCHOOL ACHIEVEMENT

In the 1960s, among the prominent explanations offered for the skewed representation of certain groups among those doing well, or, conversely, doing poorly, at school, the argument that the problem was due to cognitive, social and linguistic deficit among unsuccessful student populations (Bereiter & Engelmann, 1966; Jensen, 1969) was particularly influential. (Similar arguments are still being made today.) In other words, researchers argued that some students did poorly because they were not well-equipped (genetically, or by their environment) before entering school. It was held that the problem was due to lack of knowledge, of cognitive and social stimulation, and of cognitive and linguistic skills among certain segments of the population.

Along with other social scientists, several prominent sociolinguists (notably William Labov & John Gumperz; cf. Labov, 1972, 1982; Gumperz, 1982, 1986) attacked this argument on the grounds that sociolinguistics showed that the problem was not one of degrees of knowledge, but rather one of kind. They demonstrated that educationally unsuccessful groups certainly possessed systematic knowledge (for example, their linguistic production was perfectly grammatical, even if its rules were different from those of the standard). According to them, the problem was that schools did not recognize this knowledge, since it was different from the forms of knowledge valued by educators. This insight inspired over a decade's worth of research focussing first on discovering the nature of linguistic and cultural differences at play in a variety of settings and their consequences for educational evaluation, and second on ways of transforming schooling so as to take these differences into account in ways that might equalize chances of school success for otherwise marginalized groups.

The most influential of these studies focussed on differences between White, Black and Native American students and schools in the United States. Among these, it is important to cite the early work of Philips (1972), who showed that Native American ways of learning and of displaying knowledge were radically at variance with those of classrooms run by White teachers. In particular, Native American students were accustomed to learning by observation, to collective undertakings, and to choosing when to display competence once acquired. Teachers' insistence on individual displays of the learning process forced students to violate their cultural norms, resulting in patterns of student resistance. Michaels (1981) showed that Black students' narrative styles differed from those expected by White teachers; as a result, those teachers were actually unable to discern Black students' narrative structures. Hence, from an early age, these students were understood not as having a different competence, but as being incompetent. In addition, as Michaels and others showed (cf, Collins, 1988; Erickson & Shultz, 1982), not only were students of different backgrounds negatively evaluated, they also received differential treatment which effectively closed off for them any hope of educational success. Well-meaning attempts to "help" (such as remedial reading programs), in fact tended to increase the distance between targeted students and the kinds of knowledge they would need in order to do well in school.

On the basis of such research, a number of individually and collectively initiated action-research programs were undertaken with the intention of building into teaching and learning practices not only an awareness of linguistic and cultural differences, but also of modifying curriculum and pedagogy in order to make it more culturally compatible for minority students. Among the better-known of these is the work of Heath (1983), who examined language socialization patterns among working-class and middle-class Black and White families in the U.S. south. Based on her findings, she worked with teachers and students to increase awareness of linguistic and cultural differences at play in the community and school; her use of ethnographic techniques as learning and teaching practices might stand as one source of the more recent language awareness movement. Other significant work in this domain includes the reading programs implemented in the Hawaiian Kamehameha schools for Native Hawaiian students, which build on indigenous collective oral narrative strategies to modify literacy and literacy preparation activities in the classroom (Au & Jordan, 1981; Jordan, 1984); and the culturally compatible programs and practices implemented in a Navajo school (Vogt et al., 1993; McCarty et al., 1991). While language choice (Black English, Hawaiian, Navajo) is clearly one element of cultural compatibility, these efforts incorporate the issue of language choice into the broader context of cultural practices of teaching and learning, that is, of acquiring, constructing and displaying knowledge.

While such research has inspired many people, and many such programs seem to have met with at least a certain degree of success, they have also encountered criticism from a number of quarters (for example, Ogbu, 1993; Delpit, 1988; de Castell & Walker, 1991). What these critiques have in common is that they point out that the cultural-difference model (as it has come to be known) cannot account for some cases because it does not take into account the relationship between cultural difference and social dominance; in other words, it tends to ignore the relations of power which obtain in schooling (and in research on schooling), and to neglect schooling's contribution to social and cultural reproduction. Its primary recommendation (culturally-compatible programs and pedagogy) does not accord with minority needs to at least understand the language and culture of power (Delpit, 1988), and will not work unless students are convinced that education will actually get them somewhere (Ogbu, 1993; Erickson, 1993). It also fails to address issues faced in ethnolinguistically heterogeneous settings, whether stable or in flux.

Recent research has tried then to understand the relationship between school and community language and cultural practices as one of power, in which differences are embedded in the exercise of and resistance to the school's power to impose its values and norms on students and their families. Much of this research has in fact focussed on the issue of language choice, as one area where struggles over the value and distribution of linguistic and cultural capital may emerge most clearly. One reason for this is that research on codeswitching since the 1970s had demonstrated the prevalence of this practice in (usually officially monolingual) educational institutions in multilingual settings, and had established its effectiveness for purposes of social, discourse and conversational organization (Martin-Jones, 1995). However, by the early 1990s, this strand of research had also developed an awareness of the necessity of examining the social, economic and political constraints and processes which not only make language choice an issue in such settings, but also make them meaningful. It became clear, in other words, that language choice practices in educational settings were about, and had to be understood in terms of, social structures and processes beyond the ethnographic present and the local site (Heller, 1995a). Indeed, given the centrality of social selection in educational processes, it became clear that language choice in schools or other educational settings was at least in part about struggles of power, about, quite literally, whose voice would dominate educational discourse, about whom education is really for.

LANGUAGE CHOICE AND SYMBOLIC
DOMINATION IN EDUCATIONAL SETTINGS

Work in this area focusses both on the relationship between standard and non-standard varieties of the same language, as well as between other kinds of language varieties, more or less linguistically related. The issue of power emerges clearly in the first, since by definition what characterizes standard languages is the authority institutionally invested in them (this of course raises the question of who controls the institutions). In the second, the issue of power is connected to the relations of inequality obtaining between speakers of the languages in contact, whether due to conditions of colonization, immigration, conquest, or other processes.

Some of this work has emerged from a reflexive movement in applied linguistics, in particular among those engaged in the field of English as a Second Language. Several publications, notably Phillipson (1992) and Pennycook (1994), have focussed on the importance of moving away from examining language teaching and learning as principally technical, or universalistically cognitive, processes, and of taking into account the relations of power which inform them (this is particularly obvious in the case of English, the new global lingua franca).

Other work is emerging from other kinds of settings, notably post-colonial settings where some are beginning to question the practice of using the former colonial language as the language of instruction; from politically mobilized indigenous or long-established minorities fighting for the right to use their language as the language of instruction; and in areas of dynamic immigration, where almost every day new questions are raised about the linguistic dimensions of relations among groups. This trend is usefully captured in Martin-Jones & Heller (1996a, b), a collection of papers from a variety of such settings around the world. The collection explicitly aims to link language choice practices in interaction in educational settings to institutional processes, and to the political economic foundations of symbolic domination. The central notion is that codes represent institutional authority, or challenges to that authority, and can be drawn on in ways which serve principally to establish or resist the local, interactional order, and through that order, the larger institutional, and social, one. It is the mediation through the local interactional order which instantiates symbolic domination, since it is there that relations of power are masked through appeals to legitimizing ideologies.

For example, Heller (1995b) shows how, in French-language minority schools in Canada, the authority of the teacher is maintained through an interactional order based on a sequential organization of turn-taking, which is institutionally legitimized through the notion of "respect" ("respect" means listening silently while others talk, and talking when invited to do so). This local interactional order permits teachers to control both the form and content of talk in ways which, among other things, allow them to reproduce institutional language norms (a preference for standard, monolingual-type French). These norms are in turn legitimized through the notion that they are necessary for the maintenance of French as a minority language, and for the maintenance of the quality of that French. The unintended effect, however, is to privilege students who are speakers of the valued variety of French, members of the new middle class, as against working class speakers of the (often bilingual) vernacular, despite the fact that the schools ostensibly exist to promote the interests of all francophones, and especially those who suffer most from economic, social and political marginalization. Williams (1987), Jaffe (1993) and McDonald (1990) have made similar arguments about how the standardization of minority languages (in their cases, Welsh, Corsican & Breton) through education (as well as through related forms of linguistic research and legislation) serves the interests of emerging middle classes who benefit from political mobilization, while constructing new relations of inequality internal to the ostensibly unified minority. These cases, as well as others (see above), show clearly how language choice helps to reproduce (or, on rare occasions, to challenge) the unequal distribution of resources in the community through symbolic domination.

FUTURE DIRECTIONS

I have traced here a developing commitment to understanding language choice in education as a matter of power, as well as a commitment to examining the role of language in educational processes of social reproduction. These orientations have implications for further research, and also for educational policy and practice. Two priorities for research stand out. The first has to do with internal linkages, the second with cross-setting comparison. Current work has begun to explore the ways in which language choice as a discursive or conversational strategy is connected to its effects regarding the distribution of linguistic (and hence other cultural, or even material) resources, that is, to social and cultural reproduction. However, we still understand poorly the nature of that link, and in particular of its relationship to legitimating ideologies of language, class, ethnicity, gender and education, and to institutional structures and processes. In addition, we know we must look for institutional and ideological interstices in order to discover possibilities for resistance and change (Heller, 1995b; Martin-Jones & Heller, 1996a, b), but we do not yet really know how to look for them. Also, clearly, generalizations cannot be made without a close understanding of individual, socially- and historically-situated cases, and we are beginning to build up such a body of ethnographic work. Eventually, comparisons across cases will be necessary.

The results of such research have clear practical implications. This work fundamentally asks who education is for, who benefits from the way things are, and who is marginalized. That leaves us with the question of whether we are happy with the picture our research portrays, or whether changes are needed. Either way, such research should help us understand what policies and practices actually produce, and therefore help identify critical points of intervention. Most importantly, it shows that educational language choices are never neutral.

Ontario Institute for Studies in Education
University of Toronto, Canada

REFERENCES

Au, K. & Jordan, C.: 1981, 'Teaching reading to Hawaiian children: Finding a culturally appropriate solution', in H. Trueba, G. Guthrie & K. Au (eds.), *Culture in the Bilingual Classroom: Studies in Classroom Ethnography*, Newbury House, Rowley MA, 139–152.

Bereiter, C. & Engelmann, S.: 1966, *Teaching Disadvantaged Children in the Pre-School*, Prentice Hall, Englewood Cliffs NJ.

Bourdieu, P. & Passeron, J.-C.: 1972, *La reproduction: éléments pour une théorie du système d'enseignement*, Minuit, Paris.

Collins, J.: 1988, 'Language and class in minority education', *Anthropology and Education Quarterly* 19(4), 299–326.

de Castell, S. & Walker, T.: 1991, 'Identity, metamorphosis and ethnographic research: What kind of story is ways with words?', *Anthropology and Education Quarterly* 22(1), 3–20.

Delpit, L.: 1988, 'The silenced dialog: Power and pedagogy in educating other peoples' children', *Harvard Educational Review* 58(3), 280–298.

Erickson, F.: 1993, 'Transformation and school success: The politics and culture of educational achievement', in E. Jacob & C. Jordan (eds.), *Minority Education: Anthropological Perspectives*, Ablex, Norwood NJ, 27–52.

Erickson, F. & Shultz, J.: 1982, *The Counsellor as Gatekeeper: Social Selection in Interviews*, Academic Press, New York.

Gumperz, J.: 1982, 'Socio-cultural knowledge in conversational inference', in J. Gumperz (ed.), *Discourse Strategies*, Cambridge University Press, Cambridge, 153–171.

Gumperz, J.: 1986, 'Interactional sociolinguistics in the study of schooling', in J. Cook-Gumperz (ed.), *The Social Construction of Literacy*, Cambridge University Press, Cambridge, 45–68.

Heath, S.B.: 1983, *Ways With Words*, Cambridge University Press, Cambridge.

Heller, M.: 1995a, 'Code-switching and the politics of language', in L. Milroy & P. Muysken (eds.), *One Speaker, Two Languages: Cross-disciplinary Perspectives on Code-switching*, Cambridge University Press, Cambridge, 158–174.

Heller, M.: 1995b, 'Language choice, social institutions and symbolic domination', *Language in Society* 24(3), 373–405.

Jaffe, A.: 1993, 'Obligation, error and authenticity: Competing cultural principles in the teaching of corsican', *Journal of Linguistic Anthropology* 3(1), 99–114.

Jensen, A.: 1969, 'How much can we boost IQ and scholastic Achievement?', *Harvard Educational Review* 39, 1–123.

Jordan, C.: 1984, 'Cultural compatibility and the education of ethnic minority children', *Educational Research Quarterly* 8(4), 59–71.

Labov, W.: 1972, 'The logic of non-standard English', in W. Labov (ed.), *Language in the Inner City*, University of Pennsylvania Press, Philadelphia, 201–240.

Labov, W.: 1982, 'Objectivity and commitment in linguistic science: The case of the black English trial in Ann Arbor', *Language in Society* 11(2), 165–202.

Martin-Jones, M.: 1995, 'Code-switching in the classroom: Two decades of research', in L. Milroy & P. Muysken (eds.), *One Speaker, Two Languages: Cross-disciplinary Perspectives on Code-switching*, Cambridge University Press, Cambridge, 90–111.

Martin-Jones, M. & Heller, M. (eds.): 1996a, 'Education in multilingual settings: Discourse, identities and power, Part 1: Constructing legitimacy', *Special issue of Linguistics and Education* 8(1).

Martin-Jones, M. & Heller, M. (eds.): 1996b, 'Education in multilingual settings: Discourse, identities and power, Part 2: Contesting legitimacy, *Special issue of Linguistics and Education* 8(2).

McCarty, T., Wallace, S., Lynch, R. & Benally, A.: 1991, 'Classroom inquiry and Navajo learning styles: A call for reassessment', *Anthropology and Education Quarterly* 22(1), 42–59.

McDonald, M.: 1990, *We Are Not French*, Routledge, London.

Michaels, S.: 1981, ' "Sharing time": Childrens' narrative styles and differential access to literacy', *Language in Society* 10(3), 423–442.

Ogbu, J.: 1993, 'Variability in minority school performance: A problem in search of an explanation', in E. Jacob & C. Jordan (eds.), *Minority Education: Anthropological Perspectives*, Ablex, Norwoord NJ, 83–112.

Pennycook, A.: 1994, *The Cultural Politics of English as an International Language*, Longman, London.

Philips, S.: 1972, 'Participant structures and communicative competence: Warm springs children in community and classroom', in C. Cazden, V. John & D. Hymes (eds.), *Functions of Language in the Classroom*, Teachers College Press, New York, 370–394.

Phillipson, R.: 1992, *Linguistic Imperialism*, Oxford University Press, Oxford.

Vogt, L., Jordan, C. & Tharp, R.: 1993, 'Explaining school failure, producing school success. Two cases', in E. Jacob & C. Jordan (eds.), *Minority Education: Anthropological Perpsectives*, Ablex, Norwood NJ, 53–66.

Williams, G.: 1987, 'Bilingualism, class dialect and social reproduction', *International Journal of the Sociology of Language* 66, 85–98.

VIV EDWARDS

TEACHER-PUPIL TALK IN MULTI-ETHNIC CLASSROOMS

When children first start school, they encounter many new kinds of inter-action. They have to learn to take turns in much larger groups than they experience in a family setting; they discover that some topics of discussion are more acceptable than others; they also find that their contributions are evaluated by teachers in ways which often differ markedly from those they have experienced at home. All children, then, are expected to adapt to the new circumstances which prescribe patterns of talk in school. However, the different behaviours and expectations which distinguish children in inter-ethnic classrooms ensure that some children experience far greater cultural discontinuity between home and school than others. This is an area which has been the focus for a growing body of research in recent years.

EARLY DEVELOPMENTS

The foundations for the study of teacher-pupil talk in inter-ethnic class-rooms were laid in the development of sociolinguistics and, more specifi-cally, in the ethnography of communication in the 1970s and 1980s. The merging of interests of anthropologists and sociolinguists made it possible to construct models to explain the nature of cross-cultural differences in communication and how these sometimes lead to misunderstandings.

Early research reported in key works such as Hymes (1964) and Bauman & Sherzer (1974), and overviewed by Saville-Troike (1982) pointed to a wide range of speech events in different cultures which were explored later in educational settings. Relevant issues include discussions of when it is appropriate to speak. At the one end of the spectrum, native American groups can wait several minutes before taking a turn in the conversation; at the other end, it is perfectly acceptable in African-Caribbean societies for several people to speak at the same time. Different ways of listening have also received attention: in some cultures, people show attention by looking directly at the speaker, in others by averting their gaze. There was a growing awareness, then, of the potential for breakdown in cross-cultural communication.

The comprehensive model of politeness phenomena developed by Brown & Levinson (1978) was also to prove to be of great significance for later research. They introduced the notions of positive and negative politeness. Positive politeness strategies are often associated with Hispanic

B. Davies and D. Corson (eds), Encyclopedia of Language and Education,
Volume 3: Oral Discourse and Education, 95–103.
© *1997 Kluwer Academic Publishers. Printed in the Netherlands.*

societies; they stress intimacy and an appreciation of other members of the group. Negative politeness strategies stress social distance, deference and respect and are often linked with far eastern and native American cultures. The realisation that different groups express respect in different ways had vitally important implications for much of the research which followed.

MAJOR CONTRIBUTIONS

Philips' (1972) study of native American children in Warm Springs, Oregon was the first serious attempt to examine the effects of different patterns of communication in the classroom and paved the way for the many studies which followed. She was able to explain children's reluctance to speak out alone in front of other students or when requested by the teacher in terms of differences in 'participant structures' in school and the students' home community (see the review by Heller in this volume).

Malcolm (1979) explores this same question in an Australian context, showing how communication commonly breaks down in Aboriginal classrooms. He describes classroom interactions in terms of seven different speech acts: empty bidding in response to teacher questions (followed by silence); declined replying (after a direct elicitation from the teacher); deferred replying (after a longer than normal pause); shadowed replying (in the shadow of the next speaker); and unsolicited replying. All of these interactions are likely to be interpreted as disruptive or inappropriate by teachers unfamiliar with the discourse norms in Aboriginal communities.

Michaels & Cazden (1986) look at 'sharing time' or 'show and tell', the classroom activity where children report something that has happened to them or talk about something they have brought from home. It would seem that Black and White children in the USA approach sharing time in different ways. White children tend to have a marked beginning, middle and end to their stories, with no shifts in time and place. They use the same 'topic-centred style' as the teacher, who picks up on their topic and expands it with comments and questions. In contrast, many Black children have a 'topic associating style'. They tend to tell stories made up of a series of personal anecdotes which shift in time and place and have no explicit point. Writers such as Hyon & Sulzby (1994) and Champion et al. (1995) have subsequently questioned whether the topic associated style is, in fact, the dominant pattern for African-Americans. None the less, the findings of the earlier research underline the importance of teacher sensitivity to culturally-based discourse patterns.

White teachers sometimes feel that Black children 'ramble on' and interrupt them with inappropriate questions. Yet closer analysis shows that Black children do produce well-structured stories; the problem lies rather in the teachers' ability to recognise what they are doing. In 'sharing time' children are encouraged to be explicit and not to assume that other members of the class will know what they are talking about. This provides a valuable oral preparation for literacy: it promotes skills such as finding the most important idea, ordering events, and summarising the main point of a story. By cutting Black children short, they may well be depriving them of valuable opportunities for rehearsing written language.

Malcolm (1994) describes a similar phenomenon in an Australian setting: non-indigenous teachers frequently complain that the narrative accounts of indigenous children lack structure. However, as was the case for African-American children, the problem can be explained in terms of teachers' lack of familiarity with features of oral discourse rather than in the narratives themselves. He also identifies a culture-specific element of the narratives which he labels 'tracking': the story alternately moves and 'stops', possibly reflecting the ways in which traditional narratives have been linked to spatial geography rather than being chronologically organised.

Also in an Australian context, Malin (1990) reports a study of Aboriginal children in an Adelaide suburban school in which, despite the good intentions of the teacher, the children's strengths remained 'invisible' in the classroom context and deviations from the norm were evaluated negatively.

Jones' (1987) study of fifteen year old Pacific Island girls born in New Zealand raises similar issues. It emerges that the girls speak less and are spoken to less frequently than their European peers. They explain their unwillingness to speak out in whole class interactions in terms of their aversion to being the centre of attention. Although teachers respond by reducing their demand on the girls to speak out in public, they do not attempt to develop alternative strategies for recognising the girls' contribution as members of the class.

The findings of the New Zealand research are mirrored to some extent in two British studies undertaken with young children. Ogilvy et al. (1990) report that, although staff believed they were treating children in multi-ethnic nurseries according to their individual needs, they had fewer verbal interactions with South Asian children, failed to sustain conversations with them, spoke for them when answers were required and tended to use reduced English structures. In a second study, this time of 5–6 year old children in multi-ethnic classrooms, Biggs & Edwards (1991) show that teacher interactions with pupils from Black and South Asian families are different from those with their white classmates. They found that teachers interacted less frequently with ethnic minority students and spent less time with them discussing the tasks which had been set. Despite the acknowledged sensitivity of some teachers to issues of racism in the classroom, qualitative analysis indicated that they often behave in subtly different ways towards ethnic minority children.

Using knowledge to bring about change

The studies of pupil-teacher interaction in inter-ethnic classrooms reviewed above all deal with differences between mainstream assumptions about appropriate forms of communication in the classroom and actual classroom behaviours. Some of these studies also examine attempts to use this knowledge to influence teacher behaviours and subsequent outcomes for minority children.

Heath (1983), for instance, describes her work with teachers who could not understand why African-American children were not participating in classes in the newly desegregated town in the south east USA. One of the areas of difference which Heath identified from her anthropological fieldwork was that children were not used to being asked 'known-answer' questions about objects and events. She worked with teachers to think critically about the questions they were asking and to experiment with patterns of interaction in the classroom. For instance, teachers were advised to start with familiar content and familiar kinds of talk; to move on to new kinds of talk which none the less retained familiar content, providing peer models on audiocassettes; to encourage students to practice these new kinds of talk first on tape and then in lessons; and to talk to the children about talk itself.

Another influential initiative which led to changes in teacher behaviour is reported in Jordan's (1985) account of the Kamehameha Early Education Program (KEEP) in Hawaii. In discussing books which they had read, turn-taking rules were relaxed in order to allow children to speak without being called upon by the teacher and even to overlap with other students' contributions. This overlapping is characteristic of much Polynesian speech, including a highly stylised event called 'talk story' which uses co-narrators whose contributions overlap not only with each other but with the audience. The usual high rate of teacher praise for individuals was replaced with more indirect praise or praise intended for the group; and children were grouped 'vertically' so that more advanced students could more easily help less experienced peers. Using this approach, children were able to demonstrate a much better understanding of what they had read. Teachers also began to change their views of children as lacking in motivation or difficult to manage.

KEEP researchers, Vogt et al. (1985), confirmed the importance of cultural differences when they attempted to apply techniques developed with Polynesian students in Navajo classrooms in Arizona. Some aspects of the KEEP approach were successful. For instance, Navajo children seemed more comfortable answering questions addressed to the group as a whole; they also spoke for longer, volunteering questions and comments. However, other aspects such as vertical grouping, did not work as well.

The study underlines the importance of establishing appropriate norms of interaction for all cultures.

Cazden (1989) and May (1995) both describe initiatives which recognise and incorporate understandings of Maori and Polynesian culture into the organisation of Richmond Road, a multi-ethnic primary school in New Zealand. Children are organised into *ropu* or vertical groups for children between the ages of 5 and 11; reciprocal instruction drawing on the principle of 'whoever has knowledge teaches' is common; resources are developed co-operatively by teachers for use throughout the school (see the reviews by May in Volumes 1 and 8).

Same-ethnicity teachers

Researchers have also started to explore what happens when teachers and pupils share the same cultural and linguistic background. In a study of Amish classrooms in Pennsylvania, McDermott (1977) points to the heavy use of imperatives and direct instruction which might appear authoritarian and oppressive to outsiders. It can be argued, however, that this approach meshes well with the norms of a closed community regulated by specific routines and underpinned by common sense and mutual trust.

Erikson et al. (1983), in a study of two first grade bilingual classrooms in Chicago, point to the importance of cariño (a close and caring relationship) in Hispanic teachers' interactions with their students. This takes the form of in-group forms of address, frequent use of diminutives, reminders about interpersonal respect, demonstrations of the teachers' knowledge of students' family life and close physical behaviour. Cariño, or personalization, is, of course an example of a positive politeness strategy and stands in contrast to the privatisation strategies which characterize both Anglo and Native American classrooms, albeit in very different degrees.

Research on effective Black teachers also points to the importance of acknowledging students' cultural roots. Writers such as Foster (1991) talk in terms of connectedness, a notion closely related to cariño, which implies the presence of strong kinship bonds and a sense of mutual obligation. The firm but nurturing communicative style of Black teachers closely resembles that of Black parents. Black teachers also encourage cultural patterns of collectivity. Researchers in North America (e.g. Ladson-Billings & Henry, 1990) and Great Britain (e.g. Callender, 1995), for instance, report the use of Black communicative behaviours including participative patterns such as call-and-response, repetition, proverbs and characteristic non-verbal and paralinguistic features to establish such connectedness.

Similar observations have been made about teacher-pupil interactions in *kura kaupapa Maori*, primary schools in New Zealand organised by the Maori community (see, Corson, 1993 for a review of this area). These schools stress the importance of a holistic and co-operative relationship

with the universe. Consequently, boundaries between school subjects
reduce and learning is treated as a co-operative venture involving children,
teachers and parents.

WIDER SOCIETAL ISSUES

Another important focus for researchers has been the pattern of underper-
formance identified for many minority children whose discourse norms
differ in important ways from those of their teachers. Bourdieu (1991), for
instance, describes the ways in which schools reproduce the *status quo* by
valuing the linguistic and cultural 'capital' associated with certain social
groups.

In a stratified society, however, it is not enough to simply differentiate
between dominant and subordinate groups. Thus Ogbu (1987) contrasts
immigrant and involuntary minorities. Immigrant minorities arrive with
strong social and cultural identities and do not perceive the educational
ideology of the new country as threatening their cultural identity and tend
to do relatively well in school. In contrast, involuntary minorities who
have been present in the country for generations have been relegated to
low status positions and refuse to collude with the dominant educational
ideology which reinforces their powerlessness.

Cummins (1996) distinguishes between assimilationist and intercultural
orientations in an attempt to explain differential educational outcomes for
minority children. In the assimilationist view, the children's language and
culture are overlooked; community participation is discouraged; pedagogy
is based on the transmission of a predefined body of knowledge; and assessment is used as a tool for legitimating both this knowledge and the forms
of transmission. In contrast, educators with an intercultural orientation
strive to include children's language and culture; involve parents and community in students' learning; act as facilitators, drawing on experiences
which are relevant for the children, encouraging a critical engagement with
information; and attempt to identify those aspects of children's educational
experience which are standing in the way of their success.

PROBLEMS AND DIFFICULTIES

This overview of major studies on pupil-teacher talk points to the widespread failure of mainstream educators to recognise or take into account
differences in conversational norms in the development of the school curriculum, thus making it difficult for minority children to understand white
mainstream modes of classroom organization. It is important to remember,
however, that discourse conventions cannot simply be described in terms
of linguistic differences. Rather they are inextricably linked with different
cultural values. Indeed it is sometimes difficult to see how accommoda-

tion can be reached between groups which hold highly divergent views of education and society.

When children are taking part in bilingual education programmes or attend schools where all or most of the student population come from a given community, the presence of a teacher from the same community is an enormous asset. The situation is more complex, however, when teachers share a cultural history with only some of their students. Callender (1995) for instance, draws attention to the fact that, while Black teachers' communication is emancipatory in intent, it may be perceived as unacceptably firm by both White colleagues and White students.

Problems of a rather different nature arise when the minority community in question consider themselves to be of equal or superior status to the numerically dominant group. In an analysis of the experiences of Japanese children at school in the UK, McPake & Powney (1995) draw attention to the prevailing western view that children are active learners; that speaking and listening play a vital role in the learning process; and that teachers can use children's classroom talk to assess what they have understood. In Japanese education, in contrast, it is believed that the main way in which children learn is by listening to the teacher; children are encouraged to speak only in response to teacher questions and talk between pupils is not tolerated.

The difference in these educational philosophies has been observed to give rise to dissonant experiences in British classrooms as children struggle to make sense of contradictory notions of how they should behave. At the outset, Japanese children are reluctant to speak, partly because of limited competence in English but also for cultural reasons. Even when they become proficient speakers of English, it is rare for them to make active contributions to classroom discussion. British teachers' frustration at Japanese children's reluctance to participate is fuelled by their belief that much learning is achieved through talk. Japanese parents, for their part, expect their children to be silently respectful and are baffled by teachers' advice to encourage them to talk.

FUTURE DIRECTIONS

Our understanding of teacher-pupil talk in inter-ethnic classrooms has been revolutionised by the availability of descriptions of discourse in culturally diverse settings. There is, of course, an urgent need for both continuing study and the dissemination of research findings to practitioners.

However, providing information on linguistic differences is not enough in itself. Much work remains to be done on furthering our understanding of the wider social issues which affect classroom interaction; in identifying ways in which existing discriminatory practices can be challenged and modified; and in the development of policies for educational equity (see, for instance, Corson, 1990). Critical pedagogy (Cummins, 1996; McLaren & Sleeter, 1995) and critical language awareness (Fairclough, 1992) may well emerge as the most important focus for future research (see reviews by Goldstein in Volume 8, and reviews in Volume 6 by Wallace, and by Clark & Ivanic). Without an understanding of the power structures which govern classroom discourse, teachers and students will be ill-equipped to recognise and transform the processes which ensure that some groups are treated more favourably than others.

University of Reading
England

REFERENCES

Bauman, R. & Sherzer, J.: 1974 *Explorations in the Ethnography of Speaking*, Cambridge University Press, Cambridge.
Biggs, A. & Edwards, V.: 1994, '"I treat them all the Same": Teacher-pupil talk in multi-ethnic classrooms', *Language and Education* 5(3), 161–176.
Bourdieu, P.: 1991, *Language and Symbolic Power*, Polity Press, Cambridge.
Brown, P. & Levinson, S.: 1978, 'Universals in language usage: Politeness phenomena', in E. Goody (ed.), *Questions and Politeness: Strategies in Social Interaction*, Cambridge University Press, Cambridge.
Callender, C.: 1995, *Black Teaching Styles in Multi-Ethnic Primary Schools*, unpublished PhD thesis, University of Reading.
Cazden, C.: 1989, 'Richmond Road: A multilingual/multicultural primary school in Auckland, *New Zealand. Language and Education* 3(3), 143–166.
Champion, T., Seymour, H. & Camarata, S.: 1995, 'Narrative discourse of African American children', *Journal of Narrative and Life History* 5(4), 333–352.
Corson, D.: 1990, *Language Policy Across the Curriculum*, Multilingual Matters, Clevedon, Avon.
Corson, D.: 1993, *Language, Minority Education and Gender*, Multilingual Matters, Clevedon, Avon.
Cummins, J.: 1996, *Negotiating Identities: Education for Empowerment in a Diverse Society*, California Association for Bilingual Education, Ontario, Ca.
Erikson, F., Cazden, C., Carrasco, R. & Maldonado-Guzman, A.: 1983, *Social and Cultural Organization of Interaction in Classrooms of Bilingual Children*, final report to the National Institution of Education.
Fairclough, N.: 1992, *Criticial language awareness*, Longman, Harlow.
Foster, M.: 1991, 'Constancy, connectedness and constraints in the lives of African-American teachers', *NWSA Journal* 3(2), 233–261.
Heath, S.: 1983, *Ways with Words: Language, Life and Work in Communities and Classrooms*, Cambridge University Press, Cambridge.
Hymes, D. (ed.): 1964, *Language in Culture and Society: A Reader in Linguistics and Anthropology*, Harper & Row, New York.
Hyon, S. & Sulzby, E.: 1994, 'African American kindergartners' spoken narratives: Topic associating and topic centre styles', *Linguistics and Education* 6, 121–152.
Jones, A.: 1987, 'Which girls are "learning to lose"?', in S. Middleton (ed.), *Women in Education in Aotearoa*, Allen & Unwin, Wellington, 143–152.
Jordan, C.: 1985, 'Translating culture: From ethnographic information to educational program', *Anthropology and Education Quarterly* 16: 105–123.

Ladson-Billings, G. & Henry, A.: 1990, 'Blurring the borders: Voices of African liberatory pedagogy in the United States and Canada', *Journal of Education* 172(2), 72–88.

McDermott, R.: 1977, 'The ethnography of speaking and reading', in R. Shuy (ed.), *Linguistic Theory: What can it say about Reading?* International Reading Association, Newark, Del.

McLaren, P. & Sleeter, C.: 1995, *Multicultural Education, Critical Pedagogy and the Politics of Difference*, State Univeristy of New York Press, Albany.

McPake, J. & Powney, J.: 1995, *A Mirror to Ourselves? The Educational Experiences of Japanese Children at School in the UK*, paper presented at the British Educational Research Association Conference, Bath.

Malcolm, I.: 1979, 'The western Australian child and classroom interaction: A sociolinguistic approach', *Journal of Pragmatics* 3, 305–320.

Malcolm, I.: 1994, 'Discourse and discourse strategies in Australian aboriginal English', *World Englishes* 13(3), 289–306.

Malin, M.: 1990, 'Why is life so hard for aboriginal students in urban classrooms?', *The Aboriginal Child at School* 18(1), 9–39.

May, S.: 1995, 'Deconstructing traditional discourses of schooling: An example of school reform', *Language and Education* 9(1), 1–29.

Michaels, S. & Cazden, C.: 1986, 'Teacher/child collaboration as oral preparation for literacy', in B. Schieffelin (ed.), *The Acquisition of Literacy: Ethnographic Perspectives*, Ablex, Norwood, NJ, 132–154.

Ogbu, J.: 1987, 'Variability in minority school performance: A problem in search of an explanation', *Anthropology and Education Quarterly* 18, 312–334.

Ogilvy, C., Booth, E., Cheyne, W., Jahoda, G. & Schaffer, H.R.: 1990, 'Staff attitudes and perception in multicultural nursery schools', *Early Childhood Development and Care* 64, 1–13.

Philips, S.: 1972, 'Participant structures and communicative competence: Warm springs children in community and Classroom', in C. Cazden, V. John, & D. Hymes (eds.), *Functions of language in the classroom*, Teachers College Press, New York [reprinted by Waveland Press 1985].

Saville-Troike, M.: 1982, *The Ethnography of Communication: An Introduction*, Blackwell, Oxford.

Vogt, L., Jordan, C. & Tharp, R.: 1985, 'Explaining school failure, producing school success: Two cases', *Anthropology and Education Quarterly* 19, 276–286.

ROB GILBERT

CRITICAL ORACY AND EDUCATION FOR ACTIVE CITIZENSHIP

The role of critical oracy in active citizenship might seem obvious, since citizens' participation in decision making could hardly proceed without such oral strategies as discussing, debating, negotiating and persuading. And the idea of active citizenship clearly implies that in promoting and challenging forms of power relations or social values, participants would need a critical understanding of the consequences of arguments and actions, and their implications for the welfare of self and others. That this connection has seldom been the direct focus of research and development says something about how both citizenship and oracy have been conceptualised.

Education for active citizenship signals a concern for participation, most generally in society in all its facets, or more specifically in a polity – local, national, and/or global. In both cases, the participation envisaged is inspired by concepts of democracy and individual and community empowerment (Land & Gilbert, 1994). However, active citizenship can be seen within a liberal framework, where the aim is to promote full participation by individuals in the existing range of citizenship activities, or within an emancipatory framework, where active citizenship operates to improve social, economic, cultural and political welfare for all, giving rise to a collective project.

The emancipatory framework, driven by a commitment to social improvement, demands that reflection and action involve a constant critique of existing social arrangements in the light of changing knowledge or circumstances, and a continuing scrutiny of social relations and interactions to ensure access and participation for all. Critical oracy is an important part of this process, and an important ability for those who are to participate in the emancipatory project.

EARLY DEVELOPMENTS

Recent times have seen a remarkable resurgence of interest in education for citizenship in the production of inquiries, reports and curriculum recommendations in the United Kingdom, the United States, Canada, and Australia. However, the concepts of citizenship reflected in these documents vary, with important consequences for the potential role of critical oracy (Gilbert, 1996). In some cases, citizenship is seen as a legal status,

B. Davies and D. Corson (eds), Encyclopedia of Language and Education,
Volume 3: Oral Discourse and Education, 105–113.
© 1997 Kluwer Academic Publishers. Printed in the Netherlands.

achieved either by birth or ceremony, and implying formal rights and duties which accrue to the status of citizen. Educational programs based on this concept tend to emphasise the history of the state and its institutions as the source of protection of the rights of citizens, and promote the moral duty of citizens to be loyal to the state and its institutions in return. Hence they include neither the participatory focus of oracy, nor a critical approach to the citizen role.

A second concept defines citizenship as a particular identity formed in a set of moral and social virtues based in the democratic ideal, emphasising the kind of person one should be to be a citizen in a democratic state. The emphasis here on values and personal ideals promotes the study of moral tales and issues, and, while it might uphold participation as an ideal, its emphasis on commitment to abstract values has neglected the processes of critique and the skills of participation which might involve critical oracy.

A third view sees citizenship as public practice conducted through legal and political processes. Here citizenship is a legal and political activity, whereby people practise their formally established rights and obligations in such areas as equality under and compliance with the law, the right to vote, paying taxes, etc. This concept does give rise to oral activities in the form of mock courts, parliaments and debates, but the critical orientation is either lacking or limited to the public legal and political spheres. Recognising rights and obligations in the workplace or the home is not seen as part of being a citizen. This public/private distinction is a particular weakness in its implications for the gendered nature of conventional concepts of citizenship (Fraser 1989; Young 1987). Also, the emphasis on rules and neglect of values means that there is no basis on which the rules can be critically evaluated and improved. As a result of this focus on formal rights and obligations and the separation between the "public" and the "private" critical oracy is neglected.

Education for active citizenship emphasises a fourth concept of citizenship as democratic participation, power sharing and involvement in decision making in all aspects of life. This view promotes the right and the need for citizens to participate in decision making in the broad range of legal, political, economic, civil and private spheres according to ideals of democracy, rights and justice. Like the second concept, citizenship is centrally based in values of democratic rights, but these values must be translated into the practice of decision making in all spheres of life. In its focus on participation and critical engagement, this concept of citizenship has the greatest potential for critical oracy.

THE EARLY FOCUS ON DISCUSSION OF CITIZENSHIP ISSUES

The scope for critical oracy in many recent approaches to education for citizenship is limited, which may be one factor influencing the lack of research on the topic. This may also be because critical oracy as a form of classroom interaction challenges very longstanding practices. In their review of interaction and discourse in social studies classrooms, Wilen & White (1991) note that the predominant form of discourse in US schools remains the teacher initiation-student response-teacher evaluation (IRE) sequence, in which the teacher seeks prespecified answers to predominantly lower order questions. Young (1991) highlights the different implications for critical oracy between what he calls the 'method' classroom, where the teacher is the teller and the pupil the learning object, and the 'discourse' classroom, where the teacher is a guide and the pupil the subject of learning. In the latter classroom, the pupils engage in doing, stating and theorising, rather than practising, listening and reproducing the answers to questions which the teacher has already determined.

Much of the early work relevant to critical oracy has been aimed at challenging the IRE model by developing more open discussion models. The approach has been to identify and model the intellectual processes of critically analysing issues through discussion, though this has seldom led to any specific attention to the oral dimension of these interactions. (Indeed, a major US framework for civic education (Center for Civic Education, 1991) has a special section on 'Writing for Participation', but no corresponding recommendations for oracy.)

The most influential of this early work was the Harvard University Social Studies Project (Oliver & Shaver 1966) and its jurisprudential approach to the analysis of issues. The Harvard Project developed programs of discussion and teacher/student dialogue through which students in social studies classes could clarify 'legitimately held points of view as they bear on a public policy issue' (p. 115). What distinguished the study was its use of research on classroom interaction, and its analysis of elements of the teaching dialogue which it saw as relevant to its goals. These elements included dimensions not only of the analysis of the substantive issues, but also of social-emotional, procedural and affective aspects of the interactions. This multi-dimensional understanding of classroom treatment of issues was a significant extension to the exclusive concern for the content of discussion which had previously dominated this area. Combined with the concern for the processes of dialogue and discussion, this made the Harvard Project a significant step in the development of an explicit model of critical oracy.

Later studies applied this original work in a wider range of classroom contexts (Levin, Newman & Oliver, 1969; Newmann & Oliver, 1970), and trialed a novel series of discussion formats, such as having two teachers model dialogue skills for the class, and having small group discussions of five or six students with two teachers. In all this work the key feature was that the teacher was a listener, questioner and clarifier of issues. A comparable model was developed in the United Kingdom in the Schools Council Humanities Project (Schools Council, 1970), which specified the teacher's role as that of a neutral chairperson. Project teachers were trained in the techniques of leading discussions, with a view to increasing students' tolerance for a range of views on public issues.

While this focus on models for discussing issues has been important, a series of studies in the United Kingdom has addressed the role of talk in learning across a range of curriculum areas. Barnes, Britton & Rosen (1969) promoted the strategy of exploratory talk to connect school learning with students' knowledge derived from their other experiences. Barnes (1976) extended this work by combining the exploratory process with reflexivity and action, and introducing an additional public stage to the sequence, where reflexive discussion enters a collaborative public arena. While the terms themselves are not used, Barnes' model, which cites Freire's work on critical pedagogy (Freire, 1972), offers considerable scope for critical oracy strategies. However, the studies themselves, with their emphasis on talking to learn across a wide range of learning activities and goals, do not address any specific forms of talk which might be particularly appropriate for critical oracy. The same might be said of the UK National Oracy Project, where, apart from some consideration of gender as an issue in classroom talk, the particular forms of oracy which might be associated with critical inquiry are not considered (Norman, 1992 and see reviews by Lyle, and by Mercer in this volume).

While this work falls short of a comprehensive approach to critical oracy, there is nonetheless considerable evidence to support an emphasis on open classroom discussion and its effects on active citizenship. Harwood (1992) reports a range of studies whose generally consistent findings were that classrooms which focused on open discussion of issues and values generated positive outcomes in political interest and feelings of efficacy, confidence and commitment to participation. Similar results have been found in the relationships between classroom climate and political tolerance (Avery, Bird, Johnstone, Sullivan & Thalhammer, 1992). Ferguson (1991), in a review of largely US research, concludes that students who take part in extracurricular and school governance activities, key sites for oracy, are more likely to become civically active as adults, and that inquiry-based, activity-oriented teaching is more effective in promoting participatory attitudes and skills than are expository, didactic teaching methods.

THE LIMITATIONS OF DISCUSSION MODELS

The early developments reviewed have challenged the IRE approach by emphasising open discussion and dialogue, and have demonstrated the importance of oracy as a dimension of education for citizenship. However, they have been limited in a number of ways. First, while the work promoted the oral dimension of classroom processes, the aspect of the interactions which received most attention remained the intellectual processes of analysing issues, rather than the performative skills of oracy. This was combined with a style of discussion dominated by rules of logical thought, evidence and rational debate, and neglecting a concern for interpersonal relations, a cooperative approach to the resolution of issues, or a focus on oracy in real social contexts.

Even those curriculum models which aim to develop more open forms of interaction, as Wilen and White (1991) point out, usually rely on teacher questions as the stimulus to discussion, and may still constrain student input. Critical oracy is given little attention in such a situation, since the dominance of teacher controlled discussion strategies can deny students the power to enter into discussion as genuine participants. Wilen and White advocate greater attention to student initiated questioning, a direction more compatible with critical oracy for active citizenship.

Young (1991, p. 68) defines a critical perspective as one which focuses on improvement of human problem solving, and which 'provides *within itself* a methodology for improvements to be identified and made'. He distinguishes this from a paradigm which 'merely permits the researcher to apply some separate, essentially arbitrary normative framework (e.g.) personal values'. The early discussion strategies are clearly susceptible to this criticism, as they did not carry within their design a means for identifying and promoting the emancipatory direction in any issue.

Further, the emphasis on neutrality excluded a critical orientation and a genuine search for solutions in open discussion between teacher and students, as Singh (1988) shows in his critique of the Humanities Project. Other problems arose from the emphasis on impersonal universal rules of logic as the chief yardstick for dealing with issues. The gendered nature of these rules for dealing with social issues parallel the problems identified by Gilligan (1977) in her critique of Kohlberg's (1984) rationalist approach to moral reasoning. The emphasis on abstract, disembodied and universal concepts of justice (or, by extension, democracy, tolerance, etc.) marginalises a contextualised orientation to care, with clear gender implications.

The content of the discussion and the forms of interaction were seen to be separate dimensions of the treatment of issues. There was no consideration of the discursive features of interactions in which the substance of an issue, and the power relationships among class participants themselves, are simultaneously constructed in discourses of race, class and gender.

Finally, while jurisprudential teaching, neutral discussion and exploratory talk sought to raise, consider and clarify the various points of view on the issues under consideration, there was no explicit attempt to develop a critical approach to issues by investigating their implications for questions of democratic process or social justice. In this sense, they lacked a critical dimension.

MAJOR CONTRIBUTIONS

The most concerted attempts to develop critical oracy strategies combine the analysis of issues with critical reflection and action. An early attempt was Newmann, Bertocci and Landsness' (1977) program of skills for citizen action, which sets out strategies for developing interpersonal and group communication using both verbal and non-verbal means, and counselling and campaigning skills necessary for citizen action projects. This work moved the aim of oral work from the promotion of classroom discussion to the use of oracy in real contexts of active citizenship. More central to the notion of critical pedagogy was Shor's (1980) program which aimed to develop critical consciousness through dialogue and drama. Shor addressed more directly the reality of unequal power relations and how forms of dialectical critique are needed to understand them.

There is increasing recognition in recent work of the interpersonal and ethical dimensions of classroom talk. Bowers and Flinders (1990) argue that oral traditions accept a wider variety of knowledge sources, and with less stratified notions of authority, than literate traditions, and are therefore more open to participation. Grant (1996) illustrates how critical classroom inquiry can be based on the ethical dimension of conversation. Studies such as these show how a critical approach to citizenship is enhanced by the characteristics of the oral tradition. More importantly, they recognise the role of power relations in interaction on issues, and their attempts to address this aspect of classroom interaction, as well as its significance in the wider context of citizenship practice, gives them a critical edge lacking in earlier work, where the emphasis was primarily on sharing points of view without considering the power relations associated with them.

The connections among power relations and the analysis of issues are best revealed in those studies which use a theory of discourse as an analytical frame, for this approach shows how critique requires concern not only for the content of the topic at hand, but also for the social relations constructed in the interaction itself. A good example of this is the analysis of a history lesson (Baker & Davies, 1989) in which the teacher was attempting to develop a critical perspective on sexism by discussing with students the sexist power relations in the division of labour in medieval European life.

The authors show that, despite this avowed aim, the teacher interacted with the students in such a way that he constructed an alliance with the boys which signalled the marginal position of girls and women both in the classroom and the historical context being studied. When combined with the teacher's anachronistic explanations based on his knowledge of modern society, the result was to confirm rather than challenge the constraining sex roles being studied.

In a similar way, Grundy (1994) shows how a classroom discussion of Chinese immigration to Australia positions the students in relation to the immigrant group through the use of 'us-them' categories. Again, the anachronistic use of 'Australian' to describe the non-Chinese population immediately positions the students with this group (which is given a fictitious unity by being labelled in this way), distancing the students from the Chinese who are automatically excluded from it.

An important issue here is the position of minority language groups in developing critical oracy, for if active citizenship is to be accessible to all, the dominance of particular language regimes in linguistically diverse contexts must be addressed. (See Alloway & Gilbert, this volume.)

Theories of discourse have much to offer an understanding of critical oracy. The studies referred to here show how discourse theory can connect the substance of discussions, the longstanding concern of classroom study of citizenship issues, with the social relations of the students themselves, with the teacher, each other, and the social groups they are studying. Studying classroom interactions in this way offers important insights into how student subjectivities are constructed through the performative and perlocutionary aspects of oracy, and how students are simultaneously positioned in the discourses of power in which citizenship must be practised. In addition, this understanding can be translated into strategies for the critical analysis of classroom texts which provide a powerful resource for practising active citizenship (Janks, 1991 and see the review by Janks in Volume 1).

PROBLEMS AND DIFFICULTIES: FUTURE DIRECTIONS

Interesting new work is likely to arise from the recognition that the creation of subjectivity and the construction of power involves inscription of discourses on the body. McLaren (1989) outlines a theory of ideology as a process of production which is performatively constituted through rituals which establish 'the socially conditioned, historically acquired, and biologically constituted *rhythms and metaphors of human agency*' (p. 191). It is through our involvement in the rituals of private and public life (which are powerfully entrenched in oral routines), that our affective or visceral investments in the world construct a sense of a unified self. In McLaren's view, school instructional rituals ingrain acceptable but eros-denying dispositions in students, ignoring the body's sensuous relationship to the popular and everyday. The conventional view of ideology focuses on its semantic forms, overlooking the affective and the politics of feeling. Critical oracy, with its focus on performance in public, expressive and dramatic forms, offers possibilities to address this aspect of hegemonic relations in ways that the literate tradition has not.

The future of critical oracy in education for citizenship holds considerable promise. Citizenship is increasingly seen in terms of participation and action in real social contexts, and while this is often limited to a functional skills model of curriculum and teaching, it does recognise the role of oracy as a medium for civic participation. In addition, discourse theory provides valuable insights into the role of language in the construction of power relations among people, and resources for developing a critical approach in oracy. Finally, the recognition of the performative dimension of social life, and the embodiment of discourses in human experience, opens up new and fascinating directions for research and development.

Young's contribution to this volume makes the valuable point that critical inquiry involves both a critical hermeneutics, a theory and process of interpretation through which ideology critique can proceed, and critical agency, our capacity to 'use our skill and courage to advance our social means of development' (p. 5). The advance of critical oracy as a medium for active citizenship will depend on our ability to understand and develop the relation between these elements.

James Cook University
Australia

REFERENCES

Avery, P., Bird, K., Johnstone, S., Sullivan, J. & Thalhammer, K.: 1992, 'Exploring political tolerance with adolescents', *Theory and Research in Social Education* 20(4), 386–420.

Baker, C. & Davies, B.: 1989, 'A lesson on sex roles', *Gender and Education* 1(1), 59–75.

Barnes, D.: 1976, *From Communication to Curriculum*, Penguin, Harmondsworth.

Barnes, D., Britton, J. & Rosen, H.: 1969, *Language, the Learner and the School*, Penguin, Harmondsworth.

Bowers, C. & Flinders, D.: 1990, *Responsive Teaching: An Ecological Approach to Classroom Patterns of Language, Culture and Thought*, Teachers College Press, New York.

Center for Civic Education: 1991, *Civitas*, Center for Civic Education, Calabasas, CA.

Ferguson, P.: 1991, 'Impacts on social and political participation', in J. Shaver (ed.), *Handbook of Research on Social Studies Teaching and Learning*, Macmillan, New York.

Fraser, N.: 1989, *Unruly Practices: Power, Discourse and Gender in Contemporary Social Theory*, Polity Press, Cambridge.

Freire, P.: 1972, *Pedagogy of the Oppressed*, Penguin, Harmondsworth.

Gilbert, R.: 1996, 'Education for active and informed citizenship', in R. Gilbert (ed.), *Studying Society and Environment: A handbook for teachers*, Macmillan Education, Melbourne.

Gilligan, C.: 1977, 'In a different voice: Women's conceptions of the self and of morality', *Harvard Educational Review* 47, 481–517.

Grant, R.: 1996, 'The ethics of talk: Classroom conversation and democratic politics', *Teachers College Record* 97(3), 470–482.

Grundy, S.: 1994, 'Being and becoming an Australian: Classroom discourse and the construction of identity', *Discourse* 15(1), 16–31.

Harwood, A.: 1992, 'Classroom climate and civic education in secondary social studies research: Antecedents and findings', *Theory and Research in Social Education* 20(1), 47–86.

Janks, H.: 1991, 'A critical approach to the teaching of language', *Educational Review* 43(2), 191–199.

Kohlberg, L.: 1984, *The Psychology of Moral Development. Vol. 2: Essays in Moral Development*, Harper and Row, San Francisco.

Land, R. & Gilbert, R.: 1994, 'Education for empowerment', in T. Husen & T. Postlethwaite (eds.), *The International Encyclopedia of Education*, Pergamon, London.

Levin, M., Newmann, F. & Oliver, D.: 1969, *A Law and Social Science Curriculum Based on the Analysis of Public Issues*, Final Report Project No. HS-058, Grant No. OE310142, US Department of Health, Education and Welfare, Office of Education, Washington D.C.

McLaren, P.: 1989, 'On ideology and education: Critical pedagogy and the cultural politics of resistance', in H. Giroux & P. McLaren (eds.), *Critical Pedagogy, the State, and Cultural Struggle*, State University of New York, Albany.

Newmann, F., Bertocci, T. & Landsness, R.: 1977, *Skills in Citizen Action: An English-Social Studies Program for Secondary Schools*, University of Wisconsin, Madison.

Newmann, F. & Oliver, D.: 1970, *Clarifying Public Controversy*, Little Brown, Boston.

Norman, K. (ed.): 1992, *Thinking Voices: The Work of the National Oracy Project*, Hodder and Stoughton, London.

Oliver, D. & Shaver, J.: 1966, *Teaching Public Issues in the High School*, Houghton Mifflin, Boston.

Schools Council: 1970, *The Humanities Project: An Introduction*, Heinemann Educational, London.

Shor, I.: 1980, *Critical Teaching and Everyday Life*, Black Rose Books, Montreal.

Singh, B.: 1988, 'The teaching of controversial issues: The problems of the neutral-chair approach', in B. Carrington & B. Troyna (eds.), *Children and Controversial Issues: Strategies for the Early and Middle Years of Schooling*, Falmer Press, London.

Wilen, W. & White, J.: 1991, 'Interaction and discourse in social studies classrooms', in J. Shaver (ed.), *Handbook of Research on Social Studies Teaching and Learning*, Macmillan, New York.

Young, I.: 1987, 'Impartiality and the civic public: Some implications of feminist critiques of moral and political theory', in S. Benhabib & D. Cornell (eds.), *Feminism as Critique: Essays on the politics of gender in late-capitalist societies*, Polity Press, Cambridge.

Young, R.: 1991, *Critical Theory and Classroom Talk*, Multilingual Matters, Clevedon.

BRONWYN DAVIES

THE CONSTRUCTION OF GENDERED IDENTITY
THROUGH PLAY

Play has many meanings and many functions in our society. The understanding of play as trivial, harmless or time wasting (Thorne, 1993) is not borne out by the literature on children's play, particularly as it relates to gender differences and to the establishment and maintenance of gendered identities. Early research on children's oral play focussed on children's folklore and was blind to gender (Opie & Opie, 1959). Children's folklore has now been scrutinized for its sexist content (Factor, 1988) but also for the ways in which the rhymes are developed and changed by children in counter-sexist ways (Thorne, 1993). From the beginning of the 1980s several different approaches to play and gender have developed. One, initiated by Walkerdine (1981), draws attention to the discourses through which oppressive gender relations in children's play are facilitated in school settings. Another focuses on a variety of oral social skills in children's play and the different take-up of these skills by girls and boys. In the late 80s and 90s there is a more subtle and complex theorising of gender and of the way gender is played out. These later studies tend to make gender, and the processes through which it is established and maintained, highly problematic. Ideas about how adults might work differently with children to disrupt old patterns of gendered play become a central focus.

EARLY DEVELOPMENTS

Opie and Opie (1959, p. v) write of the invisibility of children's verbal play in the 1950s. They comment that "one of the difficulties in making the present study has been that, since this work has no true predecessor, we had first to find out what there was to find out, before we knew whether there existed a subject to study. The generally held opinion, both inside and outside academic circles was that children no longer cherished their traditional lore. We were told that the young had lost the power of entertaining themselves; that the cinema, the wireless and the television had become the focus of their attention; and that we had started our investigation fifty years too late". Despite this perception, the Opies found a rich oral tradition in use in children's play. In 1988 Factor continued this work, studying the rhymes, games, chants, insults, jokes and riddles, what she calls the "folkloric traditions of children's play" (Factor, 1988, p. xi).

B. Davies and D. Corson (eds), Encyclopedia of Language and Education,
Volume 3: Oral Discourse and Education, 115–124.
© *1997 Kluwer Academic Publishers. Printed in the Netherlands.*

Factor (1988, pp. 140–141) documents the changing pattern of chants and rhymes from the unreflected, unquestioned sexism embedded in them in the 60s to chants which both reflect and constitute new social patterns. In the 1970s, for example, she observes girls chanting:

Boys have the muscles
Girls have the brains;
Boys are the stupidest
And we won the games.

Factor (1988, p. 142) observes 'Such changes occur without adult direction. They are the result of children's acute observation and awareness of shifts in social values, their sharp ear for whatever is new and newsworthy.' She also notes that 'There are probably still boys who despise girls' play and vice versa . . . Certainly the separation of girls' and boys' play remains a feature of playground life' (Factor, 1988, p. 140).

UNDERSTANDING ''PLAY'' AND ITS RELEVANCE TO GENDER

Understanding how gender might be constituted through play requires an adequate theorizing of what play is, yet play is one of the slipperiest concepts to pin down. In whatever binary pair we locate it (such as play/work, reality/fantasy) we can immediately find exceptions. Separating out the fictional and the real is actually highly problematic when we begin to understand the extent to which play is real, and to which reality is necessarily based on what can be imagined as real. If we think of the meanings of the word "play" and what it signifies, we find "plays" as enactments of both fictional and real characters and plots which give us insight into our lived experiences. We allow ideas and concepts to "come into play" when we construct the world we take to be real. We talk of "playing the game" when we mean entering into the rules of the real world and also when we mean a contestation of physical and sporting prowess on the part of athletes who transport us into their imagined powers as we watch them, but who also live out their powers as very real, and for which they are often paid very real money in what is understood as the real world.

Definitions of play include the following. While I have presented these more or less in the order in which they appear historically, they are all still current in the research and in discourses adults mobilise when they observe children's play.

1) Play is *practising* the real, or developing mastery.
2) Play is natural and not to be interfered with. It is through play that the natural unfolding of sex/gender is facilitated (Walkerdine, 1981).
3) Play is the not-real, is fictional or fantasy based. Garvey (1990, p. 7) defines play as characteristically requiring "the players to understand that what is done is not what it appears to be". Auwarter (1986,

p. 205) observes that "To create fictionality, the children must mark some of their utterances as 'deviant', as playful or pretended, as not claiming validity in normal everyday reality. ... They must bracket the ongoing activities and key the parts within the brackets as fictional ones ... This keying, or transformation of serious, real actions into something fictional or playful, can be done in two ways: Either by marking the utterances themselves, or by creating contexts which transform utterances which look normal or mundane by any criteria, into fictional ones".

4) Play is the basis for establishing and maintaining the relations between oneself and others inside the framework of the social world as it is constructed by adults. Corsaro (1994, p. 1) compares children's talk in Italian preschools and US preschools, and finds consistent differences in communicative patterns. He reflects that friendship are "deeply embedded in children's collective, interpretive reproduction of their culture" and "socialization is not only a matter of individual adaptation and internalization, but a process of appropriation, reinvention, and reproduction". Winnicott (1971, p. 59) observes that "The precariousness of play belongs to the fact that it is always on the theoretical line between the subjective and that which is objectively perceived."

5) Play is a play on words and a play on power. Thorne (1993, p. 81), for example, describes a situation amongst third graders in which a boy she calls Ken is stalking two girls who run away from him. Another girl taunts him with "Ken can't get me". He chases her and grabs her and she says "What are you huggin' me for?" To which he replies, "I'm not" looking stunned, and he lets go. Walkerdine's work, too, reveals how preschool boys' play can be used to dominate and sexualize both girls and female teachers (See review by Alloway and Gilbert, this volume).

Research on play and gender thus begins with observations of what is taken to be natural, gradually focuses on the complex interplay between the social and the individual, then focuses on the discourses through which each of these is constructed. This is then followed by research which examines play from the children's point of view, looking at the links between play and lived and told narratives made available to the children. This research makes visible the ways in which the binary pattern of male-female is made real through imaginary stories (Davies, 1989) and begins to reconceptualize the individual/social interface in children's play (Davies et al., 1996).

OBSERVING AND THEORISING PLAY IN
RELATION TO GENDER

Curiously, one of the first social/linguistic skills teachers impart to children is a sharp distinction between the fictional and the real. It is possible to actually observe the work through which this problematic divide is set up. Paley (1986, p. 2), for example, reports a conversation between herself as teacher and a boy she calls Frederick, who is three and newly in preschool:

"Last night I saw a monster in my bed – a big white monster. Then a dinosaur." He looks around expecting encouragement.

"Then what did the dinosaur do?" Stuart asks.

"He hided downstairs. Then he went upstairs." Frederick pauses to eat his Graham cracker, watching me.

"It was a dream, Frederick," I say.

"No, teacher, listen, I want to tell you something. I saw a big white monster and then I saw a dinosaur and it was hiding by my bed under the covers and it was a monster in my room."

"Frederick, I know it really seemed like the monster was in your room, but it was all in your dream."

Frederick persists with his story and its elaboration insisting that it is not a dream, and that the monster did not want him to come to school. The teacher decides that it might have been a shadow on the wall, and Frederick rejects this as well. While the other children take his talk to be meaningful, the teacher does not. Metaphorical elaboration of his fears, imagined images so vivid they can be described as real, have no place in a preschool where fact and fantasy are being separated out – where "truth telling" as other than the fictional is being developed alongside frequent exposure to the fictions of the society *as fictions*. The very serious work of fiction writers and of poets who extend the boundaries of what is sayable and knowable is precluded in the establishment of this division in children's oral reporting of "what happened". The *work* of preschool cannot incorporate what the teacher sees to be fantasy, and so fantasy is established, through work such as Paley's, as part of the world of fantasy or play rather than the world of work.

While Paley sees play as the means by which children learn about what *already exists* as the social world, Corsaro (1985, p. 280) claims a more active role for play. 'Children not only develop social skills and knowledge as the result of interactive experiences, *they actually use their developing skills and knowledge to create and maintain social order in their life worlds.*' Corsaro analyses various play episodes in which the boys and girls reveal a knowledge of the stereotypes of male and female and yet at the same time reveal their own personal characteristics which may not at all fit the stereotypes. The children learn that they cannot expect each other to simply fall into stereotypical play although they know just how powerful the stereotypes are. Corsaro sees the power of the division between male and female as a problem posed by the adult world. He says that through play:

> children are: (a) using developing knowledge of appropriate sex-typed behaviours; (b) discovering that this knowledge must be linked or articulated with local features of the interactive scene, including characteristics of the participants and the social-ecological setting; and (c) refining and expanding their developing knowledge as a result of their interactive experience (Corsaro, 1985, p. 249).

The social/linguistic skills children require to operate the multiple features of their play have been described by Bretherton (1989) as those of co-playwrights, co-directors, and various actors. He observes that they must adopt these multiple positionings, without getting confused about which ones they or a playmate are adopting at any one point in the emergent game.

The development of the social/linguistic skills required in fantasy play would appear to be different amongst boys and girls, though it is important to emphasize that this is always a trend rather than an essential feature of the way individual girls and boys play. Black (1992, p. 225) observes:

> The communication of girls included more strategies conducive to cohesive social interaction; that is, strategies that are associated with the maintenance of social proximity and the continuation of social exchange (e.g., referring to and building upon the ideas of others). Boys, by contrast, appear to use strategies that are more likely to lead to dispersive social interaction; that is, strategies that are often followed by a disruption of play and the need to begin anew (e.g., rejecting the ideas of others).

Sheldon (1992, p. 96) similarly reports an investigation of how young girls argue during social play, showing how girls have a greater tendency to use "double voiced discourse" in which self-assertion is interleaved with an orientation towards others engaged in the play. This style is adopted more commonly by girls than by boys but is used by both groups when the context is one of a "solidarity based group". Single-voiced discourse, or bald self assertion which leads to aggressive conflict, is used by both girls and boys when their dominant concern is for themselves rather than the group as a collaborative group. Sheldon observes "We can best see how talk is gendered if we take into consideration the context in which it emerges (e.g., the sex of the speakers and what the speakers are trying to accomplish" (1992, p. 96).

Jordan, Cowan and Roberts (1995, p. 343) show how children use their knowledge of rules to gain power and autonomy within their social world.

They observe that while rules are produced by adults, they can be used by children as weapons "in struggles to achieve or resist power . . . " And while socio-dramatic play has its own rules inherent in it, "even within socio-dramatic play there is a tendency for children to rely on classroom rules for the exercise of power" since their truth is perceived as less open to challenge. An example of this, is when a girl they have called Jane finds her game in the doll corner being disrupted by boys. When the boys fail to recognise her already established positioning as mother, she controls the situation first by using the authority she has as mother and then by invoking the teacher's rules to exclude the boys:

> Maurice and Aaron rush into the doll corner. "Who's the father?" inquired Maurice. "I am," Malcolm replied quickly. "Who's the mother?" asked Maurice. "Alicia can be mum," said Malcolm authoritatively.
> "SHUT UP MALCOLM; SHUT UP," shouted Jane angrily. "NOW LISTEN, I'M THE MOTHER EVERYONE; I'M THE MOTHER. There are too many people in the doll corner. Some-one will have to go out. QUIETT. I will tell you who came in first; then the ones after that will go" (Jordan, Cowan & Roberts, 1995, p. 353).

MAKING GENDER PROBLEMATIC

Walkerdine (1981) analyses the ways in which the life worlds of children's play is created and maintained through a belief in play and gender as "natural" and innocent. The extreme misogyny of the boys in her study is invisible to the teacher. The discourses of good teaching she has access to make the boys' behaviour trivial and of little import. Kamler et al (1993) take up this point in a study of the first month of school. They show how violent and aggressive behaviour in boys is normalised through going unremarked in school, while similar behaviour in girls is not only noticed but marked as deviant. Girls (and some boys) are denied the ability to stand up to aggression in school, at the same time as they are denied the safety that prohibition of schoolboy violence would allow.

Davies (1989) takes up the poststructuralist analysis in Walkerdine's work and looks at the intertextuality of the stories preschool children play out in the playground and the fictional stories they are read. The taking up of gender identities is analysed as a locating of oneself in recognised and recognisable storylines derived from a reading of the culture and its texts. However limiting and oppressive the effects may be, gendered identity is something that is struggled for, since it is recognised as essential to becoming a competent and powerful member of any social group. This is so, despite the fact that their play runs across and between the genders, that their desire is often for the possibilities only available to the other gender, and that their competencies are not always limited to what one or other of the genders is supposed to be able to do.

Jordan and Cowan focus on the contest between boys' determination to explore narratives of masculinity involving guns, fighting, fast cars, and the teachers' attempts to exclude such play from their classrooms. "We argue that what occurs is a contest between two definitions of masculinity: what we have chosen to call 'warrior narratives' and the discourses of civil society – rationality, responsibility, and decorum – that are the basis of school discipline" (1995, p. 728). They observe that "Whereas even the most timid, least physically aggressive boys ... are drawn to identifying with the heroes of these narratives, girls show almost no interest in them at this early age. The strong-willed and assertive girls in our study ... sought power by commandeering the role of mother, teacher or shopkeeper ... " (1995, p. 732). Jordan and Cowan argue that the outlawing of the warrior narrative might be read by boys as simply one of the many constraints of school, but that equally it may be read as proof of the femininity of schooling. In the latter reading the warrior narratives become crucial discursive tools in the maintenance of male identity. Jordan also analyses the process by which the "good boys", in contrast to the "fighting boys", adopt a definition of masculinity based on avoidance of what is done by girls. "Fighting boys" who have appropriated the role of hero in the warrior narratives, cast the 'good boys' who conform to the requirements of the school as despised 'wimps' and 'sissies'. This leads the 'good boys' to adopt an alternative definition of masculinity as 'not female', and in many cases leads also to the scorn and rejection being redirected to girls as a group" (Jordan, 1995, p. 69). This can lead to playground play becoming a contestation between girls and boys. Heather, aged 11, describing her playground, says "It's like girls and boys are on different sides" (Thorne, 1993, p. 63).

Davies (1996) worked with a group of teachers who were interested in studying playground violence. They found that the oppositions were not just gendered but also between abled and disabled children. The teachers worked with all the children to ensure that they were skilled enough to play successfully on the playground equipment. They talked to the children in class about restorying themselves as competent and about restorying the playground as an exciting rather than a fearful place. They also worked with the other teachers at the school to disrupt old discourses about play-as-natural and to make visible to them the violence that was taking place. They then secured their co-operation in developing a shared set of rules for fair play in the playground, thus ensuring they felt confident in their interventions in violent play. The result was a remarkable transformation of a violent misogynist and discriminatory scene into one of skilful and collaborative play, though interestingly the dominant aggressive boys vacated the scene rather than join in this new collaborative play.

WORK IN PROGRESS

Some of the most interesting and important work in progress is that being carried out by Alloway and Gilbert who are engaged in a study of young men playing in video game arcades. While talk is not a major feature of these games they provide important insights into the enmeshing of fictional worlds with real worlds in video games. They observe that:

> "Video game texts . . . align masculinity with power, with aggres-
> sion, with victory and winning, with superiority and strength –
> and of course, with violent action. They offer positions for young
> male game players that promise success as masculine subjects.
> The video game arcade thus becomes a social arena within which
> hegemonic masculinity can be experienced and practiced. . . . In
> the virtual reality on promise within the video game, maleness
> is equated with the attainment of power and success through
> violent action" (Alloway & Gilbert, 1997, p. 97).

Alloway and Gilbert use Giroux's distinction between ritual and symbolic violence. Ritual violence is repetitive and predictable, and connected to thrill and release; it naturalises itself through the simultaneous reflection, creation and maintenance of reality. Symbolic violence, in contrast, 'asks for more complex, critical, and intellectual engagement with the issues . . . by evoking more complex emotional responses, symbolic representations of violence challenge the reader to resist, to contest, to de-naturalise cultural and textual practices that legitimate violence and that betray our potential for human connectedness' (1997, p. 99). Most of the boys were uncritical and unreflective about their experiences of the video games and were unlikely to recognise the political effects of their immersion in violent hegemonic misogynist forms of masculinity. Their talk was more likely to centre on their pleasure in winning, in being with their mates, and in the high tech aspects of video gaming. Dylan was slightly unusual in his ability to talk about the embodied nature of the experience:

> "When I'm playing the game, I'm there . . . and you get like
> demented. Like . . . I can't switch off. Like I mean like when I
> go for a block in the game I actually physically jump in the air.
> It's really quite annoying. . . . It's just, I don't know, maybe your
> brain short circuits or something. You feel like you're there. Ah,
> it's weird" (Alloway & Gilbert, 1997, p. 111).

Alloway and Gilbert's research is exploring the ways in which the body/mind is involved in *living* the imagined virtual worlds. They are developing an important theoretical model which may enable us to make more sense of the ways in which violent imaginary play is entailed in the establishment and maintenance of a violent world.

PROBLEMS AND DIFFICULTIES

The most significant problem in the research on gender and play is in recognising the complex relations between what is imagined and what becomes real. The power of the imagination is not just to shape what is real, but to lend power differentially to real players, with very real effects. Baudrillard analyses in some detail the seepage in film texts between image and reality. He says:

> More generally, the image is interesting not only in its role as reflection, mirror, representation of, or counterpart to, the real, but also when it begins to contaminate reality and to model it, when it only conforms to reality the better to distort it, or better still: when it appropriates reality for its own ends, when it anticipates it to the point that the real no longer has time to be produced as such (Baudrillard, 1987, p. 16).

A further problem is to understand the recalcitrance of the imagined self and its imagined patterns of desire in the face of new and "politically correct" admonitions from adults (Davies, 1997). Related to this is the complex task of working with children and with each other to find ways in which we can begin to imagine the unimaginable, to find ways to speak into existence imaginary worlds in which children are competent and powerful, yet able to resist becoming so at the expense of others.

FUTURE DIRECTIONS

Future research on children's play and gender is unlikely to treat play as innocent, nor to see adults as not implicated in that play. As children struggle to become members of a complex social world through making detailed readings and inserting themselves into the texts they find, they also need to come to understand the power they have to create that world and to take responsibility for the social effects of taking up one discursive practice rather than another, of finding different ways of being male or female, or neither.

Thorne (1993, pp. 5 & 173) says that play is grounded in the concept of possibility: "Within the complexities, within the 'play of gender,' indeed lie possibilities for social change". "As adults, we can help kids, as well as ourselves, imagine and realize different futures, alter institutions, craft new life stories. A more complex understanding of the dynamics of gender, of tensions and contradictions, and of the hopeful moments that lie within present arrangements, can help broaden our sense of the possible". And Alloway and Gilbert (1997, p. 113) observe that 'Where critical citizenship is honoured as a goal of education, classroom practice should be about enabling students critically to read the processes wherein they take up personal, relational and cultural meanings'.

James Cook University
Australia

REFERENCES

Alloway, N. & Gilbert, P.: 1997, 'Video game culture: Playing with masculinity, violence and pleasure', in S. Howard (ed.), *Wired Up: Young People and the Electronic Media*, Falmer Press, London, 95–114.

Auwarter, M.: 1986, 'Development of communicative skills: The construction of fictional reality in children's play', in J. Cook-Gumperz, W.A. Corsaro & Streeck, J. (eds.), *Children's Worlds and Children's Language*, Mouton de Gruyter, Berlin, 205–229.

Baudrillard, J.: 1987, *The Evil Demon of Images*, The Power Institute of Fine Arts, Sydney.

Black, B.: 1992, 'Negotiating social pretend play: Communication differences related to social status and sex', *Merrill-Palmer Quarterly* 38, 212–232.

Bretherton, I.: 1989, 'Pretence: The form and function of make-believe', *Developmental Review* 9, 383–401.

Corsaro, W.A.: 1985, *Friendship and Peer Culture in the Early Years*, Ablex Publishing Company, Norwood.

Corsaro, W.A.: 1994, 'Discussion, debate, and friendship processes: Peer discourse in U.S. and Italian nursery schools', *Sociology of Education* 67, 1–26.

Davies, B.: 1989, *Frogs and Snails and Feminist Tales. Preschool Children and Gender*, Allen and Unwin, Sydney.

Davies, B.: 1996, *Power/Knowledge/Desire. Changing School Organisation and Management Practices*, Department of Employment, Education and Training, Canberra.

Davies, B.: 1997, 'Constructing and deconstructing masculinity through critical literacy', *Gender and Education* 9(1), 9–30.

Factor, J.: 1988, *Captain Cook Chased a Chook. Children's Folklore in Australia*, Penguin, Ringwood.

Garvey, C.: 1990, *Play*, Harvard University Press, Cambridge MA.

Jordan, E.: 1995 'Fighting boys and fantasy play: The construction of masculinity in the early years of school', *Gender and Education* 7(1), 69–85.

Jordan, E. & Cowan, A.: 1995, 'Warrior narratives in the kindergarten classroom. Renegotiating the social contract?' *Gender and Society* 9(6), 727–743.

Jordan, E., Cowan, A. & Roberts, J.: 1995, 'Knowing the rules: Discursive strategies in young children's power struggles', *Early Childhood Research Quarterly* 10, 339–358.

Kamler, B. et al.: 1993, *Shaping Up Nicely: The Formation of Schoolgirls and Schoolboys in the First Months of School* Department of Employment, Education and Training, Canberra.

Opie, I. & Opie, P.: 1959, *The Language and Lore of Schoolchildren*, Oxford University Press, London.

Paley, V.G.: 1986, *Mollie is Three. Growing Up in School*, The University of Chicago Press, Chicago.

Sheldon, A.: 1992, 'Conflict talk: Sociolinguistic challenges to self-assertion and how young girls meet them', *Merrill-Palmer Quarterly* 38(1), 95–117.

Thorne, B.: 1993, *Gender Play. Girls and Boys in School* Open University Press, Buckingham.

Walkerdine, V.: 1981, 'Sex, power and pedagogy', *Screen Education* 38, 14–24.

Winnicott, D.W.: 1971, *Playing and Reality* Penguin, Harmondsworth.

HARRIET BJERRUM NIELSEN AND
BRONWYN DAVIES

THE CONSTRUCTION OF GENDERED IDENTITY
THROUGH CLASSROOM TALK

The purpose of this review is to examine the ways in which classroom talk is implicated in the construction and maintenance of the gender order. Part of being a competent member of society as it is currently organised derives from our capacity to attribute to others, and to aid others in attributing to us, the 'correct' gender. The meaning that we give to being male or female in the everyday world rests on the assumption of bipolarity of physiological differences which serves as the ground on which gendered social selves are constructed. Children learn to take up their maleness or femaleness as an element of their personal and social selves, and they do so, among other things, through learning the discursive practises in which all people are positioned as either male or female.

Children develop an emotional commitment to their gender as early as two years of age (Le Maner-Idrissi, 1996) and when they arrive in preschool, many of them already act, speak and behave according to conventional images of gender – though the content of these images can vary considerably according to culture, historical period, social class, ethnicity, age, and individual circumstances (Davies, 1989; Walkerdine, 1990). Images of gender also vary in the lifetime of any individual, and as the individual moves from one context to another. Yet classrooms can be sites where the binary, hierarchical gender order is made to seem intractable (Baker & Davies, 1989). They can also be sites where students discover ways of talking and being which liberate them from more conventional forms of gender, and where they develop a reflexive awareness of the power of discourse to shape identity and so work with the teacher to develop strategies for changing the discursive patterns through which identity and desire are constituted (Davies, 1993).

From Rousseau through to the 1950s gender differentiation had been an explicit *goal* of education. While this lost favour in the period after the second world war and the political ideology of equal rights and the educational ideology of child centred development and learning gained dominance, many of the assumptions and practices constitutive of gender difference remained remarkably intact. This was not readily apparent, however, since the language shifts and structural changes taking place suggested that gender was no longer a central defining feature of students. 'Boys' and 'girls' had become 'children' or 'students', and mixed schools became the norm in most parts of the Western world. In Nordic countries

B. Davies and D. Corson (eds), Encyclopedia of Language and Education,
Volume 3: Oral Discourse and Education, 125–135.
© *1997 Kluwer Academic Publishers. Printed in the Netherlands.*

gender segregated schools ceased to exist around the second world war and the last gender segregated classes disappeared in the 1960s. But the apparently ungendered child in the child centred ideology was actually thought of and described as a generic male – and in classroom studies 'students' were often, in fact, boys. Until around 1970 the few studies focusing on gender influences in classroom interaction criticised the treatment of boys in primary school and suggested that the teachers, being female, were unable to meet the boys' learning needs effectively (Brophy, 1985). The girls were, apparently, as invisible to the researchers as they were to the teachers. During the 1970s feminist researchers began to make girls visible in the classroom again and to reveal the problematic patterns hidden by the cloak of egalitarian educational discourses. They found that the assumed advantages enjoyed by girls at the primary level were not sustained. This led to important texts such as Spender and Sarah's edited collection *Learning to Lose* from Australia, Delamont's book *Sex Roles and the School* from England, and Wernersson's *Könsdifferentiering i grundskolan* (gender differentiation in compulsory school) from Sweden.

MAJOR CONTRIBUTIONS

The early research projects showed that the gender neutrality of the modern school was an illusion. Sex/gender had remained a major organising principle of the classroom under the claim and intention of gender neutrality. No study has shown girls receiving more individual teacher attention than boys (Croll & Moses, 1991). In the overwhelming majority of the ensuing research in the 1970s and 1980s it was found that teachers on an average pay less attention to girls than to boys (Brophy, 1985; Kelly, 1988). Kelly (1988) in a meta-analysis of 81 quantitative studies of primary and secondary schools showed that in all the countries studied, across all ages, school levels, subjects, and socio-economic and ethnic groupings, girls receive fewer instructional contacts, fewer high-level questions and academic criticism, less behavioural criticism, and slightly less praise than boys. While Brophy's (1985) review reports no differences between female and male teachers, Kelly's analysis indicated that male teachers give slightly more attention to boys than to girls. Kelly's study also shows that while girls volunteer to answer questions as often as boys, they are less likely to initiate contact. The boys initiate more contact with teachers in classroom talk, while girls tend to contact the teacher outside this context (Brophy, 1985; Bjerrum Nielsen & Larsen, 1985).

Teachers read and respond to the behaviour of boys and girls quite differently. According to Scandinavian studies (for instance Einarsson & Hultman, 1984, Bjerrum Nielsen & Larsen, 1985) a typical discourse unit in a primary school classroom talk goes as follows: Teacher asks a question, a girl raises her hand and is appointed to answer. She does so briefly and her answer is usually correct. A boy interrupts with an interesting comment on the topic and the teacher leaves the girl and engages in an exchange with the boy. Other boys then join the discussion. The girls silently wait for the next question or may use the time to whisper together on other matters. These studies also indicate that teachers tend to respond to the form of girls' contributions, and to the content of boys' contributions. Dweck et al. (1978) found in U.S. classrooms that teachers attributed boys' failures to lack of motivation significantly more often than they did with girls, and that their feedback to girls was more often of the kind which suggested that they thought the girls lacked ability. Good, Sikes & Brophy found that level of academic achievement (which other studies show will often correspond to socio-economic and ethnic background) differentiates boys more than girls: low achieving boys get more behavioural criticism, while the high achieving boys 'receive the best of everything' (1973, p. 81). In this study, low achieving girls came out as the group in the classroom talk that gets the least teacher attention. Other studies have found this to be the case for high achieving girls (Kelly, 1988; Öhrn, 1991). Boys seem to occupy their teachers minds both in and out of the classroom. When describing their students, teachers tend to describe each boy, then add: 'And the rest are girls' (Stanworth, 1983). This even applies to girls who are outspoken and active in classroom conversation. Öhrn (1991) found girls dominating the conversation in only 2 of the 7 Swedish 9th grade classrooms she studied. And in those classes the active girls were referred to by their teachers as the 'girl mafia'.

Because the boys are perceived as individuals who are either more demanding, more interesting or more unruly than the girls, the teaching is planned and executed with them in mind (Clarricoates, 1978). Generally, girls' better achievement and more cooperative style means they receive less attention: 'The overall picture of teachers' relationships to students of both sexes indicates that the girls do get some praise for their obedience and willingness to please the teacher, but that they pay a price for this by being forgotten and taken for granted, they do not exist as individuals in their teachers' minds' (Wernersson, 1977, p. 254, translated from Swedish). These differences in interaction and perception occur despite teachers' assertions that they do not treat nor wish to treat girls and boys differently. They are often unaware of their differential treatment of girls and boys and even disbelieve the evidence when confronted with it (Corson, 1993; Kelly, 1988; Whyte, 1983). For instance, Öhrn (1991) found teachers to overestimate the extent of the girls' oral activity, while the reverse applied for the boys. Boys are only judged to dominate when the gender difference is extremely marked.

DEVELOPMENTS OVER THE LAST DECADE

While the findings of gender patterns in classroom talk are quite uniform, the explanations of the relation between these patterns and the construction and formation of gendered identity have been more diverse. In the 1970s and early 80s the focus was on justice and equal rights for girls. Differential treatment, double standards in the classroom, poor self esteem in girls were all seen to lead to different educational careers for girls and boys. Girls were seen as passive victims of a patriarchal society in which women have to learn their place. Sex-role theory was often the implicit theoretical framing of the early studies: girls and boys conformed to the norms and expectations of teachers and parents, and these norms were derived from the social structures of a patriarchal society where men and women are assigned different roles and men have higher status and more power than women.

During the late 1980s and 90s, the view of children as passive recipients of social structure was questioned. Children were observed to take an active part in constructing a gendered world and to actively take up gendered patterns of discourse. Already from preschool age, children are engaged in 'category maintenance' (Davies, 1989), or 'borderwork' between the sexes (Thorne, 1993). In learning to be coherent and recognisable members of their social worlds children actively take up their assigned gender in complex patterns of conformity and resistance. Their choices are not always compatible with the way teachers and parents tell them gender should be done, nor indeed with the ways in which their parents and their teachers have taken up their gender.

The expressions and the relative importance of gendered borderwork or category maintenance work vary with age, gender and situational context. It is strongest and most inflexible in the age span from 5 to 12 years, though boys tend to demarcate themselves more fiercely from girls than the other way round, and both sexes engage more in borderwork in institutionalised or group contexts, than in more informal and personal contexts (Chodorow, 1989; Thorne, 1993). Gendered lifeworlds or cultures are formed out of the cultural and moral values that are constitutive of masculinity and femininity (Best, 1983; Jensen et al., 1984; Paley, 1984; Connell, 1989; Gilligan et al., 1990). Psychodynamic perspectives on identity formation have seen this process as creating relatively stable gendered psychic patterns of emotions, desire and fantasies, a gendered subjectivity which connects to certain forms of gendered behaviour (Chodorow, 1989; Bjerrum Nielsen & Rudberg, 1989, 1994). In these analyses the sex-role perspective has given way to a perspective that highlights girls' and (to a lesser extent) boys' agency and subjectivity and to the understanding that gender identity is shaped *by* and *within* individuals. This situates classroom talk in a broader cultural, linguistic and psychological context, as part of a process of gender identity formation. Quantitative studies of classroom talk have given way to qualitative studies of cultural meanings, the shaping of individual desires and the discursive strategies through which embodiment of self as boy or girl, both in and out of school, becomes possible.

Studies focussing on the formation of gendered identity and lifeworlds indicate that girls' cooperative and boys' competitive and individualistic discursive strategies are found and practised in their respective single sex groups. Girls like collaboration with peers and group work better than boys (Hjort, 1984; Reay, 1991). Girls and boys tend to take an interest in different aspects of the world around them, girls orienting towards human relations and conditions, boys towards more impersonal matters. Girls are more active in classroom talk when human and social issues are discussed, and the greatest male dominance is found in science classes and when the discussion concerns politics and history (Hjort, 1984; Kelly, 1988; Örhn, 1991). In classes where girls dominate, the conversation patterns tend to be different, both in regard to form and content and in the way the girls relate to classmates (Örhn, 1991, Bjerrum Nielsen & Rudberg, 1994).

These studies open up an important interpretive shift in which girls' cooperative style is no longer seen as an expression of obedience and passivity, but as an expression of their relational identity, making them both more interested in relating to the teachers as human beings and more competent in understanding their demands. The girls' interpersonal interest is also seen in their dyadic friendships where their relational competence is used both as a means of establishing contact and in fighting and betraying each other. The boys' more assertive and aggressive behaviour can be connected to their more hierarchical and competitive social life, where getting public attention and admiration from the group of boys counts more than intimate relations, and where demonstrating their superiority over girls seems to be a central point in establishing a collective male identity (Best, 1983; Paley, 1984; Connell, 1989). The Scandinavian studies show how boys take the classroom as a self-evident arena for competition, marking their difference from other boys, while girls will often have a more reluctant attitude to the public sphere of classroom talk, and look for ways to emphasise similarity in experiences and emotions. Boys fight each other in public, girls in private relations (Bjerrum Nielsen & Larsen, 1985). The subtle interplay between the priorities and social orientations of girls and boys, the structure and content of classroom discourse and the response students receive from the teacher can be seen as almost inevitably maintaining and reinforcing the traditional gender order.

Even though girls are often praised as good pupils in the primary school, perform better, and are reported to be more satisfied with school, their satisfaction with school, and teachers' satisfaction with them, seem to diminish when they reach secondary school. Several studies have indicated a serious decrease in self esteem of girls from the onset of puberty. Speaking up in class, for many of them, becomes loaded with anxiety (Lees, 1986; Gilligan et al., 1990; Örhn, 1991). The findings regarding classroom activity at adolescence display a more varied picture than the findings for earlier ages (Brophy, 1985; Lees, 1986; Öhrn, 1991). Some girls adopt a more 'masculine' approach, in line with what they perceive as being valued in school. Others respond to boys' more concerted displays of dominance by becoming silent or oppositional. In spite of the fact that girls continue to get better marks than boys, teachers often perceive girls' classroom participation to change dramatically and for the worse in adolescence (Wernersson, 1977; Davies, 1984; Hjort, 1984; Gilligan et al., 1990). The girls become less compliant to teachers, less self confident and less interested in taking part in classroom discussions (Davies, 1996).

From this age Scandinavian studies have found that the difference in the amount of behavioural criticism directed towards boys and girls disappears. The explanations given are the gradual changes in the academic demands towards more abstract knowledge, matter-of-factness, more impersonal relations to the teachers, a more competitive atmosphere, and, related to this, the limited area of application in school for the girls' interactive skills (Hjort, 1984; Brophy, 1985). The girls are neither taken seriously in regard to the male norms of school curriculum and discourse, nor given possibilities to develop their personal and social orientation. The notion of contradictory explicit and implicit norms for what is valued in school is a possible explanation: girls meet the explicit demands of obedient behaviour and lose because the more inventive and individualistic behaviour of the boys matches the implicit, but real norms for success. Bjerrum Nielsen & Larsen (1985) conclude from Scandinavia that the girls in primary school are 'the putty of the classroom': schools exploit the girls' orientation towards the interpersonal, in order to make classrooms function. When classroom norms and routines have been established, however, when a public space for communication has been established for the boys' academic encounters with the teacher and with each other, the girls are 'left over' as boring and uninteresting students.

The different social orientations of girls and boys can, however, also be seen as gender specific platforms for strategies of resistance towards the power asymmetries in the classroom. Studies of youth cultures have analysed different gendered identities as positions for gaining power and control both in relation to teachers and in peer groups. In these studies, gender and other variables such as socio-economic class or ethnicity are often more explicitly related, resulting in a more nuanced picture of different types of femininities and masculinities in the classroom. Some working class boys, for instance, oppose the middle class culture of school through macho behaviour, strengthening both their working class male identity and the likelihood that they will drop out of school (Willis, 1977; Kryger, 1988; Connell, 1989). Similarly girls' docility can sometimes be used to gain facilities or advantages, and they can use their interactive skills in order to gain influence. Adolescent working class girls have their own patterns of resistance, using more personal weapons against teachers and school routines. Teachers experience these as particularly difficult to handle and are reported to say that they would prefer to teach boys than girls this age (Davies, 1984; Jensen et al., 1984; Lees, 1986; Örhn, 1991).

While studies anchored in perspectives of social and psychological identity formation to a large extent have seen classroom behaviour and discursive strategies of girls and boys as part of a developmental process in which gendered identity is accomplished, researchers in the social-constructionist and poststructuralist traditions have challenged the idea of such fixed identities. Their focus is on the discursive practices through which culturally available meanings are taken up and lived out (Adams & Walkerdine, 1986; Walkerdine, 1990; Davies, 1989, 1993). Because gendered images, metaphors and narratives are part of the everyday, unexamined discursive practices of the classroom, they mostly pass unnoted by the teacher, even in cases where the explicit topic is sex-roles and equality of sexes (Baker & Davies, 1989).

It is not only people who are ascribed a gender, but also goals, values, skills and norms. When boys and girls are displaying the same behaviour they are not positioned in the same way in relation to that behaviour. An example is the ambivalent meanings surrounding girls performing well in school. High performance is praised by teachers, and girls who do not perform well in this way are seen as immature or difficult. At the same time, high performance is often dismissed as the product of conformity and instrumentalism (Clarricoates, 1978). As Adams & Walkerdine (1986) have demonstrated, an unruly and quite incompetent boy can be perceived by the teacher as bored but 'really' more intelligent than a cooperative and high achieving girl.

The binaries that structure Western thought (abstract/concrete, rational/ emotional, independent/dependent) are tied into the binary male/female in complex ways. Our patterns of language usage limit and shape the positions that are open to boys and girls in the discursive practices of the classroom (Davies, 1993). This has little to do with what boys and girls actually do in the classroom but it constrains the meanings that are attributed to what they do. To do gender in the classroom is to continuously negotiate, maintain or oppose these positionings offered in classroom talk.

CURRENT DILEMMAS AND FUTURE DIRECTIONS

Though both underline notions of agency and subjectivity, the perspectives of cultural or personal gender identity formation and the poststructuralist perspective challenge each other in important ways. From a poststructuralist perspective, the studies of identity formation present a stereotypical pattern of a boys' world and a girls' world, neglecting both the ongoing interaction between girls and boys (relational gender), the variation and complexity within each group (girls are not just girls, they also belong to other sociocultural categories that influence the way they express gender), and the multiplicity of identity positions and their contradictory nature within each individual. Indeed as Corson has noted there is an urgent need for research on the interplay between gender and ethnicity as it affects girls in schools (Corson, 1998).

Many of the formation studies tend to overlook the central point that there are many masculinities and many femininities both between and within the individuals. They come up with results which are too coherent and too generalised. Through ignoring the complexity of gender, the identity formation studies may actually contribute to the maintenance of the bipolarity of gender, instead of deconstructing and opposing it.

From the perspective of identity formation, on the other hand, the post-structuralist studies have largely neglected the motivational and formative dimensions of the ongoing gender constructions. Even though it is often mentioned that emotional commitment to different gender position-ings exists, constraining the ease with which new practises are created, few studies from poststructuralists add to the understanding of how such emotional commitments are developed over time, and how different and contradictory images/narratives of gender are actually lived and combined in the life of girls and boys (one exception is Davies, 1989 and 1993, in which the same children appear as preschool and then primary school children). Poststructuralist theory emphasises the positioning of self in relation to specific discourses, but does so in terms which rarely go beyond the immediate horizons of a particular interaction. The notion of agency is located as much in the linguistic system itself as in the persons using it.

Language is *neither* a means for construction of gender, *nor* an expression of gender – it is both. Studies of 'being' gendered and 'doing' gender could thus be seen as functionally related and reveal different aspects of the social process of gendered identity construction: You have *to be* someone in order *to do* something, and when you *do* something you also become someone, and this process impacts on who you *are* or who you take yourself *to be*. Studies of individuals cannot give any full account of the collective process of doing gender – something new is accomplished/created in this process. But the reverse is also true: the analysis of the collective praxis does not tell us anything about the different motives of the individuals who engage in this meaning making, what positions they choose in it, and what consequences this has for their sense of self over time. Studies of gender in classroom discourse reveal both obvious differences within each gender group and in the array of gender positionings the same girl or boy can take. At the same time, there are striking similarities within each gender group over a wide array of cultural and situational contexts in the ways girls or boys do and are their gender. A theory of gendered identity should account for both, being aware of the traps both of false similarities and false differences.

Future research must ask questions such as, in what respect must gender be part of the identity formation process? Can identity be maintained without it – and do we want to maintain it? Poststructuralist theorists imagine a world that goes beyond gendered identities. Might doing away with gender leave us once again in the gender neutral illusion of the child centred ideology, ignoring the fact that social structures of gender and power hierarchies can work quite effectively when linguistically disguised? As we develop strategies for changing images and metaphors of gender, that is, working on the gendered discourses through which gender is constructed, we cannot ever ignore the constitutive force of social structures and of individual patterns of desire. While discourse can change social structures, it does not necessarily do so – structures are held in place through many and contradictory discourses. Just so desire. New discursive strategies may or may not change desire, though an imagined possible difference is a first step towards change.

University of Oslo
Norway

and

James Cook University
Australia

REFERENCES

Adams, C. & Walkerdine, V.: 1986, *Investigating Gender in the Primary School: Activity Based Inset materials for Primary Teachers*, Inner London Education Authority, London.
Baker, C. & Davies, B.: 1989, 'A lesson on sex roles', *Gender and Education* 1(1), 59–76.
Best, R.: 1983, *We've all Got Scars: What Boys and Girls Learn in Elementary School*, Indiana University Press, Bloomington.
Bjerrum Nielsen, H. & Larsen, K.: 1985, *Piger og drenge i klasseoffentligheden* (Girls and boys in the classroom public), University of Oslo, Institute of Educational Research, report no. 2.
Bjerrum Nielsen, H. & Rudberg, M.: 1989, *Historien om jenter og gutter: kjønnsosialisering i et utviklingspsykologisk perspektiv* (The story of girls and boys: gender socialization in a developmental perspective), Scandinavian University Press, Oslo.
Bjerrum Nielsen, H. & Rudberg, M.: 1994, *Psychological Gender and Modernity*, Scandinavian University Press, Oslo.
Brophy, J.: 1985, 'Interactions of male and female students with male and female teachers', in L.C. Wilkinson & C.B. Marett (eds.), *Gender Influences in Classroom Interaction*, Academic Press, Orlando.

Chodorow, N.: 1989, *Feminism and Psychoanalytic Theory*, Yale University Press, New Haven.

Clarricoates, K.: 1978, 'Dinosaurs in the classroom – a re-examination of some aspects of the 'hidden' curriculum in primary schools', *Women's Studies Int. Quart* 1, 353–364.

Connell, R.W.: 1989, 'Cool Guys, Swots and Whimps: The Interplay of Masculinity and Education', *Oxford Review of Education* 15(3), 291–303.

Corson, D.: 1993, *Language, Minority Education and Gender*, Multilingual Matters Ltd., Clevedon.

Corson, D.: 1998, *Changing Education for Diversity*, Open University Press, London.

Croll, P. & Moses, D.: 1991, 'Sex roles in the primary classroom', In M. Woodhead, P. Light & R. Carr (eds.), *Growing up in a Changing Society*, Open University Press, London.

Davies, B.: 1989, *Frogs and Snails and Feminist Tales. Preschool Children and Gender*, Allen and Unwin, Sydney.

Davies, B.: 1993, *Shards of Glass. Children Reading and Writing Beyond Gendered Identities*, Allen and Unwin, Sydney.

Davies, L.: 1984, *Pupil Power*, Falmer Press, London.

Davies, B.: 1996, *Power/Knowledge/Desire. Changing School Organisation and Management Practices*, Department of Employment, Education and Training, Canberra.

Delamont, S.: 1980, *Sex Roles and the Schools*, Methuen, London.

Dweck, C., Davidson, W., Nelson, S. & Enna, B.: 1978, 'Sex differences in learned helplessness: II. The contingencies of evaluative feedback in the classroom: III. An experimental analysis', *Developmental Psychology* 14, 268–276.

Einarsson, J. & Hultman, T.: 1984, *Godmorgen pojkar och flickor* (Good morning boys and girls), Liber forlag, Stockholm.

Gilligan, C., Lyons, N.P. & Hanmer, T.J. (eds.): 1990, *Making Connections: The Relational Worlds of Adolescent Girls at Emma Willard School*, Harvard University Press, Cambridge.

Good, T., Sikes, J. & Brophy, J.: 1973, 'Effects of teacher sex and student sex in classroom interaction', *Journal of Educational Psychology* 65, 74–87.

Hjort, K.: 1984, *Pigepædagogik – ?* (Pedagogy for Girls – ?), Gyldendal, Copenhagen.

Jensen, P-E., Krogh-Jespersen, K., Kruse, A-M., Reinsholm, N. & Reisby, K.: 1984, *Skoleliv – pigeliv* (School life – girl life), Unge pædagoger, Copenhagen.

Kelly, A.: 1988, 'Gender differences in teacher-pupil interactions: a meta-analytical review', *Research in Education* 39, 1–23.

Kryger, N.: 1988, *De skrappe drenge – og den moderne pædagogik* (The tough guys and modern pedagogy), Unge Pædagoger, Copenhagen.

Le Maner-Idrissi, G.: 1996, 'An internal gender system at 24 months', *European Journal of Psychology of Education* XI, 301–312.

Lees, S.: 1986, *Loosing Our: Sexuality and Adolescent Girls*, Hutchinson, London.

Öhrn, E.: 1991, *Könsmönster i klassrumsinteraktion* (Gender patterns in classroom interaction), Göteborg Studies in Educational Sciences 77, University of Göteborg.

Paley, V.: 1984, *Boys and Girls: Superheroes in the Doll Corner*, University of Chicago Press, Chicago.

Reay, D.: 1991, 'Intersections of gender, race and class in the primary school', *British Journal of Sociology of Education* 12(2), 163–182.

Spender, D. & Sarah, E.: 1980, *Learning to Lose: Sexism and Education*, The Women's Press, London.

Stanworth, M.: 1983, *Gender and Schooling: A Study of Sexual Divisions in the Classroom*, Hutchinson, London.

Thorne, B.: 1993, *Gender Play: Girls and Boys in School*, Open University Press, Buckingham.

Walkerdine, V.: 1990, *Schoolgirl Fictions*, Verso, London.
Wernersson, I.: 1977, *Könsdifferentiering i grundskolan* (Gender differentiation in compulsory school), Göteborg Studies in Educational Sciences 22, University of Göteborg.
Whyte, J.: 1983, *Beyond the Wendy House: Sex Role Stereotyping in the Primary School*, Longman for School Council, York.
Willis, P.: 1977, *Learning to Labor*, Guilford.

JILL GOLDEN

NARRATIVE AND THE SHAPING OF IDENTITY

Narrative is one of the fundamental ways human beings organise their understandings of the world and their place in it. This narrative organisation happens at many levels and across many disciplines, as recent work in economics, science, psychology, history and law, as well as education, has shown (Nash, 1990). More informally, the stories that people tell – to each other, to themselves – shape the meanings that they give to their own lives and to their communities. The shaping of identity is intimately tied to the storylines that a particular society makes available and desirable to its members: from an early age children give evidence of their desire and ability to tell stories.

The use of the word "narrative" itself covers radically different understandings of what seems to be happening when people "know" or "learn" something. Most modern approaches to narrative (based on the work of linguists such as Saussure and Todorov) recognize the primacy of language in the organization of meaning – that is, that language is not a transparent medium, but imposes form and structure on experience. This common recognition can however conceal very different theoretical understandings about narrative and the shaping of identity. So any discussion of this topic needs first of all to make its theoretical basis clear.

Liberal humanism, whether secular or religious, is still the dominant discourse of Western culture. It is based on a "commonsense" understanding of the individual as a unified, rational being and is deeply rooted in the binary logic that organises Western thought into hierarchical and oppositional dualisms. Work on narrative and the shaping of identity which relies on liberal humanism ultimately assumes that each person has an "essential" self – unique, fixed and coherent, the core of each human individual. Narrative in this model might shape the surface, but not the "essence" of identity.

In this century, the move towards structuralism in many disciplines has been a (secular) seeking out of hidden rules that regulate human behaviour. Structuralist approaches in literature, for example, aim to uncover the strategies of *sameness* of form and function that underpin all narratives or myths. Structuralist approaches to narrative and identity challenge the humanist concept of the self as an autonomous agent, by laying bare the extent to which its apparently free choices are in fact predetermined by fixed rules.

B. Davies and D. Corson (eds), Encyclopedia of Language and Education,
Volume 4: Oral Discourse and Education, 137–145.
© *1997 Kluwer Academic Publishers. Printed in the Netherlands.*

Poststructuralist theory both derives from, and challenges, structuralism. It takes a radical step outside of liberal humanism by directly confronting liberal humanist ideas about the "essential self". The self is seen as 'precarious, contradictory and in process, constantly being reconstituted in discourse each time we think or speak' (Weedon, 1987, p. 33). Selfhood can be seen as 'a question of aesthetic creation rather than of the expressive liberation of some personal essence' (Macey, 1993, p. 418). Poststructuralist theory suggests that all knowledge or meaning is constructed not through fixed underlying structures within human minds or societies, but through multiple discourses circulating in language and culture. These form "storylines" within which people are positioned or position themselves in a variety of ways and through which they come to understand the world and their place in it.

EARLY DEVELOPMENTS

Scholars whose approaches to narrative theory and the shaping of identity, based on either a liberal humanist or a structuralist position, have made significant contributions to recent academic study of this field. Polkinghorne (1988) gives a detailed exposition of the main arguments about the function of narrative within the disciplines of history, literature and psychology. He provides an excellent introduction to the work of, for example, White, Ricoeur, Frye, Campbell, Barthes and Gergen. In one section, "Narrative and the self", he focuses on the role that narrative might play in the creation of identity, and suggests that 'The self is a meaning rather than a substance or a thing' (Polkinghorne, 1988, p. 152).

Bruner (1986), a psychologist, identifies narrative as one of two primary modes of human intelligence or thought (the other being logico-mathematical). He brings together a linguistic analysis of narrative and a constructivist understanding of the mind in his work on narrative and self, to explore the ways in which narrative works to endow experience with meaning. Bruner's observations are supported by the work of the neurologist Sacks (1986), for example in his account of Rebecca, a severely mentally handicapped young woman who has a "hunger for stories" which help her to organize herself as a "narrative being".

In the social sciences the collection and study of life histories has become accepted as a method to develop an understanding of the meanings people themselves give to their lives. The underlying metaphor for the narrative concept of selfhood in MacIntyre (1981) comes from drama. This dramaturgical model has been influential in sociology, taken up for example by symbolic interactionists and ethogenists.

The idea of "self as narrative" is examined from the perspective of the young child whose "self" is forming/being formed, by Miller et al. (1990). These authors start from the premise that both the experiences of self and the events in a narrative are organized with respect to time, and that narrative reproduces linguistically the process by which understanding is achieved over time. Personal storytelling by caregivers – casual anecdotes in daily settings about everyday incidents, stories which may include the child as participant or as audience – serves as a resource for young children as they come to express and understand who they are. Each culture has its own rules of narrative creation in such settings. Through them, children encounter again and again moments of personal extension (and reduction) which offer a range of potentials for their construction of self.

Other work on narrative which focuses on children and/or education (and somewhat indirectly on the shaping of identity) from a liberal humanist or structuralist position, includes Applebee's (1978) pioneering study of children's understandings and uses of story; Egan's (1979, 1988, 1990) work on the use of storytelling in teaching; Dyson's (1989) detailed study of eight children; and Fox's (1993) study of five preschool children. Within psychology, Engel's (1995) study offers a broad overview of current approaches to work with children's oral stories.

MAJOR CONTRIBUTIONS

Poststructuralist theorists like Foucault challenge dominant liberal humanist concepts about knowledge (as a unified, formal, scientific discourse organized in a natural hierarchy of power), and about identity ("the essential self" as the core of each human individual). Instead, Foucault suggests, knowledge and power are multiple, not unitary, and diffuse, not hierarchical; and identity (the "self" or subjectivity) is fluid, contradictory and precarious. For Foucault, there is no grand theory to explain human experience and meanings, no "first cause" available to human understanding as a final authority, and there is no "essential self". People are constituted *by* discourse in a multitude of ways.

Foucault introduces the concept of "technologies of the self", that is, 'the procedures ... proposed or prescribed for individuals in order to fix, maintain or transform their identity in accordance with a certain number of goals' (Foucault, in Macey, 1993, p. 417). To investigate the self means to recognise the lived experiences of *being* a particular self (with its emotional, physical and other dimensions) and at the same time to analyse the discursive production *of* that self (including its emotional, physical and other dimensions). It means paying attention to the specificities of difference as well as the continuities of samenesses. Stories, both told and lived, can be seen as "technologies of the self". Researchers using poststructuralist theory (notably in the areas of education and narrative therapy) have begun to investigate *how* stories function as "technology": how they intersect with lived experience to produce and reproduce selves.

One central feature of self-construction is the establishment and maintenance of gender, which like other aspects of identity must be accomplished within the narratives available in any culture. Researchers with a strong interest in questions of gender have found the insights offered by poststructuralist theory to be particularly valuable. Davies, for example, argues that gendered subjectivity has little to do with biological sex and much to do with storylines. She suggests that people are *interpellated* into pre-existing discourses, taking on the meanings inherent in those discourses as their own. She draws attention to the unquestioned assumptions that exist in both textual and lived narratives – for example that each character is and always has been male or female. Narrative both enables and limits children in their struggle to achieve and maintain a gender identity acceptable both to themselves and to their wider social group.

Davies also explores the idea of *how* narrative might work as a "technology of the self", through the concept of "positioning" in culturally available narratives. Production of one's sense of self, one's subjectivity, she argues, involves the following four processes:

1. Learning of the categories which include some people and exclude others, eg male/female, father/daughter.
2. Participating in the various discursive practices through which meanings are allocated to those categories. These include the story-lines through which different subject positions are elaborated.
3. Positioning of self in terms of the categories and story-lines. This involves imaginatively positioning oneself as if one belongs in one category and not in another (e.g. as girl and not boy, or good girl and not bad girl).
4. Recognition of oneself as having the characteristics that locate one as x or not x – ie the development of "personal identity" or a sense of oneself as belonging in the world in certain ways and thus seeing the world from the perspective of one so positioned. This recognition involves an emotional commitment to the category membership and the development of a moral system organized around the belonging (Davies, 1989, p. 230).

Contradictory demands (which are inevitable) are resolved by a complex interweaving of meanings, stories, emotions and experiences within discourses.

Davies & Harré (1990) use the concept of positioning to account both for a sense of continuous personal identity and a sense of discontinuous personal diversity. They argue that people (including children) make sense of their own and others' lives through stories. They both position themselves and are positioned by others in this process. Every conversation is a jointly produced story line, within which each party can accept or resist their positioning. Meaning is dependent on each participant's perception. One's sense of self is a fluid and diverse construction which shifts and changes depending on one's position within the particular storylines of the moment.

Other recent studies which explore some aspects of narrative and identity (in an educational setting, and from a poststructuralist theoretical perspective) are included in the list of references. See Walkerdine, 1981, 1984, 1989; Christian-Smith, 1988; Gilbert, 1988; Gilbert & Taylor, 1991; Lee, 1991; Mellor & Patterson, 1991; Cranny-Francis, 1992; Luke, 1993; Thorne, 1993; Davies, 1993, 1994. Recent work on masculine identity (from a poststructuralist theoretical perspective) includes White, 1992; Smith, 1992. Related work on narrative and the shaping of identity (not in an educational setting) includes Smith, 1993; Probyn, 1993; Belsey, 1994.

WORK IN PROGRESS

A search of databases in education, psychology, psychotherapy and other areas shows that research into the (oral) narrative shaping of identity continues to expand. Within some areas of psychology the development of identity is seen as the construction of life stories; psychopathology is concerned with life stories that have gone awry; and psychotherapy is an exercise in story repair (Howard, 1991).

Areas of interest are very diverse. They include: teenage mothers' narratives of self and the meanings they give to their mothering (SmithBattle, 1995); the reconstruction of identity by sufferers of Alzheimer's Disease (Crisp, 1995) or multiple sclerosis (Reissman, 1990); a North Dakota community making sense of illness (diabetes) through stories of culture, history and identity (Lang, 1989); modern Jewish identities shaped through stories of the Holocaust (Rosenman, 1990); and women (re)composing narrative life scripts that include ambition and desire (Wrye, 1994).

Work specific to the educational context includes studies of teachers' storying of their lives (Goodson, 1995); children's use of media superheroes to negotiate the symbolic and contradictory pressures of a multicultural society (Dyson, 1994) and family stories and literacy (Ott, 1993).

Poststructuralist theory is sometimes the preferred tool for analysis of data. Davies (1996) studied structures of authority and power (and the relation of this to narrative understandings of identity) amongst principals, teachers and students in a number of schools. Research funded by the *Gender Equity in Curriculum Reform Project* of the Australian Department of Employment, Education and Training (undertaken in various parts of Australia in 1991 – 1993) is now available to educators through publications such as Gilbert (1994) and Alloway (1995). Golden (1996) used poststructuralist theory to investigate the connections between children's oral storytelling and their construction of feminine or masculine gender identities.

PROBLEMS AND DIFFICULTIES

An important question which arises in any discussion of narrative and the shaping of identity (at least in a practical situation, such as education or therapy) is one of values. What are the implications of this knowledge for work with children, or clients, where the ethical implications of theory are lived out daily in personal relationships?

The traditional values of Western political, social and cultural life are strongly associated (in rhetoric if not always in practice) with "common-sense" liberal humanism – with values about individual human rights, democratic government, freedom of speech, justice and the rule of law; or certain ideas about what it means to be a person. In contrast, the relationship between poststructuralist theory and values is relatively unexplored. So although the contradictions between liberal humanism and poststructuralist theory are profound, individuals who want to use the insights of poststructuralist theory in their work (for example in the classroom) still tend to refer back (consciously or otherwise) to the ethics of versions of liberal humanism in making value judgements.

Poststructuralist theorists at this point have not taken on the task of providing an ethical guide appropriate to poststructuralist intellectual understandings (cf. Gergen, 1991; Mazzone, 1993). An articulation of values and their sources in relation to poststructuralist theory is now an important step to take. A clarification of where these values might be congruent with humanism, and where they are not, might make it easier (for teachers, for example) to use poststructuralist theory in everyday situations without slipping back into the "commonsense" of the dominant discourse.

Some recent research into the narrative construction of identity with an emphasis on ethical questions, includes an investigation into "emotional blindness" in human beings – the selective investment in caring (Scheibe, 1994); and the (re)storying that a woman with AIDS who is also a mother might do in order to lead a "responsible" life (Hassin, 1994).

A related concern is whether a focus on the narrative construction of identity might limit teachers' interest in other important political and practical issues in their work with marginalised groups (Goodson, 1995).

FUTURE DIRECTIONS

Narrative and the shaping of identity is an area of particular relevance to people with an interest, either philosophical or practical, in issues of gender, sexual preference, class and race. Research and practice continue to be undertaken based on liberal humanist, structuralist and poststructuralist theoretical frameworks.

Likely future *directions in research* include theoretical work on the question of *agency* (whether or to what extent a person is discursively positioned or actively positions her/himself in negotiating identity in a given situation); and theoretical work on the question of *desire* in lived and told stories (including the relationship between the traditional and popular narratives of the wider society, and the subjectivities of particular girls and boys, especially those belonging to marginalised groups).

Likely future *directions in practice* in relation to narrative and the shaping of identity in an educational setting can be found in recent policy statements of various Departments of Education. These have important implications for secondary English classrooms and teacher education. Innovations in practice could include the implementation of curriculum reform in English, shifts in what is seen as an appropriate pedagogy, and an ongoing review of classroom practices of writing, reading/viewing, and speaking/listening (Gilbert, 1994). Recent publications such as Dyson and Genishi (1994) indicate a growing recognition of the usefulness of work with oral narratives in the shaping of identities for children who live in modern multicultural societies.

Flinders University of South Australia
Australia

REFERENCES

Alloway, N.: 1995, *Foundation Stones. The Construction of Gender in Early Childhood*, Curriculum Corporation, Victoria.

Applebee, A.N.: 1978, *The Child's Concept of Story: Ages Two to Seventeen*, University of Chicago Press, Chicago, Ill.

Belsey, C.: 1994, *Desire. Love Stories in Western Culture*, Blackwell Publishers, Oxford.

Bruner, J.: 1986, *Actual Minds, Possible Worlds*, Cambridge, Harvard University Press, Mass.

Christian-Smith, L.: 1988, 'Romancing the girl: Adolescent romance novels and the construction of femininity', in L.G. Roman & L. Christian-Smith (eds.), *Becoming Feminine: The Politics of Popular Culture*, The Falmer Press, London, New York, Philadelphia.

Cranny-Francis, A.: 1992, *Engendered Fictions. Analysing Gender in the Production and Reception of Texts*, NSW University Press.

Crisp, J.: 1995, 'Making sense of stories that people with Alzheimer's tell. A journey with my mother', *Nursing Inquiry* 2(3), 133–140.

Davies, B.: 1989, 'The discursive production of male/female dualism in school settings', *Oxford Review of Education* 15(3), 229–241.

Davies, B.: 1993, *Shards of Glass*, Allen & Unwin, Sydney.

Davies, B.: 1994, *Poststructuralist Theory and Classroom Practice*, Deakin University Press, Victoria.

Davies, B.: 1996, *Power/Knowledge/Desire. Changing School Organisation and Management Practices*, Department of Employment, Education and Training, Canberra.

Davies, B. & Harré, R.: 1990, 'Positioning: The discursive production of selves', *Journal for the Theory of Social Behaviour* 20(1), 43–63.

Dyson, A.H.: 1989, *Multiple Worlds of Child Writers: Friends Learning to Write*, Teachers College Press, New York.

Dyson, A.H.: 1994, *The Ninjas, the X-men and the Ladies. Playing with Power and Identity in an Urban Primary School*, Center for the Study of Writing, Berkeley, California.

Dyson, A. H. & Genishi, C.: 1994, *The Need for Story: Cultural Diversity in Classroom and Community*, National Council of teachers of English.

Egan, K.: 1979, *Educational Development*, Oxford University Press, New York.

Egan, K.: 1988, *Primary Understanding, Education in Early Childhood*, Routledge, New York.

Egan, K.: 1990, *Romantic Understanding. The Development of Rationality and Imagination, 8–15*, Routledge, New York.

Engel, S.: 1995, *The Stories Children Tell. Making Sense of the Narratives of Childhood*, W. H. Freeman and Company, New York.

Fox, C.: 1993, *At the Very Edge of the Forest. The Influence of Literature on Storytelling by Children*, Cassel, London.

Gergen, K.J.: 1991, *The Saturated Self. Dilemmas of Identity in Contemporary Life*, Basic Books, USA.

Gilbert, P.: 1988, 'Stoning the romance: Girls as resistant readers and writers', *Curriculum Perspectives* 8(2), 13–18.

Gilbert, P.: 1994, *Divided by a Common Language? Gender and the English Curriculum*, Curriculum Corporation, Victoria.

Gilbert, P. & Taylor, S.: 1991, *Fashioning the Feminine: Girls, Popular Culture and Schooling*, Allen & Unwin, Sydney.

Golden, J.: 1996, *Children, Stories and Gender. A Feminist Poststructuralist Study*, Doctoral thesis, James Cook University of North Queensland.

Goodson, I.: 1995, 'Studying the self. Life politics and the study of the teacher's life and work', Paper presented at the American Education Research Association, San Francisco, California. April 18–22.

Hassin, J.: 1994, 'Living a responsible life. The impact of AIDS on the social identity of intravenous drug users', *Social Science and Medicine* 39(3), 391–400.

Howard, G.S.: 1991, 'Culture tales. A narrative approach to thinking, cross-cultural psychology and psychotherapy', *American Psychologist* 46(3), 187–197.

Lang, G.C.: 1989, ' "Making Sense" about diabetes. Dakota narratives of illness', *Medical Anthropology* 11(3), 305–327.

Lee, A.: 1991. 'Reading the differences', *English in Australia* 95, 24–35.

Luke, A.: 1993, 'Stories of social regulation: The micropolitics of classroom narrative', in Green, B. (ed.), *The Insistence of the Letter: Literacy Studies and Curriculum Theorizing*, Falmer Press, London.

MacIntyre, A.: 1981, *After Virtue: A Study in Moral Theory*, University of Notre Dame Press, Notre Dame, Indiana.

Macey, D.: 1993, *The Lives of Michel Foucault*, Hutchinson, London.

Mazzone, A.: 1993, 'The 'I' in the storm. An exploration of the concept of the self', Unpublished paper, Adelaide, SA.

Mellor, B. & Patterson, A.: 1991, 'Reading character: Reading gender', *English in Australia* 95, 4–23.

Miller, P.J. et al.: 1990, 'Narrative practices and the social construction of self in childhood', *American Ethnologist* 17, 292–311.

Nash, C. (ed.): 1990, *Narrative in Culture: The Uses of Storytelling in the Sciences, Philosophy and Literature*, Routledge, New York.

Ott, C.A.: 1993, 'Narrative and literacy. The functions of family stories and dialogues', paper presented at the Annual Meeting of the Conference on College Competition and Communication. San Diego, California. April.

Polkinghorne, D. 1988, *Narrative Knowing and the Human Sciences*, State University of New York Press, Albany NY.

Probyn, E.: 1993, *Sexing the Self. Gendered Positions in Cultural Studies*, Routledge, London.

Riessman, C.K.: 1990, 'Strategic uses of narrative in the presentation of self and illness. A research note', *Social Science and Medicine* 3(11), 1195–1200.

Rosenman, S.: 1990, 'The collective past. Group psychology and personal narratives. Shaping Jewish identity by memoirs of the holocaust', *American Journal of Psychoanalysis* 50(2), 151–170.

Sacks, O.: 1986, *The Man Who Mistook His Wife For a Hat*, Picador, London.

Scheibe, K.: 1994, 'On a certain emotional blindness in human beings', paper presented at the Annual Meeting of the American Psychological Association. Los Angeles, California. August 12–16.

SmithBattle, L.: 1995, 'Teenage mothers' narratives of self. An examination of risking the future', *Advanced Nursing Science* 17(4), 22–36.

Smith, G.: 1992, 'Dichotomies in the making of men', *Some Thoughts on Men's Ways of Being*, Dulwich Centre Newsletter, Numbers 3 & 4, 9–23.

Smith, S.: 1993, *Subjectivity, Identity and the Body. Women's Autobiographical Practices in the Twentieth Century*, Indiana University Press.

Thorne, B.: 1993, *Gender Play. Girls and Boys in School*, Rutgers University Press, New Jersey.

Walkerdine, V.: 1981, 'Sex, power and pedagogy', *Screen Education* 35, 14–24.

Walkerdine, V.: 1984, 'Some day my prince will come: Young girls and the preparation for adolescent sexuality', in A. McRobbie & M. Nava (eds.), *Gender and Generation*, Macmillan, UK, 162–184.

Walkerdine, V.: 1989, 'Femininity as performance', *Oxford Review of Education* 15, 267–279.

Weedon, C.: 1987, *Feminist Practice and Poststructuralist Theory*, Blackwell, Oxford.

White, M.: 1992, 'Men's culture, the men's movement, and the constitution of men's lives', *Some thoughts on men's ways of being*, Dulwich Centre Newsletter, Numbers 3 & 4, 33–53.

Wrye, H.K.: 1994, 'Narrative scripts. Composing a life with ambition and desire', *American Journal of Psychoanalysis* 52(2), 127–141.

JUDITH GREEN AND CAROL N. DIXON

THE CONSTRUCTION OF SOCIAL COMPETENCIES
THROUGH TALK

What counts as social competency? How are social competencies constructed in and through the everyday talk among members of a social
group? These questions guide the discussion of the conceptualization of
social competency that follows. The discussion begins with an historical
overview of the general concept of competence across time and disciplines
and then proceeds to an exploration of current perspectives to illustrate the
complexity in defining this construct.

As part of this discussion, the situated nature of social competencies
will be overviewed briefly to show that social competence is not a unitary
construct; rather its definition depends on who is asking the question,
the purpose for seeking a definition, and how such information will be
used. Through this discussion, the definition of social competency will
be revisited, and a view of competencies rather than competence will be
proposed. Underlying this view of competencies is a view of "talk" as a
form of social action within a complex array of meaning (or sign) systems
that shape and are shaped by members as they interact within and across
the everyday events of life within a group (Corson, 1995).

EARLY DEVELOPMENTS

Although the construction of social competencies through talk is a relatively recent area of study, the issue of what counts as competence is not
a new area of concern. Its roots can be traced in Western scholarship
to the time of the Greeks, and to religious texts across groups, before
and after that time (Denzin, 1977). Throughout history, scholars, both
lay and religious, have concerned themselves with defining what counts
as a competent member of society. Historically such definitions have
either implicity or explicitly used language that inscribes and privileges
an adult male position (Davies, 1989; 1993; Spender, 1982). However,
in the last two centuries, with the construction of "childhood" as a period
of development, with changes in the legal status of women and others,
with the opening of education to broad segments of society, with concerns for issues of equity and access, and with the increase in mobility
across national boundaries, the interrelated questions of what counts as
competence, and whose competence counts have received attention across
disciplines.

B. Davies and D. Corson (eds), Encyclopedia of Language and Education,
Volume 3: Oral Discourse and Education, 147–156.
© *1997 Kluwer Academic Publishers. Printed in the Netherlands.*

Underlying the dominant discourse on competency is the view that a person comes into the world incompetent and the task of adults or elders is to guide the transformation of the "incompetent" person into a competent one. This concern is visible across a variety of disciplines. For example, anthropologists seek understandings of the ways children are enculturated into or outsiders aculturated to a social group (e.g., Kimball, 1974; Mead, 1930; Ochs & Schieffelin, 1983; Schwartz, 1975). Sociologists are concerned with socialization processes and practices within and across groups (e.g., Cicourel, 1978; Corsaro & Miller, 1990; Denzin, 1977; Richards, 1974).

In contrast, psychologists have explored the acquisition and development of cognitive knowledge, social cognition, and intellectual competence of individuals (See Doise, 1996; Elbers, 1991, and Reiber & Carton, 1987 for recent discussions). Additionally, linguists have examined differences between competence and performance, in terms of both cognitive knowledge of language (Chomsky, 1968), and discourse norms – communicative competence (Hymes, 1974; Gumperz, 1982b). Thus, competence is not a unitary construct, but a situated one defined by particular disciplines, in particular ways, for particular purposes.

MAJOR CONTRIBUTIONS

The construction of social competencies through talk is an emerging area that is more interdisciplinary in nature than previous work on competence. Recent work has identified a range of perspectives from those that view social competence as residing in an individual to sociocultural perspectives that view social competency as situationally defined, as constructed over time within a social group, and as related to the opportunities for learning particular practices within a group (e.g., Vygotsky, 1934 as translated by Rieber & Carton, 1987).

At one end of this continuum, the term social competence generally implies a "fixed thing" an individual is expected to acquire or develop, and like other forms of competence, once obtained becomes a defining characteristic of an individual that applies to all contexts. From this perspective, an individual can be viewed as competent or incompetent. The dominant research approach used to assess this view of social competence involves a sociometric perspective. Kantor et al. (1993) argue that sociometric perspectives provide "a view of children's social competence as evaluated by others, not one seen in the specific accomplishment or the 'doing' of social interactions" (p. 128).

Assessments of social competence, therefore, relate to others' perceptions of social status within a group, enduring traits, and/or enduring behaviors. Thus, social competence, often viewed as social success or failure, resides with the individual as evaluated by others. Intervention research seeks to remediate or establish directly particular types of social action (e.g., singer citation).

In contrast to the focus on the individual in the sociometric perspective, the sociocultural perspective views social competence as constructed through the interactional work of people as they engage with each other in the contexts of everday life within and across times, spaces and groups (Kantor et al., 1993). Studies within this perspective range from those that view communication as the coordinated actions among members of a social group to those that view communication as a social system constructed by members of a group as they affiliate over time and work toward shared, personal or institutional goals.

Those who see communication as coordinated actions focus on interactional behaviors among members. Kantor et al. (1993) identified studies within this category that examine the quality of interactions among peers and interpret competence in light of such interactions (McDermott & Church, 1976; Monighan-Nourot et al., 1987). Effectiveness and social competence are related to one's abilities to match appropriate behavior with particular contexts.

Research from a social interactional perspective has also shown that some children or adults appear "out of tune" with others; that is, their interactional patterns do not fit those expected by other members of the group (Monighan-Nourot et al., 1987). Being interactionally "out of tune," can lead to being viewed by others as socially inappropriate, which in turn provides a basis for evaluations of these participants as socially noncompetent.

Rather than depending on rating or evaluation scales, research from a social interactional perspective depends on researcher observations of what individual members of a group are doing and the appropriateness of those behaviors to the activity. Members' behaviors in relationship to the activity, then, form the basis for examining what counts as appropriate action.

Although the social interactional perspective makes visible the dynamic and interactive nature of social competence and the fact that people in interaction make assessments of others' contributions, this work often ignores the cultural demands of group membership and the linguistic-sociocultural nature of everyday life. The difference between the interactional and sociocultural perspective can be addressed by examining two related bodies of work. The first, presented in this section, is grounded in sociolinguistics and ethnography of communication, and complements the interactional perspective. This work focuses on the role of language and culture to examine how linguistic performance and interactional patterns often lead to negative assessments of others' intellectual and/or social ability (e.g., Cazden, 1986; 1988; Gumperz, 1982a, 1986; Philips,1982), of interactional style (Tannen, 1984), and of social identity (e.g., Gumperz, 1982b;

McDermott & Church, 1976), particularly in inter-ethnic and cross-cultural settings.

For example, research from this perspective shows that when interactional patterns of a classroom do not match the social, linguistic and/or contextual presuppositions and expectations students (or teachers) bring to a classroom event (Gumperz, 1986), they may elect to remain silent, or to participate in a way that resists the expected practice (Philips, 1983; Erickson & Mohatt, 1982). This work also shows that when students do not engage in interactional practices expected by the teacher, they may be assessed as having a "bad attitude" or of being less competent than others. Further, assessment of "attitude" can lead to placement of students in particular groups and thus limits their access to opportunities for learning some forms of academic content as well as to social and academic practices.

This body of work focuses on the ways language-in-use influences others' assessment of competence and appropriate participation. (See Cazden, 1986; 1988; and Hicks, 1995 for comprehensive reviews across time.) Therefore, both the social interactional and the linguistically oriented sociocultural perspectives provide understandings of the dynamic and constructed nature of social competence and the discursive context of social competency.

WORK IN PROGRESS

Recent work from a linguistic-sociocultural perspective forms the basis for reframing social competency as social competencies. Work on social competencies focuses on the dynamic, situated and constructed nature of norms and expectations, roles and relationships, and rights and obligations within and across the events of everyday life as well as across groups (e.g., classrooms, families, and academic disciplines) and institutions. Each group or institution can be viewed as having particular ways of interacting, particular expectations for participating, and particular roles and relationships that are possible. Each, therefore, can be viewed as a small, particular culture (c.f., Spradley, 1980; Santa Barbara Classroom Discourse Group, 1992). While members have insider knowledge of these norms and expectations, and roles and relationships, a new person entering the group or institution will not have access to such knowledge automatically.

Research from this perspective has found that to enter a new group and its interactional spaces (Heras, 1993), or to participate in an ongoing group in socially appropriate ways, one must learn to read and interpret the texts of life being constructed by members, and then, to select from their communicative repertoires, socially appropriate ways of interacting (Gumperz, 1986).

Reading and interpreting an event, however, is a complex process. Individuals bring linguistic, social and contextual presuppositions to events (Gumperz, 1986). These presuppositions influence both the interpretation of the unfolding event and the choices a speaker makes in participating. Thus, what people display to others through their interactions within an event reflects a complex set of interpretations and decisions as well as what was available within their communicative repertoires. However, to understand what constitutes a person's repertoire for action involves over time observations that take into account the patterns of interaction for both the group and the individual.

The group-individual dynamic is central to understanding how social competencies are interactionally accomplished. For as Fairclough (1993) suggests, as members of a group interact, they begin constructing a text, and subsequent contributions to the text are shaped by, and then shape, the actions of those contributing to it as well as the developing text itself. From this perspective, social competencies are talked and acted into being across the local moments of life in groups. Social competencies, there-fore, do not exist separate from their context of construction. Over time, the locally constructed patterns of interaction become more or less stable within particular types of events, what Philips (1983) calls participant structures. This perceived stability, makes the expected patterns of inter-action more predictable, thus facilitating the task of selecting appropriate ways of participating.

The display of social competencies, then, is interactively accomplished, and what counts as socially appropriate actions is constructed across time and events within a group. Thus, social competencies are of a group, not of an individual. As such, they are tied to the participant structures constructed within groups for particular purposes. Knowledge of partici-pant structures, therefore, can be viewed as social, linguistic and cultural resources that members draw on when participating in subsequent events, both within and across groups and institutions. An individual's repertoire for action, therefore, reflects the past and present opportunities talked into being within and across groups.

Through such talk, members construct, and individuals have access to, the norms and expectations, rights and obligations and roles and rela-tionships that define what counts as membership and as social competen-cies (Green & Dixon, 1993; Santa Barbara Classroom Discourse Group, 1992). From this perspective, social competencies are constituted in and constructed through the talk in interactions among members of particular groups. Content of talk and ways of talking (discourse practices) constitute cultural knowledge through which group history, intertextual relationships and social practices are generated across time (Bloome & Egan-Robertson, 1993; Heap, 1991).

Further, studies in classroom settings have shown that even when members have a common history, participating in the same events does not ensure the same interpretation or the same access to opportunities to learn (Alton-Lee & Nuthall, 1992, 1993; Davies, 1990, 1993; Tuyay, Jennings & Dixon, 1995). The potential for multiple interpretations makes interaction in subsequent events a problematic aspect of everyday life (Smith, 1990) and the need for observing the negotiation of task and meanings important (Floriani, 1993). Other classroom studies have shown that student and teacher are roles that are situationally constructed as members construct a peer culture and a schooling culture (Fernie, Davies, Kantor & McMurray, 1993); and that students must simultaneously attend to and participate appropriately in both cultures. What is seen as social competency in one of these cultures may not be appropriate in the other (Bloome & Theodorou, 1988).

This body of work, although illustrative, shows that multiple groups exist within a classroom, thus placing multiple demands on students to display membership in particular ways. To be socially competent, therefore, has multiple meanings and depends on understanding to whom an individual is orienting, what they are doing, with whom, under what conditions, for what purposes, and with what outcome. Given the complex, dynamic and often overlapping group memberships, it is not possible to view social competence as a static or unitary construct. Rather, the multiple demands facing members of a group mean that multiple opportunities to display social competencies exist and that what counts as appropriate action is constantly being negotiated and renegotiated within as well as across events and groups.

PROBLEMS AND PITFALLS

The primary problems and pitfalls facing someone electing to take up the view of social competencies as constructed through talk described above are found in the area of research methods and theory-method relationships. To examine what counts as social competencies to members of a group (e.g., teachers and students in classrooms) involves extended participant observation, the purpose of which is to obtain an emic or insider understanding of the social and academic demands. To examine the role of language in constructing situated definitions of such competencies also involves over time observation. However, to explore the ways members, through their moment-to-moment interactions negotiate and construct the events of everyday life, and through this process the situated demands for participation, requires a sociolinguistic or discourse analysis approach. The choice of theories to guide these observations is also problematic, for the theories selected shape what can be seen, known, and understood (Strike, 1974).

Concern for theory-method relationships is a key problematic for anyone working in this area. It is problematic at all phases of an over time study. The theories used at the outset are orienting theories that shape initial entry, observations, data collection and data analysis. They also frame how a social contract will be written with members of the group being studied, which in turn, shapes the roles and relationships among members. For example, by selecting an ethnographic perspective grounded in cultural anthropology, a researcher will be expected to examine the question of what counts as social competencies by asking questions such as: who are the actors, what do the actors do or say, to whom? Under what conditions do actors interact, with whom, for what purposes? What are the artifacts used by actors, in what ways for what purposes and with what outcomes? What are the academic and social demands of everyday life and who has access to the opportunities constructed through such demands? And, who takes up the opportunities constructed by members of the group, under what conditions, for what purpose(s), with what outcome(s)?

Such questions provide a tool for entering a group and for identifying general patterns of life within a group, the what of daily life. However, such questions do not provide a way of examining how members, through their face-to-face interactions within and across events, construct the norms and expectations, roles and relationships, and rights and obligations that form the basis for the development and display of social competencies at both a group and individual level.

To accomplish this task requires close examination of the language or languages used by members, the practices which support or constrain that use, and how, through language, social competencies are signalled and displayed. Additionally, social competencies are not solely talked into being. Members often must display knowledge of cultural practices in written or graphic form as well as orally. Thus, to explore issues of social competencies entails a multi-faceted approach to the study of everyday life.

FUTURE DIRECTIONS

The move from social competence to social competencies entails a shift in focus from the individual in a social context to an examination of how the collective shapes and is shaped by individual members, how membership in a particular collective affords members particular opportunities and limits others, and how participation in such collectives leads to the development of particular identities, repertoires for action, and views of what counts as socially appropriate actions within and across groups and institutions.

These shifts also have consequences for the selection of topics to be explored and the ways in which questions are posed: e.g., whether or not practices in social groups are gendered, selective, inclusive, and so forth; how gendered practices among others are constructed; how literate practices shape opportunities for learning to be literate in particular ways; how members of groups construct identities – as writers, readers, scientists, mathematicians, family members or as smart, gifted, slow or talented; how access is afforded some students but not others; and how language use is socially constructed in ways that support or constrain students in using mother tongues to display to others knowledge of social competencies.

Underlying each of these questions and basic to future directions for research and theory development are the two key questions posed at the beginning of this discussion: What counts as social competencies? How are social competencies constructed in and through the everyday talk among members of a group? To move beyond a situated and local view of social competencies and to understand the repertoires for social action people develop through membership, these questions need to be examined across settings. In our global world of the future, answers to these and related questions will be needed within and across across groups, and national boundaries as well as institutions.

University of California
Santa Barbara, USA

REFERENCES

Alton-Lee, A. & Nuthall, G.: 1992, 'Children's learning in classrooms: Challenges in developing a methodology to explain "opportunity to learn"', *Journal of Classroom Interaction* 27(2), 1–8.

Alton-Lee, A. & Nuthall, G.: 1993, 'Reframing classroom research: A less from the private world of children', *Harvard Educational Review* 63(1), 50–84.

Bloome, D. & Egan-Robertson, A.: 1993, 'The social construction of interatextuality in classroom reading and writing lessons', *Reading Research Quarterly* 28(4), 304–333.

Bloome, D. & Theodorou, E.: 1988, 'Analyzing teacher-student and student-student discourse', in J. Green & J. Harker (eds.), *Multiple perspective analyses of classroom discourse*, Ablex, Norwood, NJ, 217–248.

Cazden, C.: 1986, 'Classroom discourse', in M. Wittrock (ed.), *The Handbook of Research on Teaching*, Volume 3. Macmillan, New York, 432–464.

Cazden, C.: 1988, *Classroom Discourse: The Language of Teaching and Learning*, Heinemann, Portsmouth, NH.

Chomsky, N.: 1968, *Language and Mind*, Harcourt, Brace and World, New York.

Cicourel, A.: 1978, 'Interpretation and summartization: Issues in the child's acquisition of social structure', in J. Glick & K. Alison Clarke-Stewart (eds.), *The Development of Social Understanding*, Gardner Press, Inc., New York, 251–282.

Corsaro, W. & Miller, P. (eds.): 1990, 'Interpretive approaches to children's socialization', *New Directions for Child Development*, Jossey-Bass, San Francisco, CA, 58.

Corson, D.: 1995, *Using English Words*, Kluwer, Boston.

Davies, B.: 1989, *Frogs & Snails and Feminist Tales Preschool Children and Gender*, Allen & Unwin, Sydney.

Davies, B.: 1993, *Shards of Glass: Children Reading and Writing Beyond Gendered Identities*, Hampton Press, Cresskill, NJ/Allen & Unwin, Sydney.

Denzin, N.: 1977, *Childhood Socialization*, Jossey-Bass, San Francisco, CA.

Doise, W.: 1996, 'The origins of developmental social psychology: Baldwin, Cattaneo, Piaget and Vygotsky', *The Swiss Journal of Psychology* 55(2/3), 139–149.

Elbers, E.: 1991, 'The development of competence and its social context', *Educational Psychology Review* 3(2), 73–94.

Erickson, F. & Mohatt, G.: 1982, 'The cultural organization of participation structures in two classrooms of Indian students', in G. Spindler (ed.), *Doing the Ethnography of Schooling*, Holt, Rinehart, & Winston, New York, 102–131.

Fairclough, N.: 1993, 'Discourse and text: Linguistic and intertextual analysis within discourse analysis', *Discourse and Society* 3(2), 193–218.

Fernie, D., Davies, B., Kantor, R., & McMurray, P.: 1993, 'Becoming a person in the preschool: Creating integrated gender, school culture, and peer culture positioning', *Qualitative Studies in Education* 6, 95–110.

Floriani, A.: 1993, 'Negotiating what counts: Roles and relationships, content and meaning, texts and context', *Linguistics and Education* 5(3/4), 241–274.

Gilmore, P.: 1987, 'Sulking, stepping and tacking: The effects of attitude assessment on access to literacy', in D. Bloome (ed.), *Literacy and Schooling*, Ablex, Norwood, NJ, 98–120.

Green, J. & Dixon, C.: 1993, 'Introduction to "Talking knowledge into being: Discursive and social practices in classrooms" ', *Linguistics and Education* 5(3/4), 231–239.

Gumperz, J.: 1982a, *Discourse Strategies*, Cambridge University Press, Cambridge.

Gumperz, J. (ed.): 1982b, *Language and Social Identity*, Cambridge University Press, Cambridge.

Gumperz, J.: 1986, 'Interactive sociolinguistics on the study of schooling', in J. Cook-Gumperz (ed.), *The Social Construction of Literacy*, Cambridge University Press, New York, 45–68.

Heap, J.: 1991, 'A situated perspective on what counts as reading', in C. Baker & A. Luke (eds.), *Toward a Critical Sociology of Reading Pedagogy*, John Benjamins, Philadelphia.

Heras, A.I.: 1993, 'The construction of understanding in a sixth grade bilingual classroom', *Linguistics and Education* 5(3/4), 275–299.

Hicks, D.: 1995, 'Discourse, learning, and teaching', in M. Apple (ed.), *Review of Research in Education*, American Educational Research Association Washington, DC, 49–95.

Hymes, D.: 1974, *Foundations in Sociolinguistics*, University of Pennsylvania Press, Philadelphia, PA.

Kantor, R., Elgas, P. & Fernie, D.: 1993, 'Cultural knowledge and social competence within a preschool peer cultural group', *Early Childhood Research Quarterly* 9, 125–147.

Kimball, S.: 1974, *Culture and the Educative Process: An Anthropological Perspective*, Teachers College Press, New York.

McDermott, R. & Church, J.: 1976, 'Making sense and feeling good: The ethnography of communicaiton and identity work', *Communication* 2, 121–142.

Mead, M.: 1930, *Growing Up In New Guinea*, William, Morrow, New York.

Monighan-Nourot, P., Scales, B., Van Hoorn, J., & Almy, M.: 1987, *Looking at Children: A Bridge Between Theory and Practice*, Teacher's College Press, New York.

Ochs, E. & Schieffelin, B.: 1983, *Acquiring Conversational Competence*, Routledge & Kegan Paul, London.

Philips, S.: 1983, *The Invisible Culture: Communication in Classroom and Community on the Warm Springs Indian Reservation*, Longman, New York.

Reiber, R. & Carton, A.: 1987, *The Collected Works of L.S. Vygotsky, Volume 1: Problems of General Psychology*, Plenum, New York.

Richards, M. (ed.): 1974, *The Integration of a Child into a Social World*, Cambridge University Press, Cambridge.

Santa Barbara Classroom Discourse Group (Green, J., Dixon, C., Lin, L., Floriani, A. and Bradley, M.): 1992, 'Constructing literacy in classrooms: Literate action as social accomplishment', in H. Marshall (ed.), *Redefining Student Learning: Roots of Educational Change*, Ablex, Norwood, NJ, 119–150.

Schwartz, T. (ed.): 1975, *Socialization as Cultural Communication: Development of a Theme in the Work of Margaret Mead*, University of California Press, Berkeley, CA.

Smith, D.: 1990, *The Conceptual Practices of Power: A Feminist Sociology of Knowledge*, University of Toronto Press, Toronto.

Spender, D.: 1982, *Invisible Women: The Schooling Scandal*, The Women's Press, London.

Spradley, J.: 1980, *Participant Observation*, Holt, Rinehart & Winston, New York.

Strike, K.: 1974, 'On the expressive potential of behaviorist language', *American Educational Research Journal* 11(2), 103–120.

Tannen, D.: 1984, *Conversational Style: Analyzing Talk Among Friends*, Ablex, Norwood, NJ.

Tuyay, S., Jennings, L. & Dixon, C.: 1995, 'Classroom discourse and opportunities to learn: An ethnographic study of knowledge construction in a bilingual third grade classroom', *Discourse Processes*, 75–110.

Vygotsky: 1934, 'Lectures on psychology', as translated in Reiber, R. & Carton, A. (1987), *The Collected Works of L.S. Vygotsky, Volume 1: Problems of General Psychology*, Plenum, New York, 289–359.

PAUL J. PAGLIANO

THE ACQUISITION OF COMMUNICATIVE COMPETENCE AMONGST CHILDREN WITH SPEECH AND LANGUAGE IMPAIRMENT

Fundamental to the concept of communicative competence is the ability to produce and understand ideas appropriate to the social context in which they occur, with emphasis on accuracy of idea transfer rather than mere correctness of language form or delivery. Speech impairment interferes with message transmission and may involve: a total lack of intelligible speech; articulation distortions or errors in sound production; voice deviations in pitch, volume, resonance and quality; fluency deviations in rhythm, timing and interconnectedness, or various combinations of the above. Language impairment interferes with both message transmission and reception. Language development may be absent with no recognisable receptive or expressive language. It may be delayed with language acquired later and more slowly, or interrupted with partial loss of language ability, or qualitatively disordered with bizarre or meaningless language. Speech and language impairment may also occur in combination. They are significant when they result in learning, social, economic or emotional disadvantage and/or endanger physical wellbeing. A conservative estimate is that at least 5 percent of the world's child population need specialist help to acquire communicative competence but UNICEF (1994) figures indicate less than one percent of these children even attend school.

EARLY DEVELOPMENTS

Researchers such as Itard (1962) in the early nineteenth century showed that children with communication impairment could learn if taught. In the first half of the twentieth century most children with severe communication impairment were taught in segregated institutions for individuals with intellectual, hearing, vision or physical disability. Consequently much communication impairment research appeared, often tangentially, in disability literature specific to these categories. Knowledge of communication impairment has been further complicated by research appearing in literature of a wide range of disciplines, including speech-language pathology, special education, linguistics, sociolinguistics, psycholinguistics, psychology, neurology, neurophysiology and psychiatry with a varying degree of mutual recognition and cross fertilisation. Briefly it can be said that speech and language impairments are massively diverse in type, severity

B. Davies and D. Corson (eds), Encyclopedia of Language and Education,
Volume 3: Oral Discourse and Education, 157–166.
© *1997 Kluwer Academic Publishers. Printed in the Netherlands.*

and prognosis, mostly of unknown aetiology and often occur in association with other disabilities.

Lund & Duchan (1988) summarised the historical stages of development in the latter half of the twentieth century. These reveal a focus broadening from narrow considerations of language structure to deeper concerns regarding ability to use language. Atypical and typical communication development research have had a strong complementary relationship. In the 1950s the medical model was strongly influential. Emphasis on normal language development resulted in disability being perceived as a deficit. Determining disability cause, even when successful, usually failed to inform intervention. Consequently large numbers of children were regarded as ineducable. In the 1960s behaviourism married intervention to the problem. The problem was thought to be the disordered language and language response was assumed to be under the control of stimulus and reinforcement. The didactic approach of the 1970s extended this focus to teaching the individual to request objects and actions. Sometimes vocabulary increased but functional communication development was still elusive. An alternative 1960s approach focused on language ability at four levels: phonology, morphology, syntax, and semantics. This linguistic approach became the 1970s cognitive approach with semantics the focus and identification of precursors to language acquisition the goal. The term ineducable became redundant.

MAJOR ISSUES

From ancient times children with communication impairment have been misunderstood, ridiculed, marginalised and mistreated to a greater or lesser degree by the community at large. Only recently has society started to accept the goal of all individuals with communication impairment exercising their full societal rights and responsibilities.

By far the most major contribution to the lives of children with communication impairment has been the enormous influence of the philosophy of normalisation and social role valorisation. Normalisation, or the goal of making the lives of people with disabilities as much as possible like that of others, originated in Scandinavia and has been attributed to Bank-Mikkelsen (1969). Wolfensberger (1984) developed the term social role valorisation to emphasise the valuing of people in society. In the United States of America, these philosophies have been enshrined in the 1975 Public Law 94–142, *The Education of the Handicapped Act*, and its subsequent amendments. The act is based on the principle that a student with disability must receive educational services with zero rejection, nondiscriminatory evaluation, individualised education plans, in a least restrictive environment, subject to due process, and with parental involvement. It mandated free, appropriate education, which is easily accessible, ensures equal opportunity, encourages highest potential, and enables self-sufficiency. Similar policies have been adopted internationally.

This global view of the child with disability (including communication impairment) is the result of a shift from a medical to an ecological model where children and disability are viewed in complex interaction with environmental forces. The resultant goal is to empower the child and usually involves extensive collaboration between child, family, regular class teacher, special teacher, specialists from other disciplines including speech language pathologists, and targeted community representatives. In developed countries most children with communication impairment now live at home and are educated within mainstream schools. Emphasis is on quality of life issues, from early childhood to transition from school to adult life.

Two important approaches have evolved from research on intentionality and communicative competence. The first stressed the importance of studying communication within the contexts of interaction and became the functional pragmatic approach of the 1980s, see for example Coggins & Carpenter (1981). The second investigated prelinguistic communication in infants between 9 and 18 months and spawned interest in non-symbolic competence, see for example Sugarman (1984). Examplars obtained from this research helped to define communicative competence in nonlinguistic individuals and provided the basis for expansion into the use of augmentative and alternative communication (AAC) systems. Augmentative systems support speech and language use. Alternative systems provide permanent nonvocal or nonlinguistic communication substitutes with use determined by the child's ability. AAC systems may be unaided, requiring special knowledge, or aided, requiring special equipment. Unaided techniques include gesture and facial expression. Speech reading and cued speech make maximal use of the visual components of communication. Auditory training makes maximal use of the aural components of communication. Aided systems include electronic devices or communication displays consisting of objects, photographs, words, numbers, and picture symbols pointed to in various ways to relay information. One system, Blissymbolics, originally developed as an international communication medium for non-disabled people, provides nonlinguistic children with a system that fosters creative thinking, inductive processing and concept clarification. Minspeak is a highly developed computerised icon system capable of fast representation of sophisticated individualised concepts. A variety of symbolic systems are in use, many tightly copyrighted by commercial interests. Electronic devices range from television and video teletext captioning, teletype telephones, voice output communication aids and amplification methods including FM hearing aids which suppress background noise. Bloomberg (1991) stressed the importance of matching AAC system to the needs of the child arguing that such a match is often best achieved through collaborative involvement of the multidisciplinary team.

Sign language is especially significant as it was developed for and by deaf people. Predicated on sign language are the concepts of Deaf community and Deaf culture as elucidated by Padden (1980) – concepts without strong parallel in other disability areas. Sign languages differ in different countries, but all display grammar and syntax and are regarded as natural languages. This is in distinct contrast to spoken languages rendered in sign form which are by their nature formulaic. Moores (1991) identified 'how', 'what' and 'where' as the three ongoing generic questions of deaf education. 'How' to communicate ranges from pure oral, total communication with simultaneous manual (signed spoken language) and speech, to manual (Deaf sign language and culture). 'What' to teach, or which curriculum ranges from compensatory (which involves the addition of extra resources to schools serving deaf students), oppositional (where a separate curriculum specifically for deaf students is developed) to counterhegemonic (which involves an attempt to generalise the point of view of those who are deaf to reconstruct the mainstream curriculum). 'Where' ranges from full inclusion in regular community schools to separate schooling specifically for deaf students.

Bilingual bicultural approaches have been slow to gain acceptance internationally because as Strong (1988) observed some still question if sign language is a real language, focusing on its lack of written form. The problem is further compounded by insufficient hearing parents and teachers being fluent in sign. Mason & Ewoldt (1996) claimed that deaf bilingual bicultural education and whole language proponents 'share essentially the same goal – to encourage connections between school curriculum and real life experiences and values' (p. 293). They argued that 'deaf children need access to complete languages through-the-air' (sign) 'and in written form' (p. 297). Computerised instructional approaches to teach written English to sign language users devised by Hansen & Padden (1989) also have potential to help close this literacy gap. It is largely from the basis of AAC systems, including sign that a child with communication impairment can achieve an appropriate education in his or her school of choice.

CURRENT ISSUES

The major communication impairment literature areas regarding the acquisition of communicative competence are assessment, early intervention, school age, transition, and special populations including autism, hearing impairment, cleft palate, physical and multiple disabilities. Space allows only broad themes to be addressed with particular focus on severe communication impairments.

Within the past decade researchers working with children with severe communication impairment such as Green & Cobb (1991) and Stephenson & Linfoot (1996) have begun to recognise the inextricable link between form and intention. This has resulted in a broadening of the definition of oral language to include nonvocal and nonlinguistic systems and new definitions of competency based on increase in functional skills rather than vocabulary. Furthermore it has reshaped the way communication is taught, with intentionality firmly positioned as the motivating force behind communication. These developments have in turn increased the need for greater precision in assessment information especially regarding the child's cognitive, social and motor skills.

Non-discriminatory evaluation is essential. New ethnographically sensitive assessment instruments are being developed, see for example Battle (1992), which aim to eliminate format, lexical, and/or syntactical biases against individuals. The important part of assessment is to identify the child's concomitant strengths and weaknesses regarding communicative competence and to determine appropriate educational long term goals and short term objectives. Assessment is also important in evaluating program effectiveness. Cochran and Masterson (1995) detailed potential problems and benefits of computer use in language assessment and intervention. Strengths of computer use appear to be in the areas of tools for linguistic and phonological analysis, treatment, data collection and biofeedback provision.

Early identification and intervention often reduce or even remove the communication impairment, especially when it is mild. Williams & Witzel (1994) highlighted early intervention as particularly important in children with craniofacial abnormalities such as clefts of the lip, hard and soft palate, who may require extensive treatment involving complex team collaboration with medical and dental specialists, speech-language pathologists and special educators. Generally these children have slower language, articulation, educational and literacy development. Tiegerman (1993) described chilren with autism as another group that benefit from early identification and intervention. Although children with autism form a heterogenous group, the unifying or central problem for them clearly seems to be communicative incompetence, caused by inability to integrate communicative function with other aspects of language. Children with autism experience problems initiating and completing interactions, topic maintenance, and speaker-listener roles. Early intervention focuses on individualised instruction in language-based educational orientation within a highly structured learning environment where linguistic and semantic input matches child's comprehension. Successful intervention enables entry into regular school. Some children with autism are being taught using AAC systems.

Light (1989) identified four types of communicative competence essential if AAC users are to successfully express basic needs, exchange information, establish social closeness and engage in social routines. *Linguistic competence* includes both the means to represent ideas and the knowledge of the language (or nonlinguistic) code. *Operational competence* is the individual's ability to manage specific devices or techniques used in the communication process including the means to select representation, for example eye gaze, and the means to transmit the idea, for example hands. Bradley Harris Wolf (1994) was thirteen years old before a system was designed to meet his communication limitations and break through to his rich inner world. *Social competence*, refers to the sociolinguistic, pragmatic knowledge necessary to communicate. AAC users often have little opportunity to learn social competence and the particular system used may also dictate what constitutes social competence. Goossens, Crain & Elder (1994) criticised much current AAC teaching stating that most communication was with adults not peers, with the adult lacking system fluency but dominating the interaction, asking closed-ended questions and restricting communicative range by misinterpreting or missing attempts by the child to be innovative. *Strategic competence* refers to strategies to repair communication breakdown, such as requesting additional information or recognising that message has been misunderstood. Light & McNaughton (1993) have been expanding AAC research into the area of literacy and early reading competency. Mirenda & Calculator (1993) have been conducting further research into how best to involve AAC users in school curricula especially within the mainstream. One area where strategic competence is necessary is that of facilitated communication.

Crossley (1992) reported on three case studies using a system she developed called facilitated communication where an adult provides physical support with successive approximation to help the child overcome neuromotor difficulties and communicate using a communication board. Biklin (1993) challenged current perceptions of autism as a social, cognitive disability when he reported that facilitated communication enabled the children with autism in his study to display linguistic skills not able to be observed in their verbal expression. This sparked off a vigorous debate with wide ranging legal and ethical considerations. Simon, Whitehair & Toll (1995) recommended that facilitated communications proceed only if all involved give informed consent and both a validation protocol and other potential means of communication are used. Some individuals with autism develop communicative competence to a high level as evidenced in Grandin's (1995) autobiography.

Intervention strategy paradigms currently in use include: collaborative consultation, contextual-pragmatic, curriculum-based, strategy-based, and whole language. Strategies generally emphasise message first with correction second, highlight positive achievements and provide concrete reinforcement associated with minimum frustration within a social context in the classroom, playground and community. Corrections are limited to current targets with an emphasis on skills becoming automatic. The research literature promotes whole family involvement in intervention within a context of respect for the rights and freedom of family members. Other areas of concern include self-determination and quality of life. Parmenter (1992) identified three components in a quality of life model as the individual's perception of self, functional behaviours, and social influences. Schalock (1994) argued that a paradigmatic shift is occurring reflected in the way people with disabilities are more actively expressing their views about what they want out of life. This shift has had powerful influences in the way children with communication impairment are being taught. For Mithaug (1991) special educators in the past tried too hard often missing valuable opportunities to enable children to learn from their own mistakes. He argued that children become self-determining through increased awareness of self, of needs and abilities, involvement in personal goal setting, performing a wide range of tasks well, being self-reliant, taking risks, achieving intermediate successes, taking responsibility for positive and negative results by objective self-evaluation, critical review and adjustment.

PROBLEMS AND DIFFICULTIES

The most serious and overwhelming problem worldwide is finding the resources to make provision of any specialist services for children with communication impairments. For many developing countries the goal is achieving universal primary education. Lynch (1994) in a Report to the World Bank argued that universal primary education can only be achieved with the inclusion of all children with special educational needs because the alternatives, no education or segregated education, are vastly more expensive options personally, socially and economically. This provides an enormous challenge in the area of professional teacher training. UNESCO (1994) especially through the Salamanca Agreement, has done much worldwide to promote special needs education and the inclusion of students with disabilities in regular education. However there is still an enormous gulf between rhetoric and actuality. In the developed world short term economic rationalism has limited the range and depth of service that could be provided and in many parts of the world services are actually being reduced rather than increased. This will inevitably have undesirable long term consequences. Campbell (1992) further reminds us that inequities are most exaggerated in isolated rural areas particularly those servicing children from minority groups. Currently there is a critical shortage of qualified personnel in rural areas throughout the world. There is an increased need to develop alternative modes of service delivery. Price (1995) emphasised the importance of efficient effective service delivery avoiding the accidental or ad hoc basis of many aid programs and the unrealistic time frames set for achievement of goals with little if any follow up. She suggested that national and international professional organisations could play an increased role.

Medical practices such as gene technology, antenatal screening, abortion of abnormal fetuses, operations in utero, severe prematurity, new diseases (such as AIDS), new treatments (such as cochlear implants) and euthanasia are altering the spectrum of disability. In the developing world there are problems relating to resource provision, basic health especially maternal and infant health, and the prevention of infection and malnutrition. The challenges remain considerable.

FUTURE DIRECTIONS

The biggest challenge for the future is for people with communication impairment to become full and equal members of communities, not merely live passively in them. People with communication impairment must reach into areas of prominence and responsibility so their views on communication difficulties enter mainstream awareness and debate. This heterogenous group of individuals with communication impairment does have a voice and it must be heard. In particular it is important that people with communication impairment help shape the communication impairment research literature. Several such authors have been cited in this text, for example, Padden, Wolf and Grandin.

Future research needs to focus on identifying what it is that perpetuates oppression and helplessness in the lives of individuals with communication impairment. For Woodill (1994) critical theory and social semiotics are two powerful tools which can work together to uncover, debunk, appropriate and deploy the signs of disability. He recommended more ethnographic research using these tools, more historical research into disability concept development, further study into the construct of normalcy and increased insight into how children develop an understanding of difference. Research has already started with a number of major studies recently being published such as Norden's (1994) study of the representation of disability in cinema.

Technology has the potential to both disenfranchise and empower individuals with communication impairment. As good communication skills rather than manual labour increasingly become the basis for paid employment, those without communicative competence will become even more socially disadvantaged. Conversely technology will be able to vastly expand leisure options and significantly improve many quality of life considerations for those with communication impairment. Whether most individuals will be able to afford such technology is unlikely, and is an issue for the rest of the community. The social changes predicated on this technological onslaught are predicted to be profound.

James Cook University
Australia

REFERENCES

Bank-Mikkelsen, N.: 1969, 'A metropolitan area in Denmark: Copenhagen', in R. Kugel & W. Wolfenberger (eds.), *Issues in Special Education*, Mayfield Publishing Company, Mountain View, CA, 42–50.

Battle, D.E. (ed.).: 1992, *Communication Disorders in Multicultural Populations*, Heinemann, Butterworth.

Biklen, D.: 1993, *Communication Unbound: How Facilitated Communication is Challenging Traditional Views of Autism and Ability/Disability*, Columbia University, New York, NY.

Bloomberg, K.: 1991, 'Which one for your child?', in K. Bloomberg & H. Johnson (eds.), *Communication Without Speech: A Guide for Parents and Teachers*, The Australian Council for Educational Research, Hawthorn, Victoria, 30–39.

Campbell, L. R.: 1992, 'Meeting the needs of minority children in rural settings', *Rural Special Education Quarterly* 11(2), 26–30.

Cochran, P.S. & Masterson, J.L.: 1995, 'Not using a computer in language assessment/intervention: In defense of the reluctant clinician', *Language, Speech and Hearing Services in Schools* 26, 213–222.

Coggins, T. & Carpenter, R.: 1981, 'The communication intention inventory: A system for observing and coding children's early intentional communication', *Journal of Applied Psycholinguistics* 2, 235–251.

Crossley, R.: 1992, 'Getting the words out: Case studies in facilitated communication training', *Topics in Language Disorders* 12(4), 46–59.

Goossens, C., Crain, S.S. & Elder, P.: 1994, *Engineering the Preschool Environment for Interactive Symbolic Communication: 18 months to 5 years Developmentally*, Southeast Augmentative Communication Conference Publications, Birmingham, AL.

Grandin, T.: 1995, *Thinking in Pictures and Other Reports from My Life with Autism*, Doubleday, New York, NY.

Green, M. & Cobb, L.: 1991, 'Theories of communication development', in L. Sternberg (ed.), *Functional Communication: Analyzing the Nonlinguistic Skills of Individuals with Severe or Profound Handicaps*, Springer-Verlag, New York, NY, 1–17.

Hanson, V.L. & Padden, C.: 1989, 'Interactive video for bilingual ASL/English instruction of deaf children', *American Annals of the Deaf* 134, 209–213.

Itard, J.M.G.: 1962, *The Wild Boy of Aveyron*, G. Humphrey & M. Humphrey, eds. and trans., Appleton-Century-Crofts, New York, NY, Original work published 1894.

Light, J.: 1989, 'Towards a definition of communicative competence for individuals using augmentative and alternative communication systems', *Augmentative and Alternative Communication* 5, 137–144.

Light, J. & McNaughton, D.: 1993, 'Literacy and augmentative and alternative communication (AAC): The expectations and priorities of parents and teachers', *Topics in Language Disorders* 13(2), 33–46.

Lund, N.J. & Duchan, J.F.: 1988, *Assessing Children's Language in Naturalistic Contexts*, Prentice-Hall, Englewood Cliffs, NJ.

Lynch, J.: 1994, *Provision for Children with Special Educational Needs in the Asia Region*, World Bank Technical Paper Number 261, Washington, DC.

Mason, D. & Ewoldt, C.: 1996, 'Whole language and deaf bilingual-bicultural education – naturally!', *American Annals of the Deaf* 141, 293–298.

Mirenda, P. & Calculator, S.: 1993, 'Enhancing curricular designs', in L. Kupper (ed.), *The National Symposium on Effective Communication for Children and Youth with Severe Disabilities: Topic Papers, Reader's Guide and Video Tape*, 253–280.

Mithaug, D.E.: 1991, *Self-Determined Kids: Raising Satisfied and Successful Children*, Macmillan (Lexicon Books Imprint), New York, NY.

Moores, D.F.: 1991, 'Forward', in B. Luethe-Stahlman & J. Luckner, *Effectively Educating Students with Hearing Impairments*, Longman, New York, NY, xix.

Norden, M.F.: 1994, *The Cinema of Isolation: A History of Physical Disability in the Movies*, Rutgers University Press, New Brunswick, NJ.

Padden, C.: 1980, 'The deaf community and the culture of deaf people', in C. Baker & Battison (eds.), *Sign Language and the Deaf Community*, National Association of the Deaf, Washington, DC, 89–103.

Parmenter, T.R.: 1992, 'Quality of life of people with developmental disabilities', *International Review of Research in Mental Retardation* 18, 247–287.

Price, P: 1995, ' "Love Thy Neighbour" forging links with countries in the south pacific region', *The Australasian Journal of Special Education* 19, 30–39.

Schalock, R.L.: 1994, 'The concept of quality of life and its current applications in the field of mental retardation/developmental disabilities', in D. Goode (ed.), *Quality of Life for Persons with Disabilities: International Perspectives and Issues*, Bookline Books, Cambridge, MA, 266–284.

Simon, E.W., Whitehair, P.M. & Toll, D.M.: 1995, 'Keeping facilitated communication in perspective', *Mental Retardation* 33, 338–339.

Stephenson, J. & Linfoot, K.: 1996, 'Intentional communication and graphic symbol use by students with severe intellectual disability', *International Journal of Disability, Development and Education* 43, 147–165.

Strong, M. (ed.): 1988, *Language Learning and Deafness*, Cambridge University Press, New York, NY.

Sugarman, S.: 1984, 'The development of preverbal communication: Its contribution and limits in promotion of the development of language', in R.L. Schiefelbusch & J. Pickar (eds.), *Communicative Competence: Acquisition and Intervention*, University Park Press, Balitmore, MD, 23–67.

Tiegerman, E.: 1993, 'Autism: Learning to communicate', in D.K. Bernstein & E. Tiegerman (eds.), *Language and Communication Disorders in Children*, Merrill, New York, NY, 431–481.

UNESCO: 1994, *The Salamanca Statement and Framework for Action on Special Needs Education. World Conference on Special Needs Education: Access and Quality, 7–10, June*, Ministry of Education and Services, Salamanca, Spain.

UNICEF: 1994, *State of the World's Children*, UNICEF, New York, NY.

Williams, B.J. & Witzel, M.J.: 1994, 'Cleft palate', in G.H. Shames, E.H. Wiig, & W.A. Secord (eds.), *Human Communication Disorders: An Introduction*, Merrill, New York, NY, 438–479.

Wolf, B.H.: 1994, *Trapped in Silence: The Autobiography of a Remarkable Young Man*, Bantam Books, Sydney.

Wolfensberger, W.: 1984, 'A reconceptualisation of normalization as social role valorization', *Mental Retardation* 34, 22–27.

Woodill, G.: 1994, 'The social semiotics of disability', in M.H. Rioux, & M. Bach (eds.), *Disability is Not Measles: New Research Paradigms in Disability*, L'Institut Roeher Institute, North York, Ontario, 201–226.

Section 3

Oral Language and Curriculum

CLOTILDE PONTECORVO

CLASSROOM DISCOURSE FOR THE MAKING OF LEARNING

Classroom discourse is any type of discourse which goes on in the classroom: between teacher and students, or among students with or without the teacher. Since other reviews will consider specific settings (e.g., peer groups) or domain-bound types of discourse (such as literacy, computers, or maths), I will focus here on the general aspects of classroom discourse for the facilitation of learning.

As a meeting point of social, linguistic, and educational dimensions, this field has descriptive more than prescriptive features. However changing educational settings or introducing new forms of discourse and interaction is in the foreground of this research. Often classroom discourse has been studied in cooperation with teachers who were eager to change their practices.

Basing their arguments on the heuristic constructs of Basil Bernstein (Atkinson, Davies & Delamont, 1995), sociologists (and subsequently sociolinguists) have treated classrooms as sites of social relations, as well as of power and control of access to symbolic resources (Luke, 1995). Indeed one function of classroom discourse is that the teacher controls the establishing and the maintenance of social relationships. But other goals are also achieved through discourse: first, the curriculum is implemented, i.e. the inherited knowledge is adapted in order to be transmitted to new generations; and second, the identities of participants are constituted according to the dominant positionings available in the discourses in use (Davies, 1990). This latter is a critical point when people of different backgrounds come together in schools.

Discourse in the classroom refers to a large array of symbolic tools. These are written texts, narratives, books, images and equipment: all convey sociocultural features and are part of the semiotic mediation (Wertsch, 1985) provided by schools. I will look here at teacher-student instructional conversation within this semiotic approach as analyzed in sociolinguistics, discursive psychology and conversation analysis.

EARLY DEVELOPMENTS

The antecedents of the study of classroom discourse are the studies of verbal interaction. Flanders' work (1970) launched this field of research. His system of verbal interaction was (and still is) the best known. This

B. Davies and D. Corson (eds), Encyclopedia of Language and Education,
Volume 3: Oral Discourse and Education, 169–178.
© *1997 Kluwer Academic Publishers. Printed in the Netherlands.*

approach used the Lewinian concepts of social climate and preference for democratic leadership and Rogers' construct of indirectivity for developing a system of categories for classroom interaction. By distinguishing between the direct and indirect influence of the teacher, Flanders assumes that both eliciting, using and accepting students' ideas, and using praise and encouragement increases the students' initiative and independence – an aim shared by most supporters of a democratic education and of an innovative teaching approach. This approach has been criticized because it is theoretically eclectic, combining reinforcement theory (the role of teacher's praise) with Rogers' approach of evaluating students' ideas.

The great change in this field occurred with the developments of sociolinguistics and ethnography of communication (Gumperz & Hymes, 1972) which stressed the social character of any language use and the link between language development and socialization (Ochs & Schieffelin, 1983). One of the first publications of the new approach to classroom discourse was *Functions of Language in the Classroom* (Cazden, John & Hymes, 1972) which focused on minority children's language and on differences in language use between home and school (two still prominent topics in this field). Teachers were encouraged to become ethnographers of themselves and of their classrooms. A neat distinction was thus introduced between this sociolinguistic study of classroom discourse and the former process-product study of classroom interaction, as undertaken by Flanders, (1970) and others, which looked for the relationships between talk categories and learning outcomes. The sociolinguistic research gave particular attention to all features of discourse and communication (Cazden, 1986), assuming that schools are significant social institutions in which the allocation of power, and the constitution of the student as agentic (or non-agentic) and as gendered individuals (Davies, 1990), is continuously achieved through teachers' discursive practices.

MAJOR CONTRIBUTIONS

The general perspective assumed by the sociolinguistic study of classroom discourse is interpretive. It uses the philosophical tools of hermeneutics, and attempts, as far as possible, to understand the meaning-making of the participants in the discursive activity: what conversation analysts (Sacks, Schegloff & Jefferson, 1974) have called the 'participants' categories'. It assumed, starting from the original manifesto (Cazden, John & Hymes, 1972), that this type of research can contribute to making schools better places for the development and learning of all children, in particular those who are more likely to fail at school for social and cultural reasons.

The structure of classroom discourse

One of the main contributions of the sociolinguistic approach was that of focusing on meaning negotiation and identifying the typical structure of classroom discourse. The *unmarked* or *default* pattern of discourse structure (as it is labelled by Cazden, 1988) is labelled IRE: teacher initiation, student response, and teacher evaluation. This structure was first identified in Mehan's seminal study (1979), using the videos and transcripts of Cazden's first grade classroom. Sinclair & Coulthard (1974), two British linguists working within the perspective of speech act theory, emphasized the distinction between form and function in spoken language and identified a similar pattern, IRF: teacher's initiation, student's response, teacher's feedback. This pattern was used to analyze the teacher-led lesson, a universal and more frequent classroom-speech event, in which the teacher controls the development of a topic and guides turn-taking. Indeed most analyses of classroom discourse comment on this basic speech sequence. Mehan (1979) shows that the basic IRE structure appears to be inserted within larger units, Topically Related Sets (TRS), which are part of the hierarchical arrangement of a lesson. The basic sequence establishes the topic, while one or more conditional sequences build on the topic. Several TRS constitute a phase and several phases form a lesson. Criteria of speech relevance are not governed only by the immediately preceding utterance, but by a more complex overall communicative and instructional setting.

Classroom discourse and cultural variation

From its very beginning the sociolinguistic approach to classroom discourse took a strong interest in studying cultural differences, considering school as a social context requiring – beyond and before learning – socialization to its practices and methods (see the reviews by V. Edwards and by Heller in this volume). Cultural differences appeared in classrooms in which there were both Indian and non-Indian children and led the anthropologist Philips (1972), to identify a 'participant structure'. The Indian 'invisible culture' was behind Indian children's unwillingness to participate in school discourse and explained their preference for silence in front of other students. Teachers were not aware of such cultural differences which touched everyday interaction and expressed values and beliefs through implicit norms of communication.

An important study which succeeded in changing classroom practices to accommodate the interactive patterns of minority groups was carried out by Heath (1983), who studied three communities in Piedmont and found that children were socialized into different 'ways with words'. This ethnographic study was the basis for an action-research study with students and teachers focusing on the specific narrative styles, modes of talking about events and literacy practices, which characterized the three different communities. In this case even children became involved as ethnographers of their community language practices. Other studies have shown that there are specific cultural ways of 'telling stories'. African-American children tend to tell more episodic stories, while in other minority cultures there is co-narration and speech overlapping, which are not appreciated by majority teachers. Similar cases for different minority cultures are reported in Cazden (1988). A relevant contribution to this topic has been made by Duranti and Ochs (1986) who studied literacy education in a Samoan village. They proved that not only the materials used by the missionary school but also the interactive patterns used by the teachers contrasted sharply with Samoan cultural norms. Differently from standard Western habits, Samoan family education is not child-centered and no effort is made to facilitate children's linguistic and cognitive development. The Samoan social world is adult-centered and even very young children have to adapt themselves to the requirements of adults.

The special register of classroom talk is very close to what the Western style caregivers' use with young children during play, problem-solving and book reading activities. For this reason, it has been called the 'hidden curriculum' (Cazden, 1988) because it consists of discourse which is expected but not explicitly taught at school, since most middle class children have been familiar with it from the very first years of their life. It explains the communication difficulties between teachers and children coming from different social and linguistic backgrounds.

DISCOURSE AND LEARNING

A Vygotskian perspective on meaning

The contributions we have presented before have put *meaning* and its social construction at the core of the whole research on classroom discourse (Hicks, 1995). According to the Vygotskian perspective meaning is inherently relational and is socially constituted through interaction and discourse. In school interaction it emerges as the point of encounter between conventional meanings (that are given by dictionaries and organized by disciplinary domains) and the different personal senses (to use the opposition of Vygotsky, 1934/1990) that individuals and groups elaborate through negotiation (Wertsch, 1985).

The centrality of the relational and sociocultural construction of meaning derives from the Vygotskian semiotic view according to which language is the main symbolic mediation of human thinking, learning and development. The sociolinguistic approach is thus supported by a theory which hypothesizes that intra-individual higher psychic functions are fostered by inter-individual relations through sharing a communicative intersubjective situation. While the sociolinguistic studies attempt to identify patterns of classroom discourse as expressions of underlying rules and structures – partially derived from the mechanisms of conversations discovered by the conversationalists (Sacks, Schegloff & Jefferson, 1974) – the Vygotskian perspective is more clearly oriented towards the question of how discourse can promote learning.

How can teacher talk in classroom discourse support students' reasoning and learning? Since the 1980's many new constructs have been introduced in this field under the influence of the rediscovery of Vygotskian theory (particularly the 'zone of proximal development'), the strengthening of a sociocultural developmental and instructional psychology (Cole & Cole, 1989), the theoretical and empirical attention devoted to semiotic mediation (Wertsch, 1991).

Theoretical frameworks and research trends

The new constructs are related, although in different measure, to the more general approach of meaning negotiation. Most describe the type of inter-action which can be constructed in an instructional interaction (such as scaffolding, reciprocal teaching, reconceptualization, intersubjectivity); others refer to the expected outcomes of this process (such as appropria-tion, internalization, participation). A brief presentation of each of them follows.

Scaffolding or tutoring: A social situation in which an adult offers to a child the possibility of sharing the responsibility of a complete action by doing some of the required work (Wood, Bruner & Ross, 1976). The adult offers a metaphorical scaffold to the child's activity (e.g. of making a puzzle) and progressively reduces the help. Consequently the autonomous performance of the child is gradually increased during activity until reach-ing full autonomy. The construct is particular suited to the dyadic situation of problem-solving through adult-child interaction (Wertsch, 1985).

Reciprocal teaching: A format developed by Palincsar and Brown, (1984) to improve reading comprehension in which students in small groups take turns (while collectively reading a text) in assuming the role of the teacher. They overtly use four cognitive strategies (predicting, ques-tioning, summarizing and clarifying) that result in the general ability to be critical in reading comprehension. Children are supposed to learn by acting as tutors to other children, while the teacher begins by modelling the required social behaviour and then directs and reinforces the behaviour of tutors and tutees.

Reconceptualization or recontextualization: A construct proposed by Cazden (1988) to categorize the situation in which the teacher (or the caregiver) offers to the learner an expansion or clarification, of what the child or children have just said before. It can be regarded as a content-based third part of the IRE sequence which can replace the evaluative part.

Intersubjectivity: A concept introduced and developed by Rommetveit (1985) to define an act of communication where there is a full sharing of activity and discourse between participants, who are aware that they are taking part in the same situation. Wells applied this construct to classroom discourse, showing how intersubjectivity implies at least shared attention and joint reference, and often requires long verbal negotiations to be reached (Wells, 1993a).

Internalization: In a Vygotskian framework, the process through which the desired outcome of any educational interaction is reached. Through internalization the inter-individual relationship is transformed into an intrapsychic one.

Appropriation: A construct introduced and used by Newman, Griffin and Cole (1989) as a development of a concept of Leont'ev. Appropriation is sequential and reciprocal in that teachers have to appropriate children's discourse and to show understanding of it in order to have children incorporate (or appropriate) new forms of activity and meaning. It can be considered as a less asymmetrical view of learning through discourse.

Participation: A concept introduced recently in opposition to appropriation and internalization (Matusov, 1996). Instead of addressing the question of how and what the individuals gain from sociocultural activities, the participation model assumes that such activities take place all the time. Only modes and contents of participation change. In other words not only the processes but also the outcomes of learning are socio-cultural and are observable within a variety of participation contexts.

Scaffolding, tutoring, and reciprocal teaching are generally explained within a modelling approach in which the more expert person models the required behavior for the less expert person who thus learns to produce the required behavior. Alternatively, they can be explained through a semiotic approach, in which shared meaning negotiation is understood as a necessary condition for learning a new discourse. Within this approach, the participation model rejects an individualistic view of learning. This latter perspective is akin to situated cognition for which cognitive activity is by nature interactive and knowledge is jointly constituted in groups and sociocultural settings. The pervasive social nature of thinking appears in any discourse – including classroom discourse – which does not seemingly entail cognition because it *is* cognition (Resnick, Saljö & Pontecorvo, 1996).

New approaches which hypothesize the centrality of shared and distributed meaning in any human situation mainly use the tools of conversation analysis because conversation is by definition a collaborative enterprise. Discourse is not even possible without the cooperative rules of conversation. Learning through discourse requires meaning negotiation and intersubjectivity. Indeed when a change in talk management is introduced in classroom discourse, a learning mechanism is embedded in the way in which teachers react to children's utterances by rephrasing and expanding them, and by using semantically contingent queries (Orsolini, Pontecorvo & Lumbelli, 1992).

FUTURE DIRECTIONS

At least two questions need to be clarified by future research.

The first concerns the relationships between IRE/IRF and the more recent innovative approaches to learning. The IRE genre of classroom discourse seems to be almost a sociolinguistic norm (particularly in English speaking countries, where teachers are trained to give continuous positive feedback to children). However it has also been associated with direct instruction, with 'skill and drill' modes of instruction (Hicks, 1995), and with the reduction of the student's freedom of speech (see the reviews by Young and by Lyle in this volume).

This latter view promoted innovative practices oriented at changing IRE talk as being too directive and evaluative, as a clear expression of the teachers' power and control over the students' mind and language. This experimental direction was taken by Orsolini & Pontecorvo (1992) who implemented innovative conversational strategies. The teacher was asked to replace evaluation with repetition and/or rephrasing of children's utter- ances, and to use contingent queries, i.e. queries which are semantically related to previous children's turns. Children's topical talk and extended continuations were significantly affected both by teacher's repetitions and rephrasings and by peer continuations. Teacher's evaluative talk can be replaced with other types of talk which favour children's conflicting and explanatory talk and argumentative types of reasoning (Pontecorvo, 1995). Bill, Leer, Reams & Resnick (1992) also report the case of a second grade teacher of mathematics who abandoned the standard recitation format by *revoicing* children's contributions, incorporating them in her talk and weaving their answers into her subsequent requests.

Wells (1993b) has 'reevaluated' the IRF sequence by showing that direct modes of instruction in the usual triadic form can be combined with a more open instructional conversation in which the teacher inquires about the work done by the students in a format of 'teaching for understanding'. So the IRF should be seen positively as a (neutral) and overarching form of classroom discourse that encompasses a number of different instructional functions (but see the review by Young in this volume).

Indeed the more positive approach to the IRF sequence seems to have been influenced by the Vygotskian perspective which has underlined the positive role of a competent adult in addressing the learning of the less competent student through reciprocal appropriation of their perspective

(Newman, Grifffin & Cole, 1989). However the Vygotskian reevaluation of the teaching process (which should always be in advance of spontaneous development to be useful) does not imply that any discursive strategy is equivalent as far as general learning outcomes are concerned. It remains that it is better to use a strategy which increases the discursive and learning freedom of children.

A second issue concerns the role of discourse in a constructivist approach to learning. The critical appraisal, done by Edwards and Mercer (1987), of the British Piagetian-based curriculum and of certain naive forms of instructional talk of teachers, who try to 'extract' from children laws of physics or mathematical rules, does not affect the relevant part of a constructivist learning theory (see the review by Mercer in this volume). The issue here is that it may be better in some cases to use a direct declarative form without requesting that children 'discover' everything. The rather paradoxical situation in which students have to produce 'spontaneously' exactly the utterances that the teachers are expecting can be avoided. In this case the risk is that children learn that school tasks make sense only in school and that these tasks are not at all linked with their everyday understanding (Mercer, 1992).

An emphasis on the relevance of a teacher-led discourse does not mean that children's own interpretations should be ignored. Children's experience needs to be largely used as an anchoring device for conceptual development and learning, particularly in cases in which classroom discourse is a tool for developing participation in discipline-bound domains, such as science or history (Pontecorvo & Girardet, 1993). Experiences, such as laboratory work, manipulative or observational activities, interpretation of historical documents, reading of stories, provide a shared universe of referents and alternative solutions on which collective classroom discourse can be effectively built.

Future research can better clarify the balance between guidance and freedom and the differences in domain-related genres of discourse for learning different discipline practices.

University of Rome
Italy

REFERENCES

Atkinson, P., Davies, B. & Delamont, S.: 1995, *Discourse and Reproduction*, Hampton Press, Cresskill NJ.
Bill, V.L., Leer, M.N., Pontecorvo, C., Reams, L.E. & Resnick, L.: 1992, 'From cupcakes to equations: The structure of discourse in a primary mathematics classroom', *Verbum* 1(2), 63–85.
Cazden, C.: 1986, 'Classroom discourse', in M.C. Wittrock (ed.), *Handbook of Research on Teaching*, III Edition, Macmillan, New York, 4–19.

Cazden, C.: 1988, *Classroom Discourse*, Cambridge University Press, Cambridge.

Cazden, C., John, V. & Hymes, D.: 1972, *The Functions of Language in the Classroom*, Teachers College Press, New York.

Cole, M. & Cole, S.: 1989, *The Development of Children*, Scientific American Books, New York.

Davies, B.: 1990, 'Agency as a form of discursive practice: A classroom scene observed', *British Journal of Sociology of Education* 11(3), 341–361.

Duranti, A. & Ochs, E.: 1986, 'Literacy instruction in a Samoan village', in B.B. Schieffelin & P. Gilmore (Eds.), *Acquisition of Literacy: Ethnographic Perspectives*, Ablex, Norwood, NJ, 213–232.

Edwards D. & Mercer N.: 1987, *Common Knowledge: The Development of Understanding in the Classroom*, Routledge, London.

Flanders N.: 1970, *Analyzing Teaching Behavior*, Addison-Wesley, London.

Gumperz, J.J. & Hymes, D.: 1972, *Directions in Sociolinguistics: The Ethnography of Communication*, Rinehart and Winston, Holt, New York.

Heath, S.B.: 1983, *Ways with Words: Language, Life and Work in Communities and Classrooms*, Cambrdige University Press, Cambridge.

Hicks, D.: 1995, 'Discourse, learning, and teaching', *Review of Research in Education* 21, 49–95.

Luke A.: 1995, 'Text and discourse in education: An introduction to critical discourse analysis', *Review of Research in Education* 21, 3–48.

Matusov, E.: 1996, 'When solo activity is not privileged: participation and internalization models of development', *Submitted to Human Development, Presented at the AERA Convention*, New York.

Mehan, H.: 1979, *Learning Lessons*, Harvard University Press, Cambridge, MA.

Mercer N.: 1992, 'Culture, context and the contruction of knowledge in the classroom', in P. Light & G. Butterworth (eds.), *Context and Cognition: Ways of Learning and Knowing*, Harvester Wheatsheaf, London, 28–46.

Newman D., Griffin, P. & Cole, M.: 1989, *The Construction Zone: Working for Cognitive Change in School*, Cambridge University Press, Cambridge.

Ochs, E. & Schieffelin, B.B.: 1983, *Acquiring Conversational Competence*, Routledge & Kegan Paul, Boston.

Orsolini, M. & Pontecorvo, C.: 1992, 'Children's talk in classroom discussion', *Cognition and Instruction* 9(2), 113–136.

Orsolini, M., Pontecorvo, C. & Lumbelli, L.: 1992, 'When the teacher tries to make children discuss and compare their points of view', *Verbum* 1/2, 33–61.

Palincsar, A.S. & Brown, A.L.: 1984, 'Reciprocal teaching of comprehension-fostering and comprehension-monitoring activities', *Cognition and Instruction* 1(2), 117–175.

Philips, S.U.: 1972, 'Participant structures and communicative competence: Warm springs children in community and classroom', in C.B. Cazden, V.P. John & D. Hymes (eds.), *Functions of Language in the Classroom*, Columbia Teachers Press, New York, 370–394.

Pontecorvo C.: 1995, 'Learning to argue and reason through discourse in educational settings', Invited lecture, 6th European Conference for *Research on Learning and Instruction*, University of Nijmegen, The Netherlands, August 26–31.

Pontecorvo, C. & Girardet H.: 1993, 'Arguing and reasoning in understanding historical topics', *Cognition and Instruction* 11(3–4), 365–395.

Resnick L., Säljo R. & Pontecorvo C. (eds.): 1996, *Discourse, Tools and Reasoning. Essays on Situated Cognition*, Springer Verlag, Berlin, Germany.

Rommetveit, R.: 1985, 'Language acquisition as increasing linguistic structuring of experience and symbolic behavior control', in Wertsch, J. (ed.), *Culture, Communication, and Cognition: Vygotskian Perspectives*, Cambridge University Press, Cambridge.

Sacks, H., Schegloff, E.A. & Jefferson, G.: 1974, 'A simplest systematics for the organization of turn-taking for conversation', *Language* 50, 696–735.

Sinclair, J. & Coulthard, R.M.: 1974, *Towards an Analysis of Discourse*, Oxford University Press, London.

Vygotsky, L.: 1990, *Myslenie i rec'. Psichologiceskie issledovanija* [Thought and Language], Laterza, Bari, Italy (New Italian critical edition by L. Mecacci, based on the first Russian edition; originally published in 1934).

Wells, G.: 1993a, 'Intersoggettività e costruzione di conoscenze' [Intersubjectivity and knowledge construction], in C. Pontecorvo (ed.), *La condivisione della conoscenza* [The sharing of knowledge], La Nuova Italia, Scandicci, Italy.

Wells, G.: 1993b, 'Re-evaluating IRF sequence: A proposal for the articulation of theories of activity and discourse for the analysis of teaching and learning in the classroom', *Linguistics and Education* 5, 1–37.

Wertsch, J.V.: 1985, *Vygotsky and the Social Formation of Mind*, Harvard University Press, Cambridge Mass.

Wertsch, J.V.: 1991, *Voices of the Mind: A Sociocultural Approach to Mediated Action*, Harvard University Press, Cambridge.

Wood, P., Bruner J., & Ross, G.: 1976, 'The role of tutoring in problem-solving', *Journal of Child Psychology and Psychiatry* 17, 89–100.

NEIL MERCER

EFFECTIVE EDUCATIONAL TALK

To discuss the effectiveness of the use of talk in educational institutions, it is necessary to ask what the process of education is intended to achieve. There are many possible answers to this question, and little space here to consider them. A brief answer, and one that is probably acceptable to most people involved in education, would be that it is intended to (a) enable students to realize their intellectual potential; and (b) give students access to, and understanding of, the knowledge included in the curriculum. The quality of education, as it is carried out in schools and other institutions, is very dependent on how effectively talk is used in classrooms. The Russian psychologist L.S. Vygotsky (1896–1934) described language as the principal tool by which human societies create knowledge and understanding (Vygotsky, 1978): and like all tools, language can be used with varying degrees of skill.

EARLY DEVELOPMENTS

The study of effective educational talk is not a well-defined field: research relevant to this theme is likely to be found in the broader field of research on communication in classrooms. There are two relevant, overlapping areas of research within that field. The first is the study of talk between teachers and learners, and the second is the study of talk amongst learners.

Since its beginnings, research concerned with the educational effectiveness of classroom talk has often focused on teachers' use of questions. Researchers such as Flanders (1970) working in the tradition of 'systematic observation' (whereby observers use coding schemes to place utterances in functional categories) noted the quantity and type of questions used. One of the main aims of such research was to provide teachers and teacher-educators with information which would allow for the monitoring, evaluation and improvement of practice. The study of the effective use of classroom talk received a major stimulus from the work of Barnes and his colleagues (Barnes, Britton & Rosen, 1969) in the UK during the 1960s and 1970s. Through an analysis of recorded examples of talk in classrooms, Barnes was able to show how teachers' habitual and unreflective use of 'closed questions' constrained and stifled students' intellectual contributions to the process of teaching and learning. His research encouraged many people to question the effectiveness of such normal practices, and to develop a more critical awareness of how talk was being used. In the USA,

B. Davies and D. Corson (eds), Encyclopedia of Language and Education,
Volume 3: Oral Discourse and Education, 179–186.
© 1997 Kluwer Academic Publishers. Printed in the Netherlands.

research by socio-linguists such as Hymes (1972) supported similar critical evaluations. For example, Hymes showed that teachers' talk was normally predicated upon doubtful implicit assumptions about the understanding of their pupils. Hymes' research, and that of others (such as Philips (1972) who studied Native American children in the classroom) suggested that there was often a cultural mismatch between the conversational and learning styles of children and their teachers, and that this was likely to impede the education of those children (see reviews by Tannen, Kendall & Adger, and by Heller and by V. Edwards in this volume). Much of this early research encouraged the view that talk was often not used very effectively by teachers, and that teachers were largely unaware of how and why they talked as they did.

The evaluative study of the talk of learners working together (outside the supervision of a teacher) developed much more slowly than the study of teacher-student discourse. An early major contribution was that of Barnes & Todd (1977). They recorded groups of pupils working together in British secondary classrooms, and devised an analytic scheme which enabled them to compare the extent to which talk was focused on relevant topics, ideas were presented for joint examination, and common solutions sought to problems.

MAJOR CONTRIBUTIONS

In later years, research on the effectiveness of teachers' use of talk has continued to pay much attention to their use of questions. It has become common to criticise teachers for their overwhelming reliance on questions, and especially on their use of 1closed' questions which can only be satisfied by a students providing the 'right answer' which has been predefined by the teacher. Thus Dillon (1988) and Wood (1992) have shown that one common effect of teachers' relentless questioning is to reduce the amount and variety of the verbal contributions that their pupils make in the classroom. Those researchers argue that this – and the use of 'closed' questions, in particular – must have a detrimental effect on the intellectual activity of students, and hence on their progress towards becoming more autonomous learners. Others have shown that the criteria teachers use to evaluate students' answers are often obscure to students (Edwards & Furlong, 1978; Edwards & Mercer, 1987), with the result that much time may be spent in fairly unproductive sequences of talk in which the teacher seeks to steer students towards an acceptable answer without actually telling them it. Some researchers and teacher-trainers (for example, Edwards, 1992) have argued that, in order to be most effective, teachers should try using strategies other than questions where appropriate, such as:

- making open-ended, provocative statements to students
- encouraging students to formulate their own questions about the topic of study
- maintaining silence so that students have more opportunity to generate contributions and muster up enough confidence to offer them.

More research evidence has been provided to support the view (encouraged by earlier research, as described above) that the effectiveness of teacher-pupil interactions is often limited because teachers and pupils have different cultural expectations about how to use language, so that classroom conversations are not based on mutually-understood 'ground rules' for communication. Striking examples are provided by Heath's (1983) research with children of black and white working communities in the USA, and Boggs' et al. (1985) studies of native Hawaiian children.

While research has often focused on problematic and ineffective aspects of teachers' use of talk, there have been attempts to define characteristics of good, effective practice. For example, observational research on teachers' use of questions has been used to produce manuals for teachers on the art of 'good questioning' (for example, Dillon, 1988; Brown & Wragg, 1993). Edwards & Mercer (1987) used an analysis of discourse in primary classrooms to illustrate how teachers used talk to help students perceive continuity in their educational activities, and to build a 'common knowledge' which they and their students could use effectively as a contextual basis for future activity.

Understanding of the effective use of talk in classrooms has increasingly been informed by research in cultural settings other than those of the UK and the USA (which hitherto dominated the field). This has fed into an appreciation of the potential variety of effective ways of teaching and learning. For example, Jayalakshmi's (1996) study of talk in Indian secondary English-medium classrooms has shown the continuing influence of traditional *Gurukala* and *Harikatha* styles of instruction and story-telling – styles which depended upon the unquestioned authority of a teacher as supreme arbiter of knowledge, as well as being able to perform effectively as a story-teller. While these traditional methods are of course not always used effectively (as Jayalakshmi also points out), they have served Indian scholars well for generations. Moreover, they have been combined with British influences to generate a distinct and well-established Indian style of classroom communication. Amongst other features, this style involves the frequent use of *rhetorical questions* by the teacher, marked by intonation, pauses or gestures, which the students are not expected to answer. Likewise, students contribute to the generation of a distinctive style of classroom language use by *jointly reciting* what they learn in conjunction with their teacher. (A feature of language use which used to be common in many parts of the world, though it is less so today). In southern Africa, teacher-educators such as Munjanja (1985) in Zimbabwe have argued for the effectiveness of traditional styles of teaching and learning based on narrative and debate, styles which have been devalued with the introduction of formal schooling based on European pedagogies.

Recent years have seen an increasing interest in the educational value of collaborative activity and talk amongst students. In those countries (such as Britain) where 'child-centred' approaches to classroom education became popular, it became increasingly common during the 1970s and 1980s to put children into groups to work together. Rationales could be drawn from research in developmental psychology for providing children with opportunities to work, talk and think together and the educational research on teacher's talk referred to above also encouraged many educators to think that children would benefit from working away from the dominating presence of a teacher. However, when such collaborative activity has been observed and evaluated, findings suggest that children's communications with each other were commonly fragmentary, superficial and educationally unproductive. Recent research tends to support Barnes and Todd's (1978) observation that pupils often lack a clear understanding of how they were meant to 'discuss' and 'collaborate' (Dunne & Bennett, 1990). Observational research on children working together at the computer in British primary classrooms also confirms this view, and has shown that the quality of that talk is very variable and often not very effectively applied to the task at hand (Mercer, 1995) (see review by Lyle, this volume). Observational research has also revealed that gender relations in the classroom can have a significant effect on the quality of talk and joint activity, with the dominant conversational influence of some boys reducing the effectiveness of learning experiences for other pupils (Swann, 1994). Some critics of 'child-centred' education (for example, O'Hear, 1991) have argued that peer group talk and joint activity is not an effective element of classroom education, and that teachers should be encouraged to return to the more traditional 'chalk and talk' methods of whole-class teaching. Others, however, have argued that only by giving more opportunity for pupils to talk, and by developing new approaches to talk, teaching and learning, will its educational effectiveness be improved (Norman, 1992).

WORK IN PROGRESS

One can see diverse influences of current research on the effectiveness of educational talk. The influence of earlier observational studies of talk in classrooms (such as those of Barnes, described above, and recently updated in Barnes & Todd, 1995) is still strong. A second major influence is psychological research on language and cognitive development, especially that of Bruner (for example, 1986), Rogoff (1990) and others derived from the work of the early twentieth century Russian psychologist Vygotsky

(1978). This research, mostly carried out with parents and their children rather than teachers and students, stresses the active role of the adult expert in using language to support or 'scaffold' the developing mentality of the learner. A third influence is research in linguistics on the specialized language genres or discourses used in educated 'communities of discourse' (Swales, 1990). Such research has encouraged the view that becoming educated necessarily involves being effectively socialized into specific, culturally-based ways of using language. The teaching of a curriculum subject like science, then, must pursue the aim of making students 'fluent speakers of science' (Lemke, 1990). This will involve not only the mastery of technical vocabulary, but also a grasp of other, more subtle features of the modes of discourse conventionally used by members of any academic community (such as ways of presenting information and justifying ideas). A fourth influence is that of educators concerned with the development of 'thinking skills' or 'critical thinking' in children (see Resnick, 1987; Craft, 1991 for overviews). While debate continues about quite what skills are involved in becoming able to use rational methods of enquiry within particular domains of knowledge, most accounts stress the development of ways of using talk to construct effective arguments.

One influential line of current research is that of Brown and her colleagues in California (for example Brown & Palincsar, 1989), who by drawing on such antecedents and their own experimental studies have developed a method of classroom education called 'reciprocal teaching'. Reciprocal teaching involves the use of both teacher-led and peer group activities. Its essential characteristic is that the teacher exemplifies and guides students in effective ways of using talk to interrogate written texts, share ideas, and construct rational arguments. Brown & Palincsar (1989) report that children given reciprocal teaching make striking improvements in achievement on independent learning activities involving the comprehension of written texts, and do so significantly more than children in control groups (who have been taught by teachers employing their usual methods).

In Mexico, continuing research by Rojas-Drummond and colleagues (for example Rojas-Drummond & Alatorre, 1994) in Spanish-speaking nursery classrooms has found that a method of teaching called the High/Scope Curriculum – which encourages the use of verbal strategies very similar to those of reciprocal teaching – also led to significant improvements in children's independent problem-solving. With government funding, this research has now been extended to primary schools, with the intention of identifying effective teaching strategies which can inform the process of educational reform in Mexico.

In Britain, one continuing area of applied research interest is the quality of children's discussion in collaborative activities in the classroom. This has generated research aimed at improving the quality of that talk, and in doing so converges somewhat in its aims and rationale with the other research described in this section above. Mercer (1995) has argued that one of the principal aims of education should be enabling children to become confident users of 'exploratory' talk: that is, talk in which partners reason together, engaging critically and constructively with each others' ideas. The ability to use spoken language effectively in this way is important in many social practices, including those of science, business and the law. As reported in the review which follows, researchers in mathematics education have argued for the value of such talk in the learning of mathematics. But as reported above, this kind of talk is not commonly found in classrooms. In recent and current research in primary schools, Mercer and colleagues have developed teacher-led activities which raise children's awareness of their own use of talk and require them to define explicit, shared 'ground rules' for discussion, and then combined these with computer-based activities which require the use of 'exploratory' talk. Findings of this research so far have shown that children's use of exploratory talk can be promoted, and that this is associated with significant improvements in children's performance on joint reasoning tasks (Wegerif & Mercer, 1996).

PROBLEMS AND DIFFICULTIES

Anyone concerned with evaluating the effectiveness of talk in educational settings is likely to find difficulties in reaching a satisfactory definition of what constitutes 'effectiveness', and in measuring it. While some widespread agreement might be found about the most general aims of education (as suggested in the introductory section above), any measure of how effective the use of talk is in any actual situation must move from generalizations to particular, observable features of talking and learning. For some researchers (for example, Wells, 1986; Wood, 1992), a satisfactory measure of the effectiveness of teacher-pupil talk may be a 'process' measure – such as the relative extent to which a teacher is able to elicit enthusiastic, extended contributions from students. Others (for example, Brown & Palincsar, 1989) find it necessary to make some 'outcome' measures – that is, to assess what students appear to have learned as a result of interacting with their teacher.

There are also continuing methodological problems in this field, concerned with the analysis of features of talk and their relationship to educational processes (as discussed in some detail by Edwards & Westgate, 1994; Coll, 1990). For example, as mentioned earlier, the effects of teachers' use of questions has been a popular focus for research. However, any specification of what constitutes a 'question' can easily be disputed, and identical linguistic constructions may be used in different social contexts to pursue and achieve quite different pragmatic effects. Few research methods for the analysis of the communicative process of teaching and learning are able to deal satisfactorily with the fact that in all talk, meanings depend on the continual regeneration of a context of shared understanding amongst speakers.

FUTURE DIRECTIONS

There is some agreement that the future success of this applied area of research will lie in the closer collaboration of researchers and teachers (Norman, 1992; Edwards & Westgate, 1994; Mercer, 1995). Versions of the 'action research' paradigm, in which teachers research their own practice with the aim of improving it, and/or work in close partnerships with academic researchers towards the same aim, seem to offer the most encouraging lines of development.

Regarding changes in educational practice, research described above under Work in Progress encourages the view that one positive development would be the more careful co-ordination of teacher-pupil talk and pupil-pupil talk. (Research described in the review on The Use of Talk in Mathematics, which follows, would also seem to support this view.) Teachers could spend more time helping students recognize the features and functions of 'educated' forms of discourse, while also planning for curriculum-based collaborative work in which students could develop their confidence and effectiveness in using talk to construct knowledge.

The Open University
England

REFERENCES

Barnes, D., Britton, J. & Rosen, H.: 1969, *Language, the Learner and the School*, Penguin, Harmondsworth.
Barnes, D. & Todd, F.: 1977, *Communication and Learning in Small Groups*, Routledge and Kegan Paul, London.
Barnes, D. & Todd, F.: 1995, *Communication and Learning Revisited*, Heinemann, Portsmouth, New Hampshire.
Boggs, S., McMillen, G. & Watson-Gegeo, K.A.: 1985, *Speaking, Relating and Learning: The Study of Hawaiian Children at Home and in School*, Ablex Publishing Corp., Norwood, NJ.
Brown, A. & Palincsar A.S.: 1989, 'Guided, cooperative learning and individual knowledge acquisition', in L. Resnick (ed.), *Knowing, Learning and Instruction*, Lawrence Erlbaum, New York, 393–451.
Brown, G. & Wragg, E.C.: 1993, *Questioning*, Routledge, London.
Bruner, J.S.: 1986, *Actual Minds, Possible Worlds*, Harvard University Press, London.
Coll, C.: 1990, *Aprendizaje Escolar y Construccion del Conocimiento*, Paidos, Barcelona.
Craft, A.: 1991, 'Thinking skills and the whole curriculum', *The Curriculum Journal* 2(2), 183–199.
Dillon, J.J. (ed.): 1988, *Questioning and Teaching: A Manual of Practice*, Croom Helm, London.
Dunne, E. & Bennett, N.: 1990, *Talking and Learning in Groups*, Routledge, London.

Edwards, A.D.: 1992, 'Teacher talk and pupil competence', in K. Norman (ed.), *Thinking Voices: The work of the National Oracy Project*, Hodder and Stoughton, London, 235–242.

Edwards, A.D. & Furlong, V.J.: 1978. *The Language of Teaching*, Heinemann, London.

Edwards, A.D. & Westgate, D.: 1994, *Investigating Classroom Talk* (Second Edition), The Falmer Press, London.

Edwards, D. & Mercer, N.: 1987, *Common Knowledge*, Methuen/Routledge, London.

Flanders, N.: 1970, *Analysing Teacher Behavior*, Addison Wesley, Reading, Massachusetts.

Heath, S.B.: 1983, *Ways with Words: Language, Life and Work in Communities and Classrooms*, Cambridge University Press, Cambridge.

Hymes, D.: 1972, 'On communicative competence', in J. Pride & J. Holmes (eds.), *Sociolinguistics*, Penguin, Harmondsworth, 269–293.

Jayalakshmi, G.D.: 1996, 'One cup of newspaper and one cup of tea', in N. Mercer & J. Swann (eds.), *Learning English: Development and Diversity*, Routledge, London, 36–51.

Lemke, J.L.: 1990, *Talking Science: Language Learning and Values*, Ablex, Norwood, NJ.

Mercer, N.: 1995. *The Guided Construction of Knowledge: Talk Amongst Teachers and Learners*, Multilingual Matters, Clevedon.

Munjanja, A.: 1995, 'Traditional education', Unit 1 of *Classroom Text and Discourse: A Practical Course on Language in Schools* (The LITRAID Project), The Rotary Club, Harare.

Norman, K. (ed.): 1992, *Thinking Voices: The Work of the National Oracy Project*, Hodder & Stoughton, London.

O'Hear, J.: 1987, 'The importance of traditional learning', *British Journal of Educational Studies* 35(2), 102–114.

Philips, S.: 1972, 'Participant structures and communicative competence', in C. Cazden, V. John & D. Hymes (eds.), *The Functions of Language in the Classroom*, Teachers College Press, New York, 192–212.

Resnick, L.: 1987, *Education and Learning to Think*, National Academic Press, New York.

Rogoff, B.: 1990. *Apprenticeship in Thinking*, Oxford University Press, New York.

Rojas-Drummond, S. & Alatorre, J.: 1994, 'The development of independent problem solving in preschool children', in N. Mercer & C. Coll (eds.), *Explorations in Socio-Cultural Studies, Vol. 3: Teaching, Learning and Interaction*, Infancia y Aprendizaje, Madrid, 161–175.

Swales, J.: 1990, *Genre Analysis: English in Academic and Research Settings*, Cambridge University Press, Cambridge.

Swann, J.: 1994, 'What do we do about gender?', in B. Stierer & J. Maybin (eds.), *Language, Literacy and Learning in Educational Practice*, Multilingual Matters, Clevedon.

Vygotsky, L.S.: 1978, *Mind in Society*, Harvard University, London.

Wegerif, R. & Mercer, N.: 1996, 'Computers and reasoning through talk in the classroom', *Language and Education* 10(1), 47–64.

Wells, G.: 1986, *The Meaning Makers*, Hodder and Stoughton, London.

Wood, D.: 1992, 'Teaching talk', in K. Norman (ed.), *Thinking Voices: The Work of the National Oracy Project*, Hodder and Stoughton, London, 203–214.

DAVID WESTGATE

PRECONDITIONS FOR SUCCESSFUL SMALL-GROUP TALK IN THE CLASSROOM

Much of children's talk at school serves a dual purpose. It provides contexts through which communication skills are practised; it can also play a part in cognitive, social and other development. Insights into these possibilities have encouraged many teachers, especially at the primary phase, to provide opportunities for pupils to develop through talking as well as listening. The setting most commonly assumed to be appropriate for such talk is the small group, which is further assumed to off-set limitations inherent in whole-class, teacher-led contexts. Small-group talk has, however, become associated with pupil-centred approaches and is often seen as such within wider educational debates. Some proponents of small-group talk have themselves expressed concern that unconsidered use of such talk-strategies may prejudice the case for more purposeful communication. Identifying the characteristics of successful small-group talk, and necessary pre-conditions for such success, provide the focus for much of the research reviewed here.

EARLY DEVELOPMENTS

The most significant early advances in interrelating linguistic and mental development were made in the mid-1960s by a London-based group of English teachers. The more general pedagogic implications of their work, however, were quickly apparent. Drawing upon insights from psycholinguistics, and especially upon those of Bruner and Vygotsky (e.g. through the latter's recently translated *Thought and Language* 1962), Barnes, Britton & Rosen (1969), for instance, laid the ground for a critical and cross-curricular analysis of teachers' apparently overwhelming reliance upon 'transmissional' styles of teaching. Such writers (e.g. Barnes & Todd, 1977) went on to stress, by contrast, the role which pupils' own talk, in small group settings, might have in promoting learning.

Exposition of this role has been bound up with the notion of 'oracy'. In coining the term, Wilkinson (1965) began from the same inter-related process view of talk: 'Oracy', he wrote, 'is not a "subject" – it is a condition of learning in all subjects' (p. 58). Group-talk was clearly seen as one setting in which this 'condition' might operate: 'Where children are ... placed in situations where it becomes important for them to communicate – to discuss, to negotiate, to converse. ... This is basically how oracy

B. Davies and D. Corson (eds), Encyclopedia of Language and Education,
Volume 3: Oral Discourse and Education, 187–195.
© *1997 Kluwer Academic Publishers. Printed in the Netherlands.*

grows' (p. 59). More than a decade later, MacLure et al. (1988) were still seeing 'oracy as competence' and 'oracy for learning' as closely inter-dependent. By then, too, this view was becoming internationalised (as evidenced by the work collected by Brubaker et al., 1990), most notably among groups of teachers and researchers in Australia, Canada and the USA.

Although the emerging significance of learner-talk and more generalised pedagogic arguments for group-work have to some extent converged, their different origins should not be forgotten. Concern for 'oracy' retains a focus wider than small group-talk alone; and controversies about whole-class and group-based teaching have tended to intensify issues in small-group talk on which this review will concentrate.

MAJOR CONTRIBUTIONS

Further evidence for the centrality of learner-talk came from the (UK) 'Bristol Project', under the direction of Gordon Wells. Its work, carried out between the mid-1970s and the mid-1980s, suggested particular impli-cations for small group-talk (Wells, 1989). Analysis of naturally-occurring talk between children and parents as well as teachers and co-pupils had led Wells to endorse the power of talk in externalising, shaping and extending thought; also to see a genuine communicative agenda as the driving force promoting both verbal and cognitive development. His early work, focus-ing on home and early school contexts, suggested that optimum conditions for such development involved children being taken seriouly as conversa-tional partners, especially by an adult. He drew sharp contrasts, however, between both the quantity and the quality of talk-opportunities available to young children in one-to-one interactions with parents and those occurring in busy classrooms. In addressing such issues in later papers (e.g. Wells, 1989; Chang & Wells, 1994) he has been concerned with small-group talk as a collaborative means for maximising possibilities for learning, quite broadly but especially for transition into the language of literacy (see the review by Measures, Quell & Wells in this volume).

Working in Australia, Reid et al (1991) developed parallel arguments for small-group work and talk, seeing these as constituting a basic teaching strategy for both primary and early secondary classes. In the USA, interest in talk as a foundation for literacy skills has led some early-years teachers towards development of small-group talk. Also, some liberal-minded American teachers of older students have been led to experiment with small-group talk and subsequently to claim that academic achievement, e.g. in terms of higher-level interpretation of literary texts, has shown benefits associated with such contexts. A summary and some discussion of their claims can be found in Galton & Williamson (1992).

Small-group talk, its objectives and the conditions for its successful deployment, formed a principal focus of a large-scale government-sponsored development in the UK, between 1987 and 1993. Its title, the National Oracy Project (NOP), is unsurprising in the light of the present account. Drawing its strength from regionally co-ordinated groups of teachers sharing classroom experience and innovation, it embodied in its own procedures the virtues of collaborative discussion and simultaneously represented a measure of official recognition for such underlying principles. Its contribution has been most powerfully realised through its networks of participating teachers and their schools, rather than through sponsored research. The Project nevertheless gave rise to numerous valuable studies (e.g. Des-Fountain & Howe, 1992; Phillips, 1992), and much on-going research in the area takes the NOP experience as its starting-point.

Insights emerging from the NOP with respect to small-group talk (and the practical conditions under which such talk may flourish) have been summarised by Corden (1995, p. 87) as follows:

- group work needs to be carefully planned, well structured and appropriate to the learning task
- children need to develop and understand the ground rules for small group learning
- children need to be clear about what is expected of them in terms of both working practices and expected outcomes
- appropriate and effective teacher intervention is essential
- there is a potential repertoire of roles for the teacher to adopt.

This summary emphasises purposeful, planned uses of small-group talk over less discriminating strategies. This leads to the core of the debates about the place of such talk, about definitions of its success, and about the conditions (and pre-conditions) in which such success can be realised. If small-group talk is to be carefully prepared and specifically learning-directed, how can it retain its 'exploratory' character? How are teachers to 'intervene' without so tightly prescribing the talk-agenda that pupil-participants are excluded from making the mental connections their learning requires or from talk-dependent activity such as speculating or hypothesising? Does 'successful' small-group talk have to arrive at (or include) consensus? Phillips (1988) has written persuasively of the importance of 'not sticking to the point'; Maybin (1991) highlights the role of children's *informal* talk in the social construction of personal meaning. Some critical observers of small-group talk in practice, however, (e.g. Bennet & Cass, 1989; Bennett & Dunne, 1990) have found pupils doing little more than sitting in groups and using talk for low-level 'procedural' transactions, rather than learning to manage interaction or establish directionality. Yet others, by contrast, (e.g. Fisher, 1993) stress that beneficial exploratory strategies can be taught and applied to good effect.

WORK IN PROGRESS

Work on the pre-conditions for successful small-group talk forms a significant common thread running through many current studies but is only occasionally (e.g. Hardman & Beverton, 1993; Corden, 1995) the principal focus or starting-point. The quality of such talk, the underlying competence demanded (Ward, 1993) and its impact on learning of various kinds, has nevertheless offered some generalisable insights into contextual conditions. Less attention than might have been expected has, for instance, been directed at learning within specific subject-areas. Exceptions include Gooding's studies in Australia (e.g. 1994) which have concentrated on small-group learning in mathematics. One relatively well-researched setting has been small groups talking around the computer (e.g. Fisher, 1993; Mercer, 1994); another identifiable cluster of studies has been concerned with literacy development (e.g. Short & Pierce, 1990, in the USA; Chang & Wells, 1994, in Canada; Maybin & Moss, 1993, in the UK). Gender and other equal opportunity issues have also figured (e.g. Holden, 1993). Nearly all, however, have had something to say about conditional requirements; and many have gone beyond managerial aspects to questions which have challenged basic theoretical concepts such as context and dialogue.

Attention was drawn to small-group management by critical studies already referred to. Bennett & Cass (1989) focussed, particularly, on compositional aspects, observing that groups of four and five may splinter or leave some individuals unhelpfully passive; also that groups of three, especially where one participant is of relatively high ability, may be very productive. They also contributed to the view that certain practical tasks may generate successful small-group talk among younger pupils, while older ones may respond productively to more abstract starting-points such as texts. The view that some form of shared problem-solving can be fruitful is supported by perhaps the most authoritative text on the whole topic: Barnes & Todd (1995). These authors return, almost two decades after their initial highly influential publication, to a wide-ranging summary of progress in the field, to a full discussion of issues in managing (and studying) small-group talk, and to a particularly valuable re-assessment of their own and others' theoretical perspectives.

Nearly all the studies cited in this section stress the importance of groups working in collaborative ways. They do so for reasons which transcend objectives of social development which they nevertheless recognise as important. Indeed proponents of small-group talk stress this collaborative aspect because they recognise the possibilities, inherent in dialogue, for the *co-construction* of meaning and the advantages which that can present over a merely individualist conception of knowing and learning. Barnes & Todd (1995) suggest that it is '... the prime function of group discussion to be collaborative in the development of rational thinking' (p. 88).

This 'social constructivism' may look back in part to Vygotsky and the priority he attributed to social over personal functions of language; but it has come to reflect in particular, as Barnes & Todd themselves make clear, the impact of Bakhtin's (e.g. 1981) view of dialogic discourse: the realm of utterances, not sentences, and his *dynamic* view of context. This view stresses the evolving nature of any interpersonal context through which speakers contribute, respond, build and modify, thereby creating meaning over stretches of discourse. These speech-events develop their own histories as well as reflecting others, past or possibly anticipated.

Such a 'dialogic way of coming to know' (Barnes & Todd, 1995, p. 160) depends upon speakers entering the talk 'oriented to the other', as Bakhtin (1981) puts it, being equally a speaker and a listener, and being prepared initially to handle meaning as provisional. It thus depends, too, upon participation-skills which are required for the talking into existence of such 'dialogue' but which it would be unrealistic to expect young participants to demonstrate without preparation. Hence the current widespread concern with pre-conditions defined in terms, for instance, of establishing group-work skills and explicitly valuing them (e.g. Cooper 1993). Galton and Williamson (1992) similarly write of establishing 'collaborative norms' in respect of classroom instructions. In the same vein, Fisher (1993) concludes that it is particularly 'exploratory' small-group talk which needs explicit instruction, in order to go beyond 'cumulation' of meaning, where consensual meanings are insufficiently challenged, and 'disputation' in which challenges remain unresolved. Westgate and Corden (1993) also stress the sensitivity of particular talk-events to the ways in which they are introduced; also the need for teachers constantly to reinforce the value they attach to pupil-pupil talk, given the 'shadow' (p. 119) which can so naturally be cast forward from overwhelming previous experience of teacher-dominated classroom discourse.

This view of pre-conditions for successful small-group talk lends a further perspective to the NOP conclusions, given above in Corden's (1995) formulation. If anything approaching dialogic development of understanding in Bakhtinian terms is to be encouraged (the fluidities of talk offer nothing which can be guaranteed), teachers will need to plan for more than helpful furniture-arrangement, even decide on more than group-composition. Although they will have to choose between friendship-groups, where pupils may feel at ease, and more challenging groupings, they will also have to select topics which are suitable for talk-treatment. They will need to make clear to pupils what is expected: more an engagement in a process, valuable for its own sake, than a consensual 'right answer', seen as product. Aims and 'ground rules' will need to be explicit, and the latter may benefit from prior teaching. To this end, too, teachers may choose to raise 'participants' metadiscoursal awareness' (Hardman & Beverton, 1993, p. 147) and encourage a reflexive approach where they deem it appropriate: e.g. at the secondary stage. Careful consideration will even then still be required of the interventions and support-roles for teachers to play (cf. Corden, 1992) as the talk-contexts evolve.

PROBLEMS AND DIFFICULTIES

A tension clearly exists between the potential of small-group talk, in the co-construction of understanding as well as the development of spoken competence, and classroom events in which this potential is often seen to be unrealised (e.g., Bennett & Dunne, 1990). Des-Fountain & Howe (1992) acknowledge that 'too few teachers understand, or know how to organise, true collaborative work' (p. 130). As the same writers put it, 'talk isn't simply a more sociable way for pupils to arrive at a point previously decided by the teacher' (p. 146). However, they suggest such misunderstandings can be found within talk-studies as well as among practitioners, noting a 'tendency ... to portray the group as another, smaller and safer, forum for solo talkers and listeners, whose individual contributions can ... be unravelled' (p. 140). Such arguments point towards problems in agreeing on definitions of 'successful' small-group talk.

It appears probable that a range of definitions are being operationalised by teachers and others. Some prevalent assessment practices may encourage a view of talk-events as evaluatable products: 'good' if all participants speak, 'better' if consensus is evident, 'better still' if that consensus is as intended by the teacher. The dialogic, collaborative view is very different, much subtler, less steerable, and one in which pre-conditions play a bigger part. In talk conceived in these terms, participants will typically 'finish off each others' utterances, build on each others' ideas, support and extend what the other is trying to say, create dual ... even ambiguously shifting patterns of meaning ... to the extent that it is possibly closer to the truth to talk about the construction of *joint utterance* and *joint meaning*' (Des-Fountain & Howe, 1992, p. 140; these authors provide possible examples).

An array of writing appears to support not only the value of such talk but also the preparation it requires: in terms of modelling and of carefully built-up experience and skills (e.g. Barnes & Todd, 1995; Corden, 1995; Fischer, 1993; Phillips, 1992); also of children knowing what is expected of them (Galton & Williamson, 1992) and of specific re-assurance as to the value placed upon talk-processes (Westgate & Corden, 1993). Even when delineated in such detail, such conditional requirements remain difficult to establish, and pose issues of support within any given talk-event: not least because of related problems in identifying, let alone analysing, key features of such events or of phases through which they grow.

FUTURE DIRECTIONS

If dialogic small-group talk is to establish its credentials and yield sufficiently reliably the potential learning benefits its proponents claim for it, considerable research and development is needed. The focus will need to embrace pre-conditions and talk-events themselves, and above all their inter-relationship. This will require, as Barnes & Todd (1995) suggest, a range of research styles including individual and group action-research by teachers. Studies will involve monitoring and analysis of the work of informed teachers and their pupils; it will apply and test current orthodoxies (e.g. about teaching group-talk skills) as well as being innovatory. Innovation will be required with respect to establishing climates and attitudes, inducting learners of varying ages into the skills of contributing, listening and building collaboratively, through contexts in which the teacher is present, to more free-standing ones.

Research will need to go hand-in-hand with professional development for teachers, since 'beginning to set up opportunities for students to learn through collaborative talk is much more than a change in classroom technique, ... it requires of teachers a qualitative change in their perception of their own roles and those of students in the processes of teaching and learning' (Barnes & Todd, 1995, p. 105). It is indeed a subtle and challenging agenda, requiring 'hard' evidence from contexts which by their very nature are largely unpredictable and appropriately analysed by qualitative approaches. The markers of 'quality' (or at least of qualitative differences between talk-and-learning events) must not be reductive but must do justice to shifting contextual complexities. They are, however, not yet readily to hand. It is significant that the transcript coding-system (of inter-related 'Interaction and Content Frames') which Barnes and Todd devised in relation to the data analysed for their 1977 book is reproduced in their 1995 sequel as still the best available. The theoretical work on small-group discourse analysis has simply not kept pace with that relating to other contexts, and small-group talk innovation itself has tended to be pragmatic.

Several paradoxes appear thus to need resolution. Teachers seeking openness and fluidity in their pupils' talk must devote careful prior attention to ground-rules, expectations and skills. Researchers must devise analytic tools: of a subtlety to capture key features of talk and learning in process, and of sufficient rigour to provide the hard evidence which may sustain the case for small-group talk.

University of Newcastle upon Tyne
England

REFERENCES

Bakhtin, M.M.: 1981, *The Dialogic Imagination*, University of Texas Press, Austin, Texas.

Barnes, D., Britton, J. & Rosen, H.: 1969, *Language, the Learner and the School*, Penguin, Harmondsworth.

Barnes, D. & Todd, F.: 1977, *Communication and Learning in Small Groups*, Routledge and Kegan Paul, London.

Barnes, D. & Todd, F.: 1995, *Communication and Learning Revisited*, Boynton/Cook, Portsmouth, NH.

Bennett, N. & Cass, A.: 1989, 'The effects of group composition on group interactive processes and pupil understanding', *British Educational Research Journal* 15(1), 19–32.

Brubaker, M., Payne, R. & Rickett, K. (eds.): 1990, *Perspectives on Small Group Learning*, Rubicon, Oakville, Ont.

Chang, G. & Wells, G.: 1994, *The Literate Potential of Collaborative Talk*, Micromedia Ltd., Toronto.

Cooper, H.: 1993, 'Removing the scaffolding: A case study investigating how whole-class teaching can lead to effective peer group discussion without the teacher', *Curriculum Journal* 4(3), 385–401.

Corden, R.: 1992, 'The role of the teacher', in K. Norman (ed.), *Thinking Voices*, Hodder and Stoughton, London.

Corden, R.: 1995, 'Small group work: use and abuse', *Forum* 37(3), 86–88.

Des-Fountain, J. & Howe, A.: 1992, 'Pupils working together on understanding', in K. Norman, (ed.) *Thinking Voices*, Hodder and Stoughton, London.

Dunne, E. & Bennett, N.: 1990, *Talking and Learning in Groups*, Macmillan, London.

Fisher, E.: 1993, 'Distinctive features of pupil-pupil classroom talk and their relationship to learning', *Language and Education* 7(4), 239–257.

Galton, M. & Williamson, J.: 1992, *Group Work in the Primary Classroom*, Routledge, London.

Gooding, A.: 1994, 'Recognition of effective group discussion', in G. Bell., B. Wright, N. Leeson & G. Geake (eds.), *Challenges in Mathematics Education* (Proceedings of the 17th Annual Conference of the Mathematics Education Research Group of Australia), MERGA, Lismore, NSW.

Hardman, F. & Beverton, S.: 1993, 'Co-operative group work and the development of metadiscourse skills', *Support for Learning* 8(4), 146–150.

Holden, C.: 1993, 'Giving girls a chance: Patterns of talk in co-operative group work', *Gender and Education* 5(2), 179–189.

MacLure, M., Phillips, T. & Wilkinson, A. (eds.): 1988, *Oracy Matters: The Development of Talking and Listening in Education*, Open University Press, Milton Keynes.

Maybin, J.: 1991, 'Children's informal talk and the construction of meaning', *English in Education* 25(2), 34–49.

Maybin, J. & Moss, G.: 1993, 'Talk about texts: Reading as a social event', *Journal of Research in Reading* 16(2), 138–147.

Mercer, N.: 1994, 'The quality of talk in children's talk in joint activity at the computer', *Journal of Computer Assisted Learning* 10(1), 24–32.

Phillips, T: 1988, 'On a related matter: Why "successful" small group talk depends on not keeping to the point', in M. MacLure et al. (eds.), *Oracy Matters*, Open University Press, Milton Keynes.

Phillips, T: 1992, 'Why? The neglected question in planning for small groups', in K. Norman (ed.), *Thinking Voices*, Hodder and Stoughton, London.

Reid, J, Forrestal, P. & Cooke, P.: 1991, *Small Group Work in the Classroom*, Englishand Media Centre, London: revised version of *Small Group Work in the Classroom*, Western Australian Education Department, 1982.

Short, K.G. & Pierce, K.M. (eds.): 1990, *Talking About Books: Creating Literate Communities*, Heinemann Educational, Hanover, NH.

Vygotsky, L.S.: 1962, *Thought and Language*, MIT Press, Cambridge, Mass.

Ward, A.: 1993 'Communicative competence in small group talk: Contrasting cases', *McGill Journal of Education* 28(3), 327–342.

Wells, G: 1989, 'Language in the classroom: Literacy and collaborative talk', *Language and Education* 3(4), 251–274.

Westgate, D. & Corden, R.: 1993, ' "What we thought about things": expectations, context and small-group talk', *Language and Education* 7(2), 115–126.

Wilkinson, A.W.: 1965, *Spoken English*, Birmingham University, Birmingham.

SUSAN LYLE

CHILDREN'S COLLABORATIVE TALK

Recognition of the centrality of spoken language in the processes of children's learning has led to changes in the educational status of talk throughout the English speaking world. The relationship of language to learning has been a major topic of inquiry since the late 1950s. During the 1960s psychologists identified oracy as a crucial component of learning, and during the 1970s the relationship between spoken language and thought in young children was firmly established. The foundations for the study of children's collaborative talk were laid by researchers coming from different disciplinary backgrounds including developmental psychology, sociolinguistics and classroom studies.

More recently our understanding of pupil collaborative talk has been greatly influenced by the development of social constructivist approaches to learning. Believing that knowledge creation is a shared rather than an individual experience has led to calls for a dramatic shift in classroom focus away from the traditional transmission model toward one that is much more complex and interactive. There has been a growing interest in examining the kind of social communication and interaction that leads to *collaborative* meaning making. In addition researchers have sought to consider how social, cultural and historical factors influence the contexts in which talk takes place and the kind of talk which is generated. These areas have become the focus for a growing body of research in recent years.

EARLY DEVELOPMENTS

The centrality of spoken language in the education process is widely recognised and guidelines to support teachers have appeared in most countries including Britain (Department of Education & Science, 1975), Australia (Bourke, Clark, Davis & Holzer, 1980), and Canada (Corson, 1988). Early research reported in such key works as Barnes & Todd (1977) saw pupil-to-pupil talk as beneficial to the learning process and an essential part of problem solving. Since then views on classroom talk have produced considerable consensus that pupils need worthwhile opportunities to work together in small collaborative groups in a way which enables each child to make meaning through talk, supported and challenged by their peers. Arising from this consensus a number of key issues have become a focus for research. However, classroom observation studies have shown that the

B. Davies and D. Corson (eds), Encyclopedia of Language and Education,
Volume 3: Oral Discourse and Education, 197–206.
© 1997 Kluwer Academic Publishers. Printed in the Netherlands.

benefits of collaborative talk promised by research do not materialise in school.

MAJOR CONTRIBUTIONS

In both Britain and North America research on classroom groups has taken place, although the purpose of the studies and the methods used have been fundamentally different.

In Britain the organisation of classrooms, particularly at primary level since the 1970s, are characterised by children sitting in groups. Observational surveys claim to provide descriptions of typical classroom practice consistent with the Oracle survey (Galton, Simon & Croll, 1980) in which it was exceptional to find a group working on a group task. Pupils may be seated *in* groups, but rarely worked *as* groups.

Subsequent research focused on the actual interactions of children in group settings (Bennett, Desforges, Cockburn & Wilkinson, 1984; Alexander, 1992). Findings confirmed that the typical approach of British teachers is not a group learning approach: children sit in groups, but rarely engage in collaborative styles of learning. At elementary school level (ages 5–12), groups appear to be characterised by large amounts of off-task interaction, a lack of cross gender talk and conversations of short duration.

In a project carried out in explicitly child-centred upper primary classrooms, Edwards & Mercer (1987) found that even here, the learning outcomes were controlled and directed by the teachers. Despite the apparently collaborative and active nature of the learning activities occurring, teachers played a very active role in defining and controlling the kinds of discourse permissible during the lessons.

In the US seating of children in groups is rare and much research effort has involved the implementation of experimental programmes. A key focus for this work has been in the field of cooperative learning where the emphasis has been on comparing the relative effectiveness of cooperation with more traditional styles of teaching by measuring student achievement in post-learning assessments, most commonly in mathematics classrooms. Several important cooperative learning techniques were developed and tested by researchers, and hundreds of accompanying studies have sought to document the value of cooperative learning approaches over "traditional" instruction. In a review of 122 such studies, Johnson and his colleagues (1981) claim that student achievement is at least as high, and often higher, in cooperative learning activities than individualistic efforts or competition. However, none of the studies investigated actual classroom practice: classrooms were simply used as the site in which to implement varying models of group learning. All required reorganisation of typical practice both in grouping, and often, in curriculum content. Little is known from the American studies about what actually goes on in small, cooperative learning groups that stimulates the use of appropriate cognitive processes. The focus is still on skilled performance and the mastery of subject matter as measured through individual performance rather than understanding the processes which facilitate the construction of shared knowledge and understanding through collaborative talk.

Research from both sides of the Atlantic has therefore produced a consistent picture: schools and classrooms are full of talk, but little collaborative talk between children. It is generally accepted that the Initiation/Response/Feedback (IRF) (Sinclair & Coulthard, 1975) discourse structure is a fundamental feature of all official talk in classrooms, constituting around 60% of the teaching/learning process (see reviews by Young and by Pontecorvo in this volume). Cazden (1988) explains that this practice, known as the recitation, is understood well by teachers and plays a central part in the direction and control of student learning which allows little opportunity for collaborative talk amongst peers. The movement to promote such talk has to compete against this dominant form of classroom interaction. Implementing a change from the traditional classroom to one that values talk is not a simple matter.

Investigating collaborative talk: conditions for success

Researchers have been concerned to investigate the conditions under which collaborative talk is effective. Peer interaction is a complex issue: children bring a varied set of expectations, status's, prior achievements, friendships and communication skills to their small groups. Undoubtedly, these affect their participation within the group and, in turn, mediate the effects of collaborative structures on their achievements and attitudes. A number of studies have sought to investigate the social conditions that lead to collaborative meaning making in peer group settings.

In Britain research has focused on the examination of group composition and the effect it may have on interaction. Bennett and his colleagues (1984, 1985) examined how group processes promote learning and found the group composition most widely used in the UK, namely homogeneous ability groups, is less effective than others. In the US most models of cooperative learning advocate the use of heterogeneous groups because of the beneficial effect they have on low-achieving students (Swing & Peterson, 1982).

Research into variables according to gender have been interesting. Webb (1982) found that only in groups with equal numbers of girls and boys was the achievement of girls and boys comparable. This is supported by Holden (1993) who also found that girls' abstract talk occurs when the girls outnumber the boys. Girls have also been found to like collaboration with other girls better than with boys (see review by Nielsen & Davies, in this volume). Other student characteristics which influence verbal interaction that have formed the focus of research include class (Steedman, 1982), status (Dembo & McAuliffe, 1987) race (Oakes & Lipton, 1990), ability (Brown & Campione, 1990) and age (Wood, Wood, Ainsworth & O'Malley, 1995). However, the complexity of groups makes it difficult to identify which factors have the most impact on group performance. The inter-relationship of group composition, group interaction and differing outcomes provides an interesting focus for future research.

A third area which has attracted attention has been the difficulty of implementing collaborative learning because of the dominance of the teacher's voice at the expense of students' own meaning-making voices. The power relationships which exist between teachers and learners has been identified by Wood & Wood (1988) as a major stumbling block to genuine dialogue in classroom settings. Edwards & Mercer (1987) also found overriding asymmetries between teacher and pupil, both cognitive (in terms of knowledge) and interactive (in terms of power), that impose different discursive patterns and functions. In a project designed to implement cooperative group work in British classrooms (Lewis & Cowie, 1993), teachers found it hard to accept that learning can be a cooperative rather than an individual activity and found group work conflicted with normal teaching practices.

Running alongside this work to investigate teacher control of learning is the notion that learning can be an *empowering* activity that can help learners to understand their social reality so that they might act to transform it. Located in critical theory, (the notion of critical teaching and learning and the important characteristics of critical teachers and learners is explored in the review by Young in this volume) a classroom where responsible critical inquiry takes place is one where the cultural and political nature of schooling, and the race, class, and gender backgrounds of teachers and students, as well as their prior learning histories inform the kinds of meanings that are made. This has implications for the *content* of the curriculum as well as the *processes* employed in teaching and learning. Consideration of curriculum content may well emerge as an important focus for future research.

Investigating collaborative talk: analysing discourse

Since Barnes & Todd's (1977) seminal work on collaborative talk it has been common to draw attention to the high quality of children's thinking in collaborative groups by examining the quality of the verbal interaction which takes place between children, in particular without the teacher's presence. Transcripts of talk have been produced by researchers working in experimental conditions and, more recently in the UK, from the everyday practice of classroom teachers taking part in the National Oracy Project as reported in Norman (1992).

A number of researchers, recognising that children's talk can provide a rich source of information about how meaning is negotiated in the process of learning, have turned to mainstream classrooms to carry out research. Some of the most interesting studies have involved researchers designing classroom activities, usually in consultation with the class teacher, recording groups engaged in the tasks and analysing the children's talk. Recent work confirms earlier claims that peer group discussions can enable children to make meaning beyond that which each child could make alone and that this is particularly effective when the children are engaged in discussion, argument, evaluation and sharing ideas (Lyle, 1996). Findings suggest that it is possible for classroom teachers to realise the potential of collaborative talk in the classroom if they pay attention to a number of variables including the construction of the group, the nature, content, organisation and demand of the tasks, the role of the teacher, and the curriculum area (Galton & Williamson, 1992).

In recent years a number of classroom-based projects have emerged to facilitate *computer-supported collaborative learning*. In Canada, Scardamalia and Bereiter's (1991) computer-supported learning environments (CSILE) programme sought to identify opportunities in which cumulative knowledge building and reflection can take place between a networked community of learners. In the UK, the Spoken Language and New Technology (SLANT) project (Wegerif & Mercer, 1996) has provided data on the content and quality of children's talk whilst working together at the computer. This kind of engagement, described by the authors as "exploratory talk", is particularly useful to help children actively participate in educated discourses. In the US, Ahern's (1994) study of computer-mediated small group discussion found it was possible to design computer-mediated-communication systems that encourage participation and maintain sustained reciprocal interaction without teacher presence. Research into the effects of new technology on the dynamics of group interaction and its transformative potential is likely to be an important area for continued investigation.

An important finding of the SLANT project is the importance of respect between collaborating students and the mutual right to participate. In this context friendship was identified as an important factor in supporting exploratory talk. This finding is supported by Lyle's (1996) research into the social factors relevant to successful exploratory talk and Steedman's (1982) account of collaborative writing between girls.

Curriculum area has also been identified as an important consideration when investigating classroom talk. In the US Lehr (1991) has identified story as an impetus for children's thinking and meaning-making. Numerous studies present evidence of children of different ages and abilities participating in rich discussions of works of literature. In a classroom-based investigation across grade levels in elementary schools Leal (1992) demonstrated ways in which the child, the text, and peers each influence the construction of meaning during literary discussions. Wells' (1989) work in literacy development supports Leal's (1992) and Lyle's (1996) findings that children construct knowledge by bringing what they know to new information and using this to extend or modify their initial understanding.

There is, therefore an increasing body of research to support the view that the cognitive processes most necessary for deep level understanding can occur through collaborative interaction with others. Many studies also emphasise the benefits for meaning making if teachers can suspend their role as authorities on meaning and help the students clarify their understanding.

PROBLEMS AND DIFFICULTIES

This overview of major contributions to understanding children's collaborative talk highlights the gap between mainstream practice and the growing understanding of the power of talk to help learners make meaning in educational settings. Mercer (1995) has suggested that the educational value of any classroom talk between children hinges on how well the teacher has set up activities and the nature of the tasks. An important factor hindering the adoption of collaborative learning groups is teachers' beliefs that learning is an individual rather than a cooperative activity. This is clearly true for many areas of the curriculum. Identifying which aspects of learning are best suited to collaborative group tasks is an important area which needs more research. As Edwards (1993) notes, teachers have an overriding practical concern with achieving order and control, both behavioural and cognitive, and with "doing" the curriculum. They are faced with the dilemma of having to elicit from children precisely what the curriculum determines shall be taught. The power imbalance between teachers and children means the former have authority to privilege their preferred speech style at the expense of children's voices. How can students actively construct their understanding when it is 'the teacher who knows the answers, asks most of the questions, asks questions to which she already knows the answers' (Edwards & Mercer, 1987). How this can be overcome will continue to be an area of interest to researchers.

FUTURE DIRECTIONS

Prawat and Floden (1994) recently identified two important strands in social constructivist approaches to peer collaboration. On the one hand are the advocates of co-operative learning who see the teacher's role as facilitating and managing learning in cooperative groups through establishing the ground rules, defining the task, structuring interaction and providing incentives for students to work together. Their goal is to free the teacher to circulate and monitor each group's progress, providing advice or assistance as needed.

On the other hand, are those who wish to re-establish the importance of the teacher's involvement in collaborative discussions and emphasise the skills required to do it well. This includes selecting topics and planning tasks which generate fruitful discourse between children. During activities teachers must observe the children before deciding what intervention will best help them to make progress. Any intervention should be contingently responsive to the needs of the learners and should probe the limits of children's understanding. When teachers do this the children begin to use disciplinary-based cognitive tools to examine ideas which have the potential to transform their thinking. Examples of this style of collaborative talk are increasing; one example can be found in the philosophy for children programme (Lipman, 1988). This approach sees development and understanding best achieved in dialogue between peers, facilitated by their teacher. In a number of studies in the US, Brown, Campione, Palinscar and their colleagues have developed and evaluated a *Community of Learners* project in which pupils engage in activities which are essentially dialogic in nature. A central part of this approach is "reciprocal teaching", which involves the development of a minilearning community engaged in interpreting texts (Brown & Campione, 1990).

Orsolini and Pontecorvo (1992) also argue for the presence of the teacher in small group work and present conversations of young children and their teacher engaged in collaborative talk to support this. The discussions are characterised by the instructional aims of facilitating children's topical talk and arguing. Children are expected to express and consider different points of view; the teacher's role is limited to repetitions and rephrasing of the children's contributions to promote talk.

Calls for teachers to engage with children as co-collaborators in meaning making have been greatly influenced by the ideas of Vygotsky. Recently Bakhtin's work on the role of dialogicality in the construction of understanding has added an important dimension to the investigation of children's collaborative talk (see review by Measures, Quell & Wells, in this volume). The concept of dialogical meaning making allows the learner to play an active role in developing a personally constructed understanding of the curriculum through a process of dialogic interchange. A sociocultural approach to learning, it may provide an important framework to examine the epistemological and power dimension of schooling and for suggesting ways in which the relations between individual and society, between culture and thought, and between knowledge and power might be redefined.

Future theoretical developments

Discourse is the characteristic feature of human life. Edwards (1990) has put forward a view of learning as a "discourse" between people, a shared experience which is dependent on the dialogue and quality of relationships in which the child participates. Corson (1995) draws our attention to the importance of discursive psychology and the insights it is beginning to provide on the world as a discursive construction. Bruner (1996) argues that cultural psychology alerts us to the importance of "situatedness" in learning, and emphasises that learning is an interactive process in which people learn from each other. Young's (1988) work on critical pedagogy has focused attention on Habermas's theory of communicative action, suggesting it is a theory of interaction where meaning is arrived at dialogically and therefore must be understood as socially situated. Corson (1993) has stressed the importance of critical dialogue in the growth of knowledge and consciousness of the world around us.

If we accept that the social world is a discursive construction and the mind is embedded in contexts which have unique historical, political, cultural, social and interpersonal determinants then language is at the heart of cognitive activity and dialogue the key to learning. The implications of this for classroom practice is revolutionary. If classrooms are to become places where collaborative talk between peers is an accepted teaching strategy, where all (including teachers) can learn, change and grow, approaches to teaching and learning must value personal experience and feelings as essential elements in the learning process as well as cognitive growth. Knowledge will not be something which is already established but negotiated as students create meaning dialogically. Pupils bring with them different cultural meaning systems through which they make sense of the world. Children's collaborative talk has the potential to allow pupils to experience the different ways in which people use language to make meaning out of educational text. Content will reflect a fuller and clearer representation of the world as students struggle to make sense of global interdependence and its implications for ecological and social integrity in the future. Collaborative talk could offer a pedagogical addition with emancipatory potential to current authoritarian models of teaching and learning.

Swansea Institute of Higher Education
Wales

REFERENCES

Ahern, T.C.: 1994, 'The effect of interface on the structure of interaction in computer-mediated small-group discussion', *Journal of Educational Computing Research* 11(3), 253–250.

Alexander, A.: 1992, *Policy and Practice in Primary Education*, Routledge, London.

Barnes, D & Todd, F.: 1977, *Communication to Curriculum*, Penguin, Harmondsworth.

Bennett, N. & Desforges, C.: 1985, *Recent Advances in Classroom Research*, Scottish Academic Press, Edinburgh.

Bennett, N., Desforges, C., Cockburn, A & Wilkinson, B.: 1984, *The Quality of Pupils' Learning Experience*, Lawrence Erlbaum Associates, New Jersey.

Bourke, S.F., Clark, M.L., Davis, D.F & Holzer, F.: 1980, *Oracy in Australian Schools*, ACER, Melbourne.

Brown, A.L. & Campione, J.C.: 1990, 'Communities of learning and thinking, or a context by any other name', in D. Kuhn (ed.), *Developmental Perspectives on Teaching and Learning Thinking Skills*, Karger, Basle, 108–126.

Bruner, J.S.: 1996, *The Culture of Education*, Harvard University Press, Cambrige, MA.

Cazden, C.B.: 1988, *Classroom Discourse: The Language of Teaching and Learning*, Portsmouth, Heinemann Educational Books, New Hampshire.

Corson, D.: 1988, *Oral Language Across the Curriculum*, Multilingual Matters, Clevedon, OH.

Corson, D.: 1993, 'Discursive bias and ideology in the administration of minority group interests', *Language in Society* 22, 165–191.

Corson, D.: 1995, *Using English Words*, Kluwer Academic Publishers, Dordrecht.

Dembo, M. & McAuliffe, T.: 1987, 'Effects of perceived ability and grade status on social interaction and influence in cooperative groups', *Journal of Educational Psychology* 79, 415–423.

Department of Education & Science: 1975, *A Language for Life* (Report of the Bullock Committee of Inquiry) HMSO, London.

Edwards, D. & Mercer, N,: 1987, *Common Knowledge: The Development of Understanding in the Classroom*, Routledge, London.

Edwards, D.: 1990, 'Classroom discourse and classroom knowledge', in C. Rogers & P. Kutnick (eds.), *The Social Psychology of the Primary School*, Routledge, London.

Edwards, D.: 1993, 'But what do children really think? Discourse analysis and conceptual content in children's talk', *Cognition and Instruction* ii(3/4), 207–225.

Galton, M., Simon, B. & Croll, P.: 1980, *Inside the Primary Classroom*, Routledge & Kegan Paul, London.

Galton, M. & Williamson, J.: 1992, *Group Work in the Primary Classroom*, Routledge, London.

Holden, C.: 1993, 'Giving girls a chance: Patterns of talk in co-operative group work', *Gender and Education* 5(2), 179–189.

Johnson, D.W. Maruyama, G. Johnson, R. & Nelson, D.: 1981, 'Effects of cooperative, competitive, and individualistic goal structures on achievement: A meta-analysis', *Psychological Bulletin* 89(1), 47–62.

Leal, D.J.: 1992, 'The nature of talk about three types of text during peer group discussions', *Journal of Reading Behaviour* XXIV(3), 313–338.

Lehr, S.: 1991, *The Child's Developing Sense of Theme*, Teachers' College Press, New York.

Lewis, J. & Cowie, H.: 1993, 'Cooperative group work: promises and limitations: A study of teachers' values', *Education Section Review* 77–84.

Lipman, M.: 1988, *Philosophy Goes to School*, Temple University Press, Philadelphia, PA.

Lyle, S: 1996, 'An analysis of collaborative group work in the primary school and the factors relevant to its success', *Language and Education* 10(1), 13–32.

Mercer, N.: 1995, *The Guided Construction of Knowledge: Talk Amongst Teachers and Learners*, Multilingual Matters, Clevedon.

Norman, K (ed.): 1992, *Thinking Voices: The Work of the National Oracy project*, Hodder & Stoughton, Sevenoaks, Kent.

Oakes, J. & Lipton, M.: 1990, *Making the Best of Schools: A Handbook For Parents, Teachers and Policymakers*, Yale University Press, New Haven.

Orsolini, M. & Pontecorvo, C.: 1992, 'Children's talk in classroom discussions', *Cognition and Instruction* 9(2), 113–136.

Prawat, R.S .& Floden, R.E.: 1994, 'Philosophical perspectives on constructivist views of learning', *Educational Psychology* 29(1), 37–48.

Scardamalia, M. & Bereiter, C.: 1991, 'Higher levels of agency for children in knowledge building: A challenge for the design of new knowledge media', *The Journal of the Learning Sciences* 1, 37–68.

Sinclair, J.M. & Coulthard, R.M.: 1975, *Towards an Analysis of Discourse*, Oxford University Press, Oxford.

Steedman, C.: 1982, *The tidy house: Little Girls' Writing*, Virago, London.

Swing, S. & Peterson, P.: 1982, 'The relationship of student ability and small-group interaction to student achievement', *American Educational Research Journal* 19, 259–274.

Webb, N.M.: 1982, 'Group composition, group interaction, and achievement in cooperative small groups', *Journal of Educational Psychology* 74, 475–484.

Wells, G.: 1989, 'Language in the classroom: Literacy and collaborative talk', *Language and Education* 3(4), 251–273.

Wegerif, R. & Mercer, N.: 1996, 'Computers and reasoning through talk in the classroom', *Language and Education* 10(1), 47–64.

Wood, D. & Wood, H.: 1988, 'Questioning versus student initiative', in J.T. Dillon (ed.), *Questioning and Discussion: A Multidisciplinary Study*, Norwood, Ablex.

Wood, D., Wood, H., Ainsworth, S. & O'Malley, C.: 1995, 'On becoming a tutor: Towards an ontogenetic model', *Cognition & Instruction* 13(4), 565–581.

Young, R: 1988, 'Critical teaching and learning', *Educational Theory* 38(1), 47–59.

VIVIAN DE KLERK

INTERACTION PATTERNS IN UNIVERSITY EDUCATION

Much of the learning taking place in tertiary institutions takes place through verbal intercourse, and the traditional mode of such discourse is the lecture, complemented more recently by the seminar. Such modes of discourse are inherently historical, built up by previous exposure to and experience of discourse types which reinforce the norms of existing social structures and practices, and limit the potential for change.

The specifics of the "ideal" learning experience, and views on acceptable teaching methods and relationships, depend on what one sees as the goal of learning and how one measures success and achievements. When these are challenged, the traditional methods of teaching are challenged, and practices which were hitherto seen as successful appear ineffective and ill-adapted. Current socio-demographic trends and changing views about what constitutes knowledge and in particular, recognition of the importance of the subjective experience of individuals, the organised background knowledge which leads them to expect, predict and notice certain aspects in interpreting what they see, hear and learn has had a profound effect on thinking about teaching methodology in tertiary institutions. These changes have lead to a shift from top-down, individualistic approaches to bottom-up, inquiry-based approaches, dependent on meaningful interaction. The steady shift to the view of knowledge as an individual construction resulting from interaction has grown steadily and the effect on tertiary educational methodology has been increasing learner-centredness and small group work.

EARLY DEVELOPMENTS

Socrates' dialogues with his students, performed in order to get them to see the flaws in their thinking and to come to his conclusion, could be seen as a precursor to more formal lecturing techniques. The lecture has a long history as the central method of University instruction, having its origins in fifth century pre-Christian academy, where Plato and his students gathered; as practised in mediaeval Europe and the Muslim East, the lecture changed slowly from a carefully crafted (often rehearsed) example of the art of oratory, to the reading of and commentary on a book or manuscript (which only the lecturer possessed); its usefulness was so much taken for granted that it developed its own inertia and ceased to be questioned.

B. Davies and D. Corson (eds), Encyclopedia of Language and Education,
Volume 3: Oral Discourse and Education, 207–216.
© *1997 Kluwer Academic Publishers. Printed in the Netherlands.*

Only during the 18th century did the practice of teaching became a pedagogic question, owing to the rise of scientism and rationalism. The lecture-recitation-examination approach, dominated by the authoritative teacher and stressing limitless assimilation of facts was challenged by attempts to develop intellectual capacity by discussion, and debates. Lecturing involves a continuous formal exposition, a monologue on a prepared and self-chosen topic, physically removed from silent listeners, and therefore sheltered from the hazards of improvisation and interruptions; lectures are highly dependent on the style, personality and communication skills of the lecturer, and by the 1940s, with higher education more widely available, along with books, television and radio, and with the appointment of more and more young and inexperienced lecturers, strong criticism from students regarding the efficiency of lecturing resulted in several studies (reviewed in Bligh, 1972, pp. 5–11) being carried out to assess the efficiency of lectures (cf. Verner & Dickinson, 1968; Costin, 1972).

A host of new factors now impinging on tertiary education have accelerated this process because increased levels of prosperity, population growth, explosion of knowledge, increase in numbers of professions, and changes in mass media technology have led to increasingly widespread scepticism about previously accepted values and traditional practice. The growth in concern for equity in educational opportunity for all social classes, sexes, ethnic and racial groups, and the increasing accessibility of tertiary education have changed Universities and Colleges from being elitist and selective to being mass institutions, with multilingual and multicultural student populations from a range of different cultural and social backgrounds. This has, in turn, had a direct effect on curricula and teaching methodology.

MAJOR CONTRIBUTIONS AND WORK IN PROGRESS

Various writers on the topic (McLeish, 1968) have shown that the advantages of using lectures are that immature learners learn more readily through listening than reading and lectures can be valuable in introducing a subject or in updating an area which is constantly changing and where texts are not readily available; also lectures can awaken critical skills, inspire and arouse interest and be aesthetically pleasing, and they are more economical than tutorials or seminars in covering ground and disseminating information to a wide audience (Johnson et al., 1991, p. 85).

However, recent research has shown that many University students are unable to cope with the technical and scholastic demands made on their use of language, and the problem goes beyond the superficialities of jargon to the operation of a highly complex code of transmission. Academics as a group traditionally use certain discourse norms which operate as a given, and in terms of which students are assessed. The low level of tertiary students' comprehension of the language of their lecturers is confirmed in several studies (Parry, 1989; Dunkel et al., 1989, p. 547), which reveal how crucial linguistic misunderstanding is in higher education, and highlight the determining role of linguistic background in academic success. Non-native speakers are at a particular disadvantage in a lecture or seminar environment, insofar as it affects their note-taking, conceptualisation, participation and recall.

On the whole, evidence strongly suggests that lecturing is not a particularly effective mode of teaching: Menges (1988) discusses low lecture-recall rates from research studies in the 1920s; research showed that an unacceptably high loss of information occurs in the way teaching was conducted in French Universities in the 1960s (Bourdieu, 1994, p. 3); investigations in the 1960s revealed rapid fall-off of attention and assimilation after 10 minutes (Penner, 1984) and low levels of recall after 24 hours (Verner & Dickinson, 1967; Goolkasian, 1979), as well as low levels of effect in promoting thinking or changing attitudes (Bligh, 1972); lecturers need to take into account the limits of listeners' short term memory and the importance of rate of delivery (Curzon, 1985) suggests a rate of 110 w.p.m., with anything over 200 w.p.m resulting in rapid decline of assimilation).

Added to this problem is the fact that many lecturers have little feel for the total set of concepts and information students are required to master, and overestimate the level of intellectual development of school-leavers, expecting levels of sophistication in appreciation of the nature and interpretation of evidence, relativism and abstraction far beyond their capacity (Entwistle, 1990).

Critics see the lecture as autocratic and top-down, discouraging the partnership essential to facilitation of learning, and ineffective because it lacks any feedback: the spatial and social distance between teacher and student are seen as barriers to interaction, as is the use of powerful academic discourse, which serves as a further exclusionary technique. The lecture approach views knowledge as an external object, with teaching a matter of transmission, and this view is seen as 'one of the most intractable obstacles to the development of effective teaching' (Stones, 1983, p. 3), resulting in no crossover or application of anything learned in the classroom. Recent changes in thinking about knowledge and learning as the active construction of meaning (cf. Pastoll, 1992, p. 5; Cowie et al., 1994) have led to the demystifying of academic discourse and the deconstruction of the power of the lecturing mode of delivery in favour of dialogue with small groups of students in order to promote genuine understanding.

The small-group seminar, associated with older English Universities, requires a very generous staff-student ratio, but offers opportunities for active learning and substantive conversation essential for authentic achievement across all educational levels and subjects. The view that knowledge is socially constructed by 'consensus among the members of a community of knowledgeable peers' (Bruffee, 1993, p. 3) – something people construct collaboratively by talking together and reaching agreement through the negotiation of meaning, has received growing support (Cohen, 1994; Slavin, 1990; Pastoll, 1992). Such collaborative learning, with students all participating in a clearly assigned open-ended task, allows for the exploration and expression of diverse ideas and experiences in non-threatening cooperative company in order to deepen understanding, critical judgement and acknowledge differing perspectives (Cowie et al., 1994). This approach in tertiary education can be seen as a process of cultural change (Bruffee, 1993, p. vii).

Unlike the dependence of the lecture on the solo performance of the lecturer, seminars need collective activity for success, and free flow of argument is important, with members pooling knowledge in a cooperative search for understanding. If interaction leads to conceptual learning and deepening of understanding, then those groups which allow equitable interaction and cooperation among students of different statuses and backgrounds would be most likely to enjoy a climate conducive to learning.

Unfortunately, however, the potential for failure of the tutorial is high: the gradual transition to joint responsibility and full participation rights at tertiary level means that students have to learn new conventions in which they have equal rights with the tutor to the floor and their contribution is seen as valuable. This goes counter to conventions learned at school, where discourse conventions are significantly different from casual conversation. Mundane, everyday conversation is finely-tuned linguistic behaviour in which participants take turns to exchange information and provide evidence of shared interpretations: turn-taking operates on a local turn-by-turn basis, with allocation, length and content locally managed by participants; these are not fixed or pre-specified, but governed by a rule system which has been carefully described by conversation analysts, foremost among them Sacks, Schegloff & Jefferson (1974).

It is widely accepted that the rules of turn-taking in school contexts are adjusted so as to ensure differential participation rights and the open-endedness and permutability is controlled to make for a minimisation of gap and overlap (McHoul, 1978). Teachers are traditionally seen as providers of new information, models of correct performance and selective reinforcers of student efforts; interruptions are usually exclusively their right, and they alone may continue indefinitely without fear of interruption or select the next student speaker; if a student speaks, the next turn will revert to the teacher again. The identities of teachers and students and the relationships between them are at the heart of the educational system and depend on the durability of the discourse patterns used.

At tertiary level, each brings to the classroom his/her own past experiences and expectations for a certain conventionalized behaviour of teacher and learner, in accordance with historical precedents, and the shift to a participatory form of discourse can be problematic because a host of factors militate against success: tutors are often loath to give up their powerful speaking rights and overdependence on the leader is also possible, with perceived tutor expertise being a barrier to discussion in that students may fear seeming ignorant or the tutor may offer solutions too hastily, not giving students a chance to formulate a response; the size of the group may discourage participation from less confident members, and inappropriate spatial arrangements may have a negative effect. Unless all the participants are equally prepared (via pre-reading etc.) and there are very clear aims, poor management skills by the tutor can result in the degeneration of small group sessions into loose discussion or domination by "star" speakers.

There is obviously going to be strong competition for the right to speak, as speaking turns are highly desirable, from everyone's points of view: for the tutor, the right to speak offers opportunities to explain and inform and indirectly to assert the dominant role that tutors traditionally fill (studies suggest very high levels of teacher/tutor interruption at tertiary level (Reynolds, 1990; de Klerk, 1995)); from the student's point of view, the right to speak offers an opportunity to display knowledge, interest and understanding to peers but more importantly to the tutor who holds the power to assess the student's academic progress. Apart from significantly aiding the learning process, the opportunity to speak also allows students to explore areas of vagueness or aspects which are controversial, and to express an opinion and persuade others of its validity in the face of opposition. Clearly, it is in everyone's interest to speak as much as possible. However, in tutorials we are not dealing with homogeneity: participants often have significantly different cultural backgrounds and gender and ethnicity are important factors in determining predisposition to engage in formal discourse and likelihood of success (Bashiruddin, 1990, p. 78). Those who are most at risk in such a competitive speaking environment are women and cultural minorities, because their language practices differ from those of the dominant groups and they are most likely to be routinely repressed, dominated or disempowered.

The unspoken underlying dispositions and attitudes which underlie behaviour tend to pervade the social system, making it difficult for those with alternative norms (such as females or members of ethnic or linguistic minorities) to participate as equals. Those with power tend to want to reinforce the system which gives them that power, to utilise 'the social and cultural resources available to them, and in particular the largely inherited qualities which they derive from their social milieu' (Bourdieu, 1994, p. 96). It has been shown that those with more power (either from status, social convention or numerical advantage) have special linguistic rights which tend to upset the otherwise ideal symmetry that verbal interaction would reflect: the powerful have been shown to be more talkative, less self-effacing, less compliant, and less likely to abandon positions taken (Smith, 1987). By subtly imposing their definition of what is possible, right, rational and normal in discourse (and because minority groups are inclined to accept such norms uncritically), an unjust reality is often constructed.

This is particularly pertinent to discourse norms in tertiary educational institutions, as those groups who have alternative dispositions and discourse tendencies will have less purchase on the culture of education and be at a greater disadvantage than others. As Corson (1993, p. 9) puts it, 'the readiness of minority language or non-standard speakers to stigmatise their own language means that they often condemn themselves to silence in public settings for fear of offending norms which they themselves sanction'.

Gender and ethnicity have received increasing scholarly attention in recent years, in order to investigate their importance in determining equity in discourse participation. A large body of work has accumulated over the past few decades which provides evidence for the existence of separate "genderlects", into which we are socialised and which we accept as the norm, thereby reinforcing them in our own practice. Female norms of interaction have been shown to be less individualistic, more collectivist, valuing equal, collaborative participation to create and maintain connections with others and to acknowledge and support contributions from others. Thus women typically appear to facilitate conversation by offering evidence of active listening through minimal responses, asking questions, and acknowledging and building on each other's utterances; evidence shows that females participate more actively when led by fellow females (Holmes, 1988; Sommers & Lawrence, 1992).

On the other hand, empirical research suggests that males' communication style is based on competitive efforts to control conversation by trying to seize turns, possibly through interruption or topic shifts, and then speaking for longer than women (Condravy, 1991, p. 16; McConnel-Ginet et al., 1980).

If active participation is a prerequisite for educational success, then competitive (disruptive) behaviour is the mode of interaction which will bring most rewards. The implication for discourse at tertiary level is that while small group work might be ideally suited to girl's preferred style of learning, i.e. a cooperative negotiation of meaning (Oxford, 1993), the competitive norm of male conversation means that the less aggressive female participants will have less access to the floor and decreased opportunities for learning. The differing habits of conversation of females will significantly disadvantage them in educational interaction and there is strong pressure for them to conform and assimilate if they wish to succeed in a man's world.

In addition to gender being a significant variable in discourse, increasingly, tertiary education involves intercultural interaction, which has significant implications as far as discourse is concerned, because cultural groups can differ significantly in terms of the norms that influence their behaviour and perceptions, and particularly their approaches to education and preferred style of learning. Different perceptions of the role and rights of teacher and students, the norms of conversational interaction, the aims of education and the nature of knowledge can lead to significant misunderstanding and frustration. The power and status of different groups determine the results of intergroup contact (Goodman, 1994 p. 144), and studies focusing on ethnicity and culture have revealed that those for whom the current conventions are regarded as the norm will be at a distinct advantage, while those from foreign cultures, because of their lack of familiarity with the norm will be less likely to utilise opportunities for participation (Shapiro, 1984). Power relations, gender and cultural norms systematically decrease opportunities for particular students to benefit from the system and individuals accustomed to discourse norms which run counter to the norms of the dominant group would obviously be disadvantaged. This is likely to reinforce preexisting stereotypes about lesser competence of minorities in the group's experience, making the effects of cooperation far less desirable than many proponents of the technique would have us believe, because status, gender and cultural differences lead to disproportional interaction patterns and the reinforcement of the status quo.

Research into seminar interaction patterns (de Klerk, 1995; Hunt, 1996) revealed how competitive such small-group discussions can be in terms of winning the floor: talk was at a premium, and analysis of the nature of turn-types shows that by far the majority of turns resulted from self-selection and of these, the majority were non-valid or violative turns. Students who won a more-than-fair proportion of the floor *and* who interrupted and displayed assertiveness and willingness to participate tended to belong to dominant social groups (males, or cultural insiders or mother-tongue speakers with privileged educational backgrounds).

FUTURE DIRECTIONS

While the Hale report (1964) states that the lecture has an essential place and cannot be replaced by reading combined with discussion because of its economy in terms of staff time and topic coverage, it seems clear that additional instructional methods are gaining in popularity, and that their efficiency also needs to be closely monitored. In the previous century the educative process was part of western cultural imperialism, taking the form of training in and assimilation of western norms, values and behaviours. Today the ability to participate appropriately in academic discussion depends on mutual understanding and cooperation regarding certain entrenched discourse "norms", and such cooperation reinforces existing norms and power relations, ensuring their continued existence because they are naturalized and achieve the status of "common sense" (Candlin, 1987, p. 24; Corson, 1993).

Instead of viewing verbal interaction as harmonious and cooperative, researchers will need to link it to wider social processes and relationships and to explicate its role in confirming and consolidating or challenging and changing the organisations which shape it. Viewing oral discourse at tertiary level as a kind of social struggle which could result in change, both in the mode of discourse and of wider social and cultural domains will require increasing attention to be given to what these discourses are and how they operate, and ongoing research into patterns of interaction will be a priority.

In the light of current socio-political changes which are affecting both gender and race relations, and of the international debate with regard to the possible marginalisation of certain sub-groups in academic institutions generally, research needs to focus on the extent to which normalized differences in discourse habits advantage or disadvantage certain groups, and the extent to which these norms are being challenged. Ethical questions are raised concerning whether the discourse patterns of less-powerful groups should be changed, encouraging assimilation, or whether plurality should be fostered by sensitising tutors and students to the different norms of each group.

The efficacy of current teaching methods in rapidly changing tertiary contexts also deserves attention. Efforts to improve teaching and learning at tertiary levels have been hampered by the lack of a coherent theoretical framework (Entwistle, 1990, p. 668), leading to disproportionate stress on methods of instruction and not enough emphasis on independent studying techniques and perceptions about the aims underlying learning. There has been a growing recognition of the need to consider students' experiences of the overall academic context in which they learn and develop intellectually (Marton et al., 1984), and the educational effects of the increasing focus on collaborative learning and on the need to provide opportunities to develop the skills now demanded by society will need to be monitored.

With the steady trend in many Universities (especially in Africa) towards higher proportions of ESL students from impoverished educational backgrounds, there will also need to be increasing focus on creating an environment to facilitate students' development of academic literacy, especially for students from disadvantaged educational backgrounds or cultural minorities. In order to enable academics to take responsibility for running courses more conducive to developing academic literacy among their students, the vital role that oral discourse plays in developing an understanding of concepts and constructing knowledge needs greater attention, as does the nature of different subject-specific academic discourses.

Rhodes University
South Africa

REFERENCES

Bashiruddin, A., Edge, J. & Hughes-Pelegrin, E.: 1990, 'Who speaks in seminars? Status, culture and gender at durham university', in R. Clark, N. Fairclough, R. Ivanic, N. McLeod, J. Thomas & P. Meara (eds.), *Language and Power*, Centre for information on language teaching and research for the British Association of Applied Linguistics, 74–84.

Bligh, D.A.: 1972, *What's the use of lectures?*, Penguin, Harmondsworth, England.

Bourdieu, P., Passeron, J-C. & Saint Martin, M.: 1994, *Academic Discourse*, Polity Press, Cambridge.

Bruffee, K.A.: 1993, *Collaborative Learning: Higher Education, Interdependence, and the Authority of Knowledge*, John Hopkins University Press, Baltimore, USA.

Candlin, C.E.: 1987, 'Beyond description to explanation in cross-cultural discourse', in L.E. Smith (ed.), *Discourse Across Cultures*, Prentice Hall, New York, 22–35.

Cohen, E.G.: 1994, 'Restructuring the classroom: Conditions for productive small groups', *Review of Educational Research* 64(1), 1–35.

Condravy, J.C.: 1991, 'Women's talk in a women's studies reading and discussion group: A descriptive study of cooperation and competition', Unpublished doctoral thesis, Indiana University of Pennsylvania USA.

Corson, D.: 1993, *Language, Minority Education and Gender*, Clevedon: Multilingual Matters.

Costin, F.: 1972, 'Lecturing versus other methods of teaching: A review of research', *British Journal of Educational Technology* 3(1), 4–30.

Cowie, H., Smith P.K., Boulton, M. & Laver, R.: 1994, *Cooperation in the Multi-ethnic Classroom – The Impact of Cooperative Groupwork on Social Relations in Middle Schools*, David Fulton (Publishers) Ltd., London.

Curzon, L.B.: 1985, *Teaching in Further Education*, Cassell, London.

de Klerk, V.A.: 1995, 'The discourse of post-graduate seminars', *Linguistics and Education* 7, 157–174.

Dunkel, P., Mishra, S. & Berliner, D.: 1989, 'Effects of note-taking, memory and language proficiency on lecture learning for native and non-native speakers of English', *TESOL Quarterly* 23(3), 34–49.

Entwistle, N.: 1990, 'Teaching and the quality of learning in higher education', in *Handbook of Educational Ideas and Practices*, Routledge, London.

Goodman, N.: 1994, 'Intercultural education at the university level: Teacher-student interaction', in Richard W. Brislin & T. Yoshida (eds.), *Improving Intercultural Interactions: Modules for Cross-cultural Training Programmes*, Sage Publications, Inc., CA, 129–147.

Goolkasian, P.: 1979, 'Memory for lectures', *Journal of Educational Psychology* 71.

Hale Report: see University Grants Committee.

Holmes, J.: 1988, 'Sex differences in seminar contributions', *BAAL Newsletter* 31, 33–41.

Hunt, S.: 1996, 'An investigation into patterns of interaction in small group teaching at Rhodes University, with particular emphasis on the effects of gender and mother-tongue', unpublished Masters dissertation, Rhodes University, Grahamstown.

Johnson, D.W., Johnson, R.T. & Smith, K.A.: 1991, *Cooperative Learning: Increasing College Faculty Instructional Productivity*, ASHE-ERIC Higher Education Report No

4. The George Washington University, School of Education and Human Development, Washington, DC.

Marton, F., Hounsell, D.J. & Entwistle, N.J. (eds.): 1984, *The Experience of Learning*, Scottish Academic Press, Edinburgh.

McConnel-Ginet, S., Borker, R. & Furman, N. (eds.): 1980, *Women and Language in Literature and Society*, Praeger, New York.

McHoul, A.: 1978, 'The organisation of turns at formal talk in the classroom', *Language in Society* 7, 183–213.

McLeish, J.: 1968, *The Lecture Method*, Institute of Education, Cambridge.

Menges, R.: 1988, 'Research on teaching and learning: The relevant and the redundant', *Review of Higher Education* 11(3), 259–268.

Oxford, R.L.: 1993, 'Gender differences in styles and strategies for language learning: What do they mean? Should we pay attention?', *Georgetown University Roundtable on Languages and Linguistics*, 541–557.

Parry, S.: 1989, 'Achieving academic literacy: Disciplined discourse', *Higher Education Research and Development* 8(2), 147–159.

Pastoll, G.: 1992, *Tutorials that Work: A Guide to Running Effective Tutorials*, Arrow Publishers, Cape Town.

Penner, J.: 1984, *Why Many College Teachers Cannot Lecture*, Charles C. Thomas, Springfield, Illinois.

Reynolds, M.: 1990, 'Classroom power: Some dynamics of classroom talk', in Clark et al., 122–136.

Sacks, H., Schegloff, E.A. & Jefferson, G.: 1974, 'A simplest systematics for the organisation of turn-taking for conversation', *Language* 50, 696–735.

Shapiro, M. (ed.): 1984, *Language and Politics*, Blackwell, Oxford.

Slavin, R.E.: 1990, *Cooperative Learning: Theory, Research and Practice*. Prentice Hall, Englewood Cliffs, NJ.

Smith, L.E.: 1987, *Discourse Across Cultures*, Prentice Hall, New York.

Sommers, E. & Lawrence, S.: 1992, 'Women's ways of talking in teacher-directed and student-directed peer response groups', *Linguistics and Education* 4, 1–36.

Stones, E.: 1983, 'Further education and pedagogy', *Journal of Further and Higher Education* 7(2), 3–11.

University Grants Committee: 1964, *Report of the Committee of University Teaching Methods* (Chairman: Sir E. Hale), H.M.S.O., London.

Verner, C. & Dickinson, G.: 1967, 'The lecture – an analysis and review of research', *Adult Education* 17, 85–100.

PETER SCRIMSHAW

CHILDREN'S TALK AND COMPUTERS

The development of an interest in computers and children's talk is understandably quite recent. It grows out of the convergence of four main strands of related research, namely the development of a social constructivist theory of the relationship between language and learning, the growth of classroom discourse analysis, largely experimental studies of cooperative learning amongst children, and non-language related research on computers and children's learning (see the reviews by Snyder in Volume 8 and by Abbott in Volume 2).

EARLY DEVELOPMENTS

The work of Vygotsky (1962, 1978) has led to a flourishing US school of research in which the classroom implications of his work were explored within a broadly social constructivist but not language-related framework (see for example Moll, 1990). Vygotsky's ideas were also developed, but in a somewhat different direction, by Edwards & Mercer (1987), Cazden (1988) and later others, such as the contributors to Hicks (1996). These researchers too explored classroom life but their emphasis upon the primacy of language in the learning process led them to use discourse analysis as a major tool.

Given their concern for context, most of the research of the social constructivists was classroom-based. A separate strand of work was the usually experimental or quasi-experimental research carried out in the USA into children's cooperative learning (see for instance Foot et al., 1990). Much of this research gave no particular emphasis to talk, but it provided a clearer picture of the internal complexities of the notions of cooperation and collaboration.

The final influence upon research into children's talk round computers was the work done on children learning with computers. In the early 80s much of the academic work on this drew upon constructivist perspectives that emphasised individual action and development, notably exemplified by the work of Papert (1980). While his approach was strongly Piagetian, other contributors, for instance O'Shea & Self (1983), wrote within the broader framework of the newly emerging area of cognitive science. From both these viewpoints however the educational focus for research was the interaction between the learner and the computer, with a consequent emphasis upon software design and individual learning. For obvious

B. Davies and D. Corson (eds), Encyclopedia of Language and Education,
Volume 3: Oral Discourse and Education, 217–227.
© *1997 Kluwer Academic Publishers. Printed in the Netherlands.*

reasons this did not lead to any great interest in classroom talk, but it did emphasise the significance of active learning and of the diversity of kinds of software even then available.

However for financial reasons as much as any commitment to a cooperative view of learning, children shared computers in classrooms from the outset. Consequently when attempts were made to apply and research the theories of Papert and others in working classrooms by Canadian and US researchers such as Pea & Scheingold (1987), Olson (1988) and Schofield (1995), there was a strong movement towards seeing learning in the wider classroom context, with a corresponding growth of interest in the teacher's role, and that of the group working round a computer. These studies tended to be naturalistic in design, but they too made relatively little explicit reference to classroom talk.

None of these lines of development led directly to a concern with computers and children's talk. However in the late 80s and early 90s researchers began to find ways of approaching this topic by combining ideas and research techniques drawn from these four approaches. While some attempt has been made to draw these strands together, notably by Crook (1994) no single research paradigm for the area has yet evolved, although as indicated below there are some signs of productive convergence.

To date two main lines of attack have emerged. One is to use a quantitative and largely experimentally based approach, in which predesigned coding schemes are used to analyse talk round the computer. The other is to rely upon a naturalistic classroom-based paradigm, in which emergent and fairly general talk categories are developed, supplemented in some cases by a more detailed analysis based upon some form of discourse analysis. For simplicity these two approaches are labelled below as the quantitative and qualitative approaches respectively.

MAJOR CONTRIBUTIONS AND WORK IN PROGRESS

Researchers working within a quantitative framework (e.g. Bennett & Cass, 1988; King, 1989) tend to use multilevel hierarchical classifications with numbers of subcategories, and take single utterances (or some other small element of talk) as the unit of analysis. As far as content goes they vary considerably in the names and details of their classifications, but generally separate off-task and on-task talk, and subdivide the latter into cognitively and socially oriented categories, with task management sometimes distinguished as another major grouping.

By contrast researchers working within a naturalistic and classroom-based paradigm (e.g. Scrimshaw, 1993; Mercer, 1995; Wegerif & Scrimshaw, 1997) take broadly defined kinds of talk as the main object of analysis. They have identified three kinds of children's talk as being of particular educational importance. These have been variously characterised since Fisher first suggested them, but Mercer (1995) distinguishes them as follows:

– Disputational talk, which is characterised by disagreement and individualised decision making. This kind of talk is characterised by short exchanges made up of assertions and challenges.
– Cumulative talk, in which speakers build positively but uncritically upon what the other has said. This talk is characterised by repetitions, confirmations and elaborations.
– Exploratory talk, in which partners engage critically but constructively with each other's ideas. In this kind of talk knowledge is made more publically accountable and reasoning is more visible.

Workers operating within this qualitative framework use common ethnographic techniques, such as the provision of vignettes and thick description, but some have also investigated ways of using or extending Sinclair and Coulthard's IRF structures to analyse talk amongst children (Fisher, 1993; Wegerif, 1996).

These attempts have led in turn to the suggestion (Wegerif & Mercer, 1997) that these three kinds of talk, although originally drawn inductively from classroom observation, actually differ from each other on four distinct levels. Firstly they involve participants orienting themselves socially towards each other in fundamentally different ways. Secondly the ground-rules for each of the three forms of discourse differs. Thirdly the speech acts used need to be considered according to their apparent function in the immediate context, and finally the linguistic surface details of the talk needs to be noted.

Wegerif & Mercer (1997) argue that there is a degree of play between each of these levels. Thus, for example, the occurrence of particular terms in the talk may suggest that certain speech acts are probably being performed, but does not guarantee it. This, if true, means that quantitative analyses of the occurrence of either specific terms (e.g. 'because') or of speech acts (e.g. questioning) provide useful indicators of what is happening educationally, but need to be supplemented by linked analyses of the same talk at the level of ground-rules and overall orientation. This in turn suggests that the different ways that children work round the computer and the related variations in talk are very closely linked, and that both are usefully characterised in terms of the distinctions between exploratory, cumulative and disputational talk, at least where the researcher is centrally concerned with cognitive learning.

What this analysis therefore offers is a provisional way of relating the findings from quantitative studies to those arising from the qualitative approach. It must be said that the number of studies available of either kind is small, and those that have been carried out are often based upon

small groups. Conclusions must therefore be very tentative. Nevertheless a provisional picture is beginning to take shape concerning:
- the effect of the computer on attention and motivation,
- the different ways that children work round the computer, and the variations in talk that result,
- the effects of using different types of software on children's talk
- gender differences,
- the importance of the role of the teacher in supporting educationally productive talk.

One finding that emerges strongly is that children tend to exhibit a very high proportion of on-task talk when using computers (Cummings, 1985; Bennett & Cass, 1988; Teasley, 1995; Kampulainen, 1996). One study (Hoyles et al., 1991) also found that pairs using spreadsheets and Logo software produced a substantially higher level of on-task talk than they did when working at a pencil and paper task, which matches the experience of many teachers that computer use, even after children have had several years of exposure, remains a strong motivator.

How talk (especially cognitively oriented talk) is related to different forms of software has also been explored. Within on-task talk, cognitively oriented contributions are often substantial. Cummings (1985) found more than half the total talk in his study of pupils' use of a simulation was related to logical reasoning. Wild & Braid (1996) reported a similar level where word processing was involved, but gained much higher levels with a simulation program, while Bennett & Cass (1988), also using a simulation, found that instructional talk (a mainly cognitive category) was by far the largest present in their data.

Nevertheless, what specific kinds of cognitively oriented contributions arise varies considerably depending in part upon the software used. Hoyles and her co-workers (1991) found that inter-pupil discussion round computers served a scaffolding role in helping the pupils to make mathematical generalisations. However working with paper and pencil provided no such support, and within the two computer related contexts using Logo assisted with the process of mathematical generalisation itself, whereas when using the spreadsheet it was the pupil's actions and gestures that became important.

In another study where pupils used eight different programs (Anderson et al., 1993) the distinction between open and closed software proved important. Broadly speaking open programs can be characterised as ones where control rests largely with the user (such as word processing or drawing packages) as against those, such as drill and practice and simulation packages, where the user's possible responses are tightly constrained. This study indicated that closed packages tended to generate more mechanistic speech behaviours, whereas open packages generated less of these behaviours, but seemed to leave pupils unclear as to what else to do. Programs in the middle of the open-closed spectrum produced the most mechanical behaviour, rather as if they produced confusion and subsequent regression. A rather different picture emerges from Kampulainen's study (1996) of Finnish and British children involved in cooperative wordprocessing. She found relatively little differences between the two groups in terms of the distribution of kinds of talk, but in both cases cognitively oriented talk tended to be relatively low-level and context-bound rather than exploratory.

An early qualitative study (Fisher, 1993) suggested that open-ended software was accompanied by more varied and wide ranging talk than was more highly structured packages. But was this accompaniment a result of these differences? The rather diverse findings from the quantitative research summarised earlier would indicate that there are other factors that need to be considered too. This was supported by a later study in which Wegerif (1996) used a mixture of quantitative and qualitative methods to reanalyse Fisher's data. He concluded that highly structured packages can sometimes support exploratory talk better than open ended packages may do, given approapriate kinds of teacher intervention.

Another major issue that has been explored concerns the ways in which groups are organised to reach their decisions when using computers, and with what effects. There is evidence (Teasley, 1995) that children who are asked to talk together as they work round computers generate better hypotheses than groups asked to remain silent; while more specifically an early study by King (1989) showed that groups that asked more task-related questions, that spent more time on strategy and that reached higher levels of elaboration in their strategies were most successful at solving a graphics task using Logo. The question then is what kinds of group organisation best support the generation of such talk.

Bennett & Cass (1988) have identified the ability mix within groups as an important factor with, for example, groups containing both high and low achieving children seeking and generating more explanations than homogeneous groups, but with a higher number being erroneous. Wild & Braid (1996) by contrast found that in mixed ability groups the higher ability children took the lead and thus needed to produce a lower proportion of socially oriented talk, whereas in the homogeneous high ability groups such talk was more frequent, apparently because the children needed to use it to build a more cooperative climate.

Another study, however (Hoyles et al., 1991), indicated that the match of task to children was also important. There the level of joint decision making that occurred was affected by the extent to which the task set was within the children's zone of proximal development; where the task was too hard or too easy one child of the pair would tend to become dominant, rather than their working together at the problem.

Gender differences form an important subtheme within this work on grouping. Bennett & Cass (1988) found that girls spoke slightly more than boys despite being outnumbered in nearly all groups, while Cummings (1985) found that girls spoke more than boys, but also a higher proportion of irrelevant talk. However the genre mix within groups appears to be important here. Thus Tolmie & Howe (1993) found that boys and girls did equally well in terms of the amount of relevant discussion generated in single gender pairs, with mixed pairs discussing less. However the boy pairs were better at linking predictions to explanations than girl pairs, while conversely the all-girl pairs did better at generalisation. Given that both generalisation and linking predictions to explanations are important scientific competences, this indicates that both groups were using less than optimal approaches.

Using a cloze procedure program Underwood (1994) found the same beneficial effect on discussion for single sex pairs, and better performance on the task, although there the girl pairs outperformed the boys.

One way of interpreting these results is that the differences between science and language tasks alone might be creating differences between boys' and girls' talk. However the different effects associated with different kinds of software outlined earlier suggest that there may be interactions between gender and software features too. Indeed Littleton et al. (1993) have shown that quite small presentational changes in a simulation program (i.e. replacing pirates by 'honey bears' as the main characters) substantially altered the relative performances of boys and girls despite the two versions having the same underlying task structure.

The role of gender differences has also been explored by Swann (1997) and Watson (1997a), both analysing single classroom sessions using a mix of quantitative and qualitative methods similar to that advocated by Mercer and Wegerif. Swann's conclusion is that simple notions of male dominance are hard to sustain, at least in the case she considers, but that talk needs to be seen as involving a complex network of negotiations operating on several levels, with different children dominant in different aspects and stages of the activity. This was largely supported by Watson's study too, in which children who had been given explicit training in methods of cooperating showed much less tendency to gendered differentiation in their talk than might have been anticipated.

Overall the picture that emerges so far is one in which the computer and the kind of software used impacts differentially upon achievement in ways that depend upon a wide range of interacting elements in the situation. These include the general social orientation that the children have towards the task and each other (with gender and ability (or possibly perceived ability) as significant influences), the nature of the ground rules needed to make effective cooperative use of the specific kind of software involved, the extent to which these ground rules are explicitly understood and the manageability and explicitness of the task set.

What all this in turn implies is that successful and productive talk and learning round the computer will not occur unless the teacher is actively involved in the process. An early experimental study (Emihovich & Miller, 1988) showed how successful scaffolding of learning using Logo involved the teacher using metacognitive prompts to help transfer responsibility for learning to the children. Anderson and Tolmie's work (1993) revealed that children have different kinds of difficulties in dealing with open and closed programs, which suggests that the teacher's role as scaffolder will also need to differ.

The qualitative studies available also strongly support the belief that the teacher is indeed crucial in framing and monitoring the activity to ensure that it supports educationally productive talk. These studies also indicate that the teachers and researchers can help achieve this by setting out to provide explicit instruction on the ground-rules for cooperative discussion (Mercer & Fisher, 1992; Dawes, 1997) or by designing both software and pedagogy together to promote exploratory talk (Wegerif & Dawes, 1997; Watson, 1997b).

PROBLEMS AND DIFFICULTIES

Three generic difficulties in language research are: establishing a workable and theoretically defensible relationship between quantitative and qualitative methodologies, deciding what level of detail in classification and coding categories is optimal, and identifying research processes and topics that encourage a productive relationship between theory and practice. All of these issues are alive in this area at present, although recent work from within the quantitative framework by Wild (1996) and by Wegerif & Mercer (1997) starting from the qualitative end of the spectrum suggests that some productive convergence of these perspectives is emerging.

However, there are also some problems more specific to the area of computers and talk. One is that the range of studies is small, and very largely focussed upon English-speaking groups working in English-speaking classrooms. Much of the work too is with children in the middle age ranges of schooling. Secondly the communicative status of the computer itself remains problematic. It has an interactive quality that makes it hard to establish a standard set of conventions for researching and representing the computer's contributions to classroom interactions.

Finally, and most importantly, the impact of information technology on language is different from the impact that it has upon other curriculum areas, for in the case of language introducing these technologies fundamentally redefines the subject itself (Adams et al., 1997). What constitutes talk, and its relationship to reading writing, and listening is being reconceptualised as new technologies emerge, redefining those activities just as the invention of film and television redefined theatre-based conceptions of drama. Word processing is not the same as handwriting, at the levels of physical activity, text construction, composition planning or editing. Electronic mail has points of similarity with conversation and conventional letter writing, but is a different genre from both, while videoconferencing is not the same form of discourse as telephone conversation or face to face discussion. Novels written as electronic hypertexts are not the same as linear printed texts, nor are the relationships between their creators and readers identical in the two cases. The practical and theoretical implications of all these changes for teaching and learning (not to mention the effects of their interactions with each other) will be considerable.

FUTURE DIRECTIONS

Nearly all the research reported above has been concerned with children talking around a single computer that they share between them. However other very different possibilities emerged in the 80s and early 90s. One innovation is the appearance of portable laptop or handheld computers, some of which are significantly cheaper than conventional desktop systems. Another is the development of within-school networks (see for example Scardamalia & Bereiter, 1992 and 1994) and more recently still the growth of external networks (such as the Internet). A third is the continuing development (but much slower diffusion) of more expensive technologies such as video conferencing and multimedia.

These changes, individually and in combination, seem likely to produce the following effects:

- increased availability of handheld computers, provision being enough in some schools to allow one per child in a class or group,
- extension of computer-related discourse to children in cultures (and classroom cultures) very different from those in Europe or the USA.,
- the growing use of (largely monolingual) computers in bilingual settings,
- disintegration of the barriers between home and school learning (for some children, in some schools, in some societies) as the Internet creates national and international learning networks between schools, homes, universities and commercial organisations such as publishers and television companies, with corresponding changes in the forms of discourse that mark learning and teaching, as the educational relationships between teacher, outside expert, parent and learner become progressively more complex,
- the teacher's role will move from that of information source to that of coordinating and scaffolding the support that a variety of adults (and other children) will be providing for learners, in schools and beyond, through various forms of electronic communication,

– continuing technology-led development of new interrelationships between talk, writing, reading and listening, creating new opportunities and problems for the teaching of first (and subsequent) languages,
– cross-cultural communications through the Internet (both in schools and more significantly through the home) will alter the boundaries of children's speech communities, with significant longterm impacts upon the form and content of their face to face communications within their own immediate communities.

All of these changes create considerable opportunities for research, and may well have a theoretical and practical significance for language teaching and learning that extends well beyond the concerns of those with an immediate interest in information technology itself.

The Open University
England

REFERENCES

Adams, A., Tweddle, S., Clarke, S., Scrimshaw, P. & Walton, S.: 1997, *English for Tomorrow*, Open University Press, Buckingham.
Anderson, A., Tolmie, A., McAteer, E. & Demissie, A.: 1993, 'Software style and interaction around the computer', *Computers in Education* 20(3), 235–250.
Bennett, N. & Cass, A.: 1988, 'The effects of group composition on group interactive processes and pupil understanding', *British Educational Research Journal* 15(1), 19–32.
Cazden, C.: 1988, *Classroom Discourse*, Heinemann Educational Books Inc. Portsmouth NH.
Crook, C.: 1994, *Computers and the Collaborative Experience of Learning*, Routledge, London and New York.
Cummings, R.: 1985, 'Small-group discussions and the microcomputer', *Journal of Computer Assisted Learning* 1(3), 149–158.
Dawes, L.: 1997, 'Teaching talking', in R. Wegerif & P. Scrimshaw (eds.), *Computers and Talk in the Primary Classroom*, Multilingual Matters Ltd, Clevedon, 189–195.
Edwards, D. & Mercer, N.: 1987, *Common Knowledge: The Development of Understanding in the Classroom*, Methuen and Co Ltd., London.
Emihovich, C. & Miller, G.: 1988, 'Talking to the turtle: A discourse analysis of logo instruction', *Discourse Processes* 11, 182–201.
Fisher, E.: 1993, 'Characteristics of children's talk at the computer and its relationship to the computer software', *Language and Education* 7(2), 97–114.
Foot, H.C., Morgan, M.J. & Shute, R.H. (eds.): 1990, *Children Helping Children*, John Wiley.
Hicks, D. (ed.): 1996, *Discourse, Learning and Schooling*, Cambridge University Press, Cambridge.
Hoyles, C., Healy, L. & Sutherland, R.: 1991, 'Patterns of discussion between pupil pairs in computer and non-computer environments', *Journal of Computer Assisted Learning* 7, 210–228.
Kampulainen, K.: 1996, 'The nature of peer interaction in the social context created by the use of word processors', *Learning and Instruction* 6(3), 243–261.
King, A.: 1989, 'Verbal interaction and problem-solving within computer-assisted co-operative learning groups', *Journal of Educational Computing Research* 5(1), 1–15.

Littleton, K., Light, P., Barnes, P., Messer, D. & Joiner, R.: 1993, 'Gender effects and software effects in computer-based problem solving', Paper presented at the Society for Research in Child Development, New Orleans, March.

Mercer, N.: 1995, *The Guided Construction of Knowledge: Talk amongst Teachers and Learners*, Multilingual Matters, Clevedon.

Mercer, N. & Fisher, E.: 1992, 'How do teachers help children to learn? An analysis of teachers' interventions in computer-based tasks', *Learning and Instruction* 2, 339–355.

Moll, L.C. (ed.): 1990, *Vygotsky and Education: Instructional Implications and Applications of Sociohistorical Psychology*, Cambridge University Press, Cambridge.

Olson, J.: 1988, *Schoolworlds/Microworlds: Computers and the Culture of the Classroom*, Pergamon Press, Oxford.

O'Shea, T. & Self, J.: 1983, *Learning and Teaching with Computers*, Harvester Press, Brighton.

Papert, S.: 1980, *Mindstorms: Children, Computers and Powerful Ideas*, Basic Books, New York.

Pea, R. & Scheingold, K. (eds.): 1987, *Mirrors of Minds: Patterns of Experience in Educational Computing*, Ablex Publishing Corporation, Norwood, NJ.

Sinclair, J. & Coulthard, R.: 1975, *Towards an Analysis of Discourse: the English used by Teachers and Pupils*, Oxford University Press, London.

Scardamalia, M. & Bereiter, C.: 1992, 'Text-based and knowledge-based questioning by children', *Cognition and Instruction* 9(3), 177–199.

Scardamalia, M. & Bereiter, C.: 1994, 'Computer support for knowledge – building communities', *The Journal of the Learning Sciences* 3(3), 265–283.

Schofield, J.W.: 1995, *Computers and Classroom Culture*, Cambridge University Press, Cambridge.

Scrimshaw, P. (ed.): 1993, *Language, Computers and Classrooms*, Routledge, London.

Swann J.: 1997, 'Tinker Town: Reading and rereading children's talk around the computer', in R. Wegerif & P. Scrimshaw (eds.), *Computers and Talk in the Primary Classroom*, Multilingual Matters Ltd., Clevedon, 133–150.

Teasley, S.D.: 1995, 'The role of talk in children's peer collaborations', *Developmental Psychology* 31(2), 207–220.

Tolmie, A. & Howe, C.: 1993, 'Gender and dialogue in secondary school physics', *Gender and Education* 5(2), 191–209.

Underwood, G.: 1994, 'Collaboration and problem solving: Gender differences and the quality of discussion', in J. Underwood (ed.), *Computer Based Learning: Potential into Practice*, David Fulton Publishers, London.

Vygotsky, L.S.: 1962, *Thought and Language* (E. Hanfmann, G. Vakar, Trans.), MIT Press, Cambridge, Mass.

Vygotsky, L.S.: 1978, *Mind in Society: The Development of Higher Psychological Processes*, edited by M. Cole, V. John-Steiner, S. Scribner and E. Souberman, Harvard University Press, Cambridge.

Watson, M.: 1997a, 'The gender issue: Is what you see what you get?', in R. Wegerif & P. Scrimshaw (eds.), *Computers and Talk in the Primary Classroom*, Multilingual Matters Ltd, Clevedon, 151–167.

Watson, M.: 1997b, 'Improving group work at the computer', in R. Wegerif & P. Scrimshaw (eds.), *Computers and Talk in the Primary Classroom*, Multilingual Matters Ltd, Clevedon.

Wegerif, R.: 1996, 'Collaborative learning and directive software', *Journal of Computer Assisted Learning* 12(1), 22–32.

Wegerif, R. & Dawes, L.: 1997, 'Computers and exploratory talk: An intervention study', in R. Wegerif & P. Scrimshaw (eds.), *Computers and Talk in the Primary Classroom*, Multilingual Matters Ltd., Clevedon, 227–239.

Wegerif, R. & Mercer, N.: 1997, 'A dialogical frame work for researching peer talk', in

R. Wegerif & P. Scrimshaw (eds.), *Computers and Talk in the Primary Classroom*, Multilingual Matters Ltd, Clevedon, 49–61.

Wegerif, R. & Scrimshaw, P. (eds.).: 1997, *Computers and Talk in the Primary Classroom*, Multilingual Matters Ltd., Clevedon.

Wild, M.: 1996, 'Investigating verbal interaction when primary children use computers', *Journal of Computer Assisted Learning* 12(2), 66–77.

Wild, M. & Braid, P.: 1996, 'Children's talk in cooperative groups', *Journal of Computer Assisted Learning* 12(4), 216–232.

SUSAN E.B. PIRIE

THE USE OF TALK IN MATHEMATICS

The statement 'talk is but one element of language use' becomes highly significant when considering mathematics classrooms. Whereas in other areas of the curriculum the words and syntax used in oral discourse are closely related to those employed in written communication, this is untrue for mathematics. Here the written forms are symbolic rather than verbal, and one cannot therefore assume that notions concerning relationships between oral and written language derived from other disciplines will necessarily transfer to the learning and teaching of mathematics. The learning process becomes more complex, because, for understanding to take place, children have to construct mathematical meanings from experiences that, at least initially, are embedded in everyday language and "everyday language" can have slippery, changing meanings sometimes encompassing more, sometimes less, than the sought after mathematical meaning. Only after this can mathematical symbols be introduced (Pirie, 1997). There is no one-one correspondence between the written and the oral. Indeed, this is not the only linguistic transition that the mathematics learner is expected to master. Mathematics also has its own verbal register, which is composed of a combination of mother-tongue words, many with distorted or specialised meanings, and additional new vocabulary, quite specific to mathematics (Pimm, 1987). Consider the differences between: "Four threes are twelve", "the product of three and four is twelve", and $3 \times 4 = 12$. From the perspective of the teacher, how can one know what and how much understanding is encapsulated in students' own use of the mathematics register, unless the students can also express themselves in everyday language and function with the symbolic representation? The three facets of mathematical language are inextricably woven together.

EARLY DEVELOPMENT

Historically, the connections between language and the teaching of mathematics tended to be thought of purely in terms of symbolic representations, teacher talk and students' factual answers. The interest in the value of oral communication is thus a comparatively new one. 'In general ... mathematics classrooms are places where you do mathematics not where you communicate or discuss mathematical meanings' (Bishop, 1985, p. 27). There have even been attempts to produce textbook series that aim to teach mathematics pictorially and symbolically without any

B. Davies and D. Corson (eds), Encyclopedia of Language and Education,
Volume 3: Oral Discourse and Education, 229–238.
© *1997 Kluwer Academic Publishers. Printed in the Netherlands.*

verbal distractions, but such ventures overlooked the fact that the meaning that students bring to the symbols will of necessity be grounded in their earlier, verbal experiences.

Among the earliest publications to address the value of classroom discourse including that in mathematics lessons, were those of Barnes, notably Barnes, Britton & Torbe (1969) which became influential in raising awareness of the power of analysing talk in the mathematics classroom (see also the section on Early Developments in the review on Effective Educational Talk). Aiken in 1972, and Austin and Howson in 1979 set out to review research into language and mathematical education. The paucity of published research in this area, however, led Austin and Howson (p. 175) to suggest that 'in most classrooms the teacher does most of the talking and that few pupils respond' – a statement which continued to be true for many years to come. Not withstanding this state of affairs, in the early 1980s researchers in places as far apart as Britain, Japan, France and America, were starting to focus their interest on talk, and attempting to describe oral situations that they felt needed further exploration. The problem at this time was that there was little or no understanding of the specific nature of mathematical talk and so in 1982 Harvey et al endeavoured to 'document rather than philosophise and theorise' the phenomenon (p. iv). A growing interest in both problem solving and small group work was also fuelling the attention being paid to talk, but it was without a doubt the governmental Cockcroft Report (1982) which brought the role of discussion in the mathematics classroom to the forefront of British teachers' awareness, in a manner similar to the effect that the National Council of Teachers of Mathematics (NCTM) Standards documents were to have on teachers in America nearly a decade later. While challenging the automatic assumptions of the efficacy of pupil-pupil discussion, two early responses to Cockcroft sought to clarify the nature and effects of the phenomenon and laid the ground work for much of the research that was to follow (Hoyles, 1985; Pirie & Schwarzenberger, 1988).

MAJOR CONTRIBUTIONS

The study of talk in mathematics can be approached from three different perspectives: it is possible to examine the talk itself, qua talk, or to explore it as a medium through which teaching and learning can happen, or to use the analysis of talk as a vehicle for the exploration of other classroom events. In the first of these approaches, the actual words the students and teachers use, the explanations they give, their familiarity with the register, the occurrence of unorthodox language, and the use of metaphors are all of concern. There is a need for informal language to precede formal expression and Richards (1991, pp. 15–16) contrasts the 'language of mathematical literacy' with what he calls "number talk", illustrating how teachers and students can be merely "exchanging words" rather than communicating. An alternative approach to the analysis of classroom talk is taken by both Goos et al. (1996) and Wood (1997), who seek to elicit patterns of effective discussion from the classes they study, with a view to better understanding this complex phenomenon. In all this work it must, however, be remembered that any talk analysis is dependent on a personal interpretation (Laborde, 1996).

One aspect of talk to which some attention has been paid is that of unorthodox words, coined by teachers and students, to express, with greater meaning for themselves, the mathematical concepts they are seeking to construct (Pirie, 1991; Rubenstein, 1996; Pirie, 1997). The argument being made here is that in teacher-directed, orthodox-language classes the students appropriate the teacher talk, however little they understand it, whereas the freedom to create personal language allows for greater expression of mathematical comprehension. Similarly, it is conjectured, there may be value in student "side-talk" which usually passes unnoticed by teachers and researchers alike (Pirie & Schwarzenberger, 1988; Cazden, 1988). The student's need for oral words to verbalise both written symbols (Usiskin, 1996) and actions that are no longer being performed (Perrin-Glorian, 1990) illustrates one facet, self-communication, of the fundamental communicative nature of language.

Bishop (1985, p. 27) comments that communicating is 'concerned with sharing mathematical meanings and connections. We can only share ideas by exposing them, and "talk" is clearly a most important vehicle'. The framework for teaching and learning through talk, that is provided by problem solving and group work, facilitates not only thinking aloud and spontaneous verbalisation but also genuine mathematical discussion. Forman & Cazden (1985) and Bartolini-Bussi (1997) consider such discussion from the Vygotskian perspective of "scaffolding". The belief is that through the need to verbalise their mathematical working, at the same time as seeing the problem from another's perspective, students will clarify, recognise incongruities in, and then reorganise their own thinking (Hatano, 1988). Hoyles et al. (1991), however, illustrate the different attitudes that boys and girls have to the resolution of disagreements.

There has been a return to the study of the role of teachers' talk, but this no longer focuses on the asking of routine questions demanding correct answers, rather on the higher-order, "why?" questions. Hoping to find the key to 'how classroom discourse relates to learning', Hiebert & Wearne (1993, p. 397) state that 'if students are challenged to explain the reasons for their responses, ... they will engage in deeper reflective, integrative thought'. Verbal explanation and justification is taking the place of formal proof in classroom mathematics, but whereas the structure of proofs could be routinely committed to memory, teachers must encourage opportunities for oral practice before students will become adept at expressing their mathematical reasoning on paper. This situation will of course make teachers more vulnerable to the exposure of their own, sometimes shaky, mathematical understandings, and Thompson & Thompson (1994) are concerned with the way that one 'teacher's conceptualisations ... were encapsulated' in language that 'undermined his effort to help the student understand' (p. 279). Despite the claims of the power of cognitive conflict to enhance learning (Gooding & Stacy, 1993), other research has shown that a conflict situation cannot always be presumed to produce enhanced mathematical understanding (Pirie, 1991). If, nonetheless, talk is seen as on the whole valuable to the learning of mathematics, then oral discussion must also have a role to play in the compiling of evidence for assessment.

WORK IN PROGRESS

The third focus of research is that of gaining access and insight into other classroom phenomena through the examination of classroom discourse. Historically this has been mainly focused on classroom management, in particular on the allocation of teacher attention and questions, although equally accessible are the negotiation and adoption of roles in discussion, and the indications of the balance of power among classroom participants (Cobb, 1994; Cooper et al., 1996). Although largely anecdotal, beneficial affective features are claimed for classroom talk, resulting in reduced math-anxiety and increased interest.

In recent years the technology of audio- and video-recording has enabled deeper analysis of other aspects of classroom life as revealed by examination of student and teacher talk. A greater voice is being given to teachers investigating the practice of teaching through analysis of recordings made in their own classrooms. Access to the thinking processes of students, has been made easier through the ability to recall for the students, by video-replay, the precise words that they used in an earlier situation, thus further enabling, the exploration of the effects of discussion on learning.

In 1988, Hatano cited several studies that had 'found that peer discussion and decision making facilitate meaningful learning, understanding and cognitive growth' (p. 62). If one accepts that under certain conditions classroom talk is beneficial, then the question becomes 'what are the mechanisms by which such meaningful learning can occur?'. One major continuing research thrust lies in this area of the growth of mathematical understanding. Through detailed study of both student-student and student-teacher classroom dialogues, Kieren and Pirie are seeking to construct a theory that will offer language with which to talk about and understand such growth. (For an overview see Pirie & Kieren, 1994.) One of the features of the theory, evident from the study of any student discussion, is that which has been termed "folding back". It is clear that mathematical growth does not, and indeed cannot, proceed along the straight path which has often been the assumed ideal route, moving ever outward to more sophisticated understanding. Students return repeatedly to earlier understandings, to build "thicker" foundations on which to construct their growing understanding. Such insights could only have been gained through the study of classroom talk, since the final, presented, written mathematics, whether that of students or mathematicians, rarely shows any trace of its genuine construction. Since this is the case, current research questions include the exploration of verbal teacher interventions which might facilitate such growth (Abele, 1997).

For several years now, Cobb et al., have been working on another aspect of the mathematical classroom, also concerned with the building of mathematical meaning for children, and also through the close analysis of classroom talk. Many researchers have made the claim that discussion builds common meanings within a classroom. Through both joint and individual research projects, Cobb et al., have been seeking to explain how the social norms are constituted within a classroom, that facilitates the negotiation and construction of taken-as-shared meanings. (For an overview see Cobb et al., 1992.) In the classrooms where they conduct their research, attention is paid to the verbal roles played by the teacher, and the acceptance by the children of personal obligations orally to challenge one another, to explain their own thinking, and to justify their mathematical assertions. Discussion occurs both in small groups and whole class situations, and although the classrooms are few and admittedly "special", there seems little doubt that their findings could have lasting impact on the use of talk in other mathematics classrooms.

PROBLEMS AND DIFFICULTIES

One long-standing concern has been the teaching of mathematics in languages, particularly those of the African nations, which did not have words for much of the mathematical register as it had evolved in Western cultures (Austin & Howson, 1979). For example, in Hausa there was no word for triangle, in Sinhala there was no way to distinguish between different four-sided shapes and in Swahili there was no word for diagonal (Gibbs & Orton, 1994). Traditionally this was not seen as a problem, as mathematics was 'delivered' in English. The UNESCO recommendation that early education should be in the first language of all children, however, exposed the inadequacies of these languages to convey mathematical concepts. A common way to deal with this problem was to import specific words such as "minuend" and "subtrahend" into the classroom (words that are totally unfamiliar to most native English speakers). This does not, of course, deal with the need for concepts to be grounded in everyday language. The problem is more than simply one of not having, and therefore importing, the vocabulary of modern technology; the lack of language can denote a lack of concept or traditional ability to make specific distinctions within that culture.

Watson (1988) discusses in detail this cultural "handicap" (p. 266) as it impinges on the learning of Aboriginal Australians. Notions of "self" and the traditions of learning within their culture are at odds with the teaching with seeks to impose semantic structures and registers born of Western mathematics. Currently students must wrestle with their bicultural experiences and the degree with which they successfully achieve some form of bridge between these differing cultures determines their ability to integrate with "European Australians". Studies of South American students (Nunes, Schliemann & Carraher, 1993) have focused on the thriving mathematical "street culture" that exists and have focused on ways in which this culture could be profitably linked to formal learning. Such international ethnomathematical studies of local and oral traditions in non-dominant cultures are increasing, both in scope and depth, our understanding of what it means to learn mathematics. Paradoxically, however, increasing Western interest in children's autonomous classroom talk and group problem solving has lead to the discounting of other oral practices, notably those of Eastern nations. Rote learning and group recitation do not of themselves automatically imply or produce lack of mathematical understanding, as can be seen by the supremacy of Asian students in international competitions.

More recently, cultural problems have been identified as arising within large inner-city schools, particularly in Australia and Canada, where recent immigration policies have resulted in classrooms in which English is a second language for a large number of students from a variety of first languages. Dawe & Clarkson (1996) have looked at the complex ways in which children at elementary schools switch between their first language and English when doing mathematics, and have uncovered the phenomenon, of which many teachers were unaware, that although children can translate a problem word for word, it is not until they have done this that they are able to understand the mathematics that is required of them. It also seems important to know how this impinges on their learning of the symbolic language of mathematics. For all children there is a tension between the precise language, and the multi-faceted nature, of any mathematical concept. Take, for example, the mathematical notion of "product". (A notion which incidentally has only a tenuous connection with the everyday language meaning of the word.) Fundamentally, the product of two integers and the product of two vectors are the same concept, yet to the learner the difference seems far from superficial. Many children have no realisation of the commonalty of meaning between the uses of the word "square" to describe a shape and to describe a number. It is, however, a perceived problem, rather than a realistic difficulty, that children have problems with learning the words of the mathematics register. Even 5 year-olds can handle with ease the far more complicated names for pterodactyl, and brontosaurus! The challenge for teachers is to reveal the intended power of mathematical language to be precise, unambiguous, brief and manipulable, through the clumsy, imprecise, personal language of oral discourse.

FUTURE DIRECTIONS

The current focus on oral language in the mathematics classroom has led to an increased awareness of the metaphorical ways in which we present mathematics and it is within these metaphors that the basic images lie, from which students construct new mathematical learning. Early notions of subtraction are dependant on the physical action of "taking away" some elements of a group of objects. However, the verbalisation of "5–2" as "five take away two" does not imply any actual removal of the symbols, it is a metaphorical reference to a related physical act. The importance of the study of metaphor lies in the fact that it can inhibit later learning. To give one simple example: too strong an adherence to the metaphorical meaning of "take away" results in "2–5" being articulated as "two take away five" and the conclusion that "it is not possible to subtract two from five" because one cannot physically perform such an act of "taking away". Little is known about the effects of other such grounding metaphors on the mathematical misconceptions that students build.

A widely accepted definition of discussion is that it is 'purposeful talk on a mathematical subject in which there are genuine pupil contributions and interaction' (Pirie & Schwarzenberger, 1988). Research over the past twenty years has focused on student and teacher talk, and yet "interaction" implies that there must also be listening. To date, however, little research has been undertaken that focuses on how students and teachers listen (Pirie, 1996). One approach to this area could be through hermeneutics, broadly defined as the art of interpretation. Although 'well-developed theories of the relationships between teaching and learning ... do not yet exist' (Hiebert & Wearne, 1993, p. 394), for teaching to lead to learning there must at the very least be consensual interaction. In his book on teaching mathematics, Davis (1996) deals in detail with hermeneutical listening and its effect on the mathematical curriculum, opening up a possible new perspective on the classroom. Here may lie the way to greater understanding of the power of higher order questions to promote learning.

There is little doubt that certain kinds of talk in the mathematics classroom can engender more effective mathematical understanding. What we must now explore and define are the mechanisms that, within the complex interactions that form the classroom environment, provide such effective discourse. We need to examine imaginatively the talk which we consider "effective", seeking to elicit the essential elements needed to foster growth of understanding. The future for mathematics education lies not in facts but in ideas. Technology in the 21st Century will take charge of the routine and facilitate the implementation of ideas. The teacher's role lies in educating students in the processes of conjecturing, explaining and justifying their ideas, and classroom talk has a major part to play in such education.

University of British Columbia
Canada

REFERENCES

Abele, A.: 1997, 'Pupil language – teacher language: Two case studies and the consequences for teacher training', in M.G. Bartolini-Bussi, A. Sierpinska & H. Steinbring (eds.), *Language and Communication in the Mathematics Classroom*, National Council of Teachers of Mathematics, Reston, VA.

Aiken, L.: 1972, 'Language factors in learning mathematics', *Review of Educational Research* 42, 359–385.

Austin, J.L. & Howson, A.G.: 1979, 'Language and mathematical education', *Educational Studies in Mathematics* 10(3), 161–197.

Barnes, B., Britton, J. & Torbe, M.: 1969, *Language, the Learner and the School*, Penguin Books, Harmondsworth, England.

Bartolini-Bussi, M.G.: 1997, in M.G. Bartolini-Bussi, A. Sierpinska & H. Steinbring (eds.), *Language and Communication in the Mathematics Classroom, National Council of Teachers of Mathematics*, Reston, VA.

Bishop, A.: 1985, 'The social construction of meaning – a significant development for mathematics education?', *For the Learning of Mathematics* 5(1), 24–28.

Cazden, C.: 1988, *Classroom Discourse: The Language of Teaching and Learning*, Heinemann, New York.

Cobb, P.: 1994, 'A summary of four case studies of mathematical learning and small group interaction', *Proceedings of the 18th International Conference on the Psychology of Mathematics Education (Lisbon)* II, 201–208.

Cobb, P., Wood, T., Yackel, E. & McNeal, B.: 1992, 'Characteristics of classroom mathematics traditions: An interactional analysis', *American Education Research Journal* 29(3), 573–604.

Cockcroft, W.H.: 1982, *Mathematics Counts*, Her Majesty's Stationery Office, London.

Cooper T.J., Bleicher, R.E. & Atweh, B.: 1996, *Gender, Social Class and Classroom Talk, Oral Presentation at Working Group 1 (Communication) of the 8th International Congress for Mathematics Education (Seville)*.

Davis, B.: 1996, *Teaching Mathematics: Toward a Sound Alternative*, Garland Publishing, New York.

Dawe, L. & Clarkson, P.: 1996, 'Through the child's eyes: Classroom communication in mathematics in Australian multilingual classrooms', *Oral Presentation at Working Group 1 (Communication) of the 8th International Congress for Mathematics Education (Seville)*.

Forman, E.A. & Cazden, C.B.: 1985, 'Exploring Vygotskian perspectives in education: The cognitive value of peer interaction', in J.V. Wertsch (ed.), *Culture, Communication and Cognition: Vygotskian Perspectives*, CUP, Cambridge, 323–347.

Gibbs, W. & Orton, J.: 1994, 'Language and mathematics', in A. Orton & G. Wain (eds.), *Issues in Teaching Mathematics*, Cassell, New York, 95–116.

Gooding, A. & Stacy, K.: 1993, 'Characteristics of small group discussion reducing misconceptions', *Mathematics Education Research Journal* 5(1), 60–73.

Goos, M., Galbraith, P. & Renshaw, P.: 1996, 'When does student talk become collaborative mathematical discussion?', *Proceedings of the 19th Annual Conference of the Mathematics Education Group of Australia, MERGA*, Melbourne, 237–244.

Harvey, R., Kerslake, D., Shuard, H. & Torbe, M.: 1982, *Language, Teaching and Learning: 6. Mathematics*, Ward Lock, London.

Hatano, G.: 1988, 'Social and motivational bases for mathematical understanding', in G.B. Saxe & M. Gearhart (eds.), *Children's Mathematics*, Jossy-Bass, San Francisco, 55–70.

Hiebert, J. & Wearne, D.: 1993, 'Instructional tasks, classroom discourse and students' learning in second-grade arithmetic', *American Educational Research Journal* 30(2), 393–425.

Hoyles, C.: 1985, 'What is the point of group discussion in mathematics?', *Educational Studies in Mathematics* 16, 205–214.

Hoyles, C., Sutherland, R. & Healy, L.: 1991, 'Children talking in computer environments: New insights into the role of discussion in mathematics learning', in K. Durkin & B. Shire (eds.), *Language in Mathematical Education: Research and Practice*, Open University Press, Milton Keynes, England, 162–175.

Laborde, C.: 1996, 'Putting mathematics into language and language into mathematics', *Proceedings of the 20th International Conference on the Psychology of Mathematics Education (Spain)* 1, 63–70.

Nunes, T., Schliemann, A.D. & Carraher, D.W.: 1993, *Street Mathematics and School Mathematics*, Cambridge University Press, Cambridge.

Perrin-Glorian, M.J.: 1990, 'Reflexions sur le role du maitre dans les situations didactiques', *Proceedings of the 14th International Conference on the Psychology of Mathematics Education (Mexico)* II, 209–216.

Pimm, D.: 1987, *Speaking Mathematically*, Routledge & Kegan Paul, London.

Pirie, S.E.B.: 1991, 'Mathematical discussion: Incoherent exchanges or shared understandings?', *Language and Education* 5(4), 273–286.

Pirie, S.E.B.: 1991, 'Peer discussion in the context of mathematical problem solving', in K. Durkin & B. Shire (eds.), *Language in Mathematical Education: Research and Practice*, Open University Press, Milton Keynes, England, 143–161.

Pirie, S.E.B.: 1996, 'Is anybody listening?', in P.C. Elliott & M.J. Kenney (eds.), *Communication in Mathematics, K-12 and Beyond*, National Council of Teachers of Mathematics, Reston, VA, 105–115.

Pirie, S.E.B.: 1997, 'Crossing the gulf between thought and symbol – language as (slippery) stepping stones', in M.G. Bartolini-Bussi, A. Sierpinska & H. Steinbring (eds.), *Language and Communication in the Mathematics Classroom*, National Council of Teachers of Mathematics, Reston, VA.

Pirie, S.E.B. & Kieren, T.E.: 1994, 'Growth in mathematical understanding: How can we characterise it and how can we represent it?', *Educational Studies in Mathematics* 26(2–3), 165–190.

Pirie, S.E.B. & Schwarzenberger, R.L.E.: 1988, 'Mathematical discussion and mathematical understanding', *Educational Studies in Mathematics* 19(3), 459–470.

Richards, J.: 1991, 'Mathematical discussions', in E. von Glasersfeld (ed.), *Radical Constructivism in Mathematics Education*, Kluwer, Netherlands, 13–51.

Rubenstein, R.N.: 1996, 'Strategies to support the learning of the language of mathematics', in P.C. Elliott & M.J. Kenney (eds.), *Communication in Mathematics, K-12 and Beyond*, National Council of Teachers of Mathematics, Reston, VA, 214–218.

Thompson, P.W. & Thompson, A.G.: 1994, 'Talking about rates conceptually, part I: A teacher's struggle', *Journal for Research into Mathematics Education* 25(3), 279–303.

Usiskin, Z.: 1996, 'Mathematics as a language', in P.C. Elliott & M.J. Kenney (eds.),

Communication in Mathematics, K-12 and Beyond, National Council of Teachers of Mathematics, Reston, VA, 231–243.

Watson, H.: 1988, 'Language and mathematics education for aboriginal-Australian children', *Language and Education* 2(4), 255–273.

Wood, T.: 1997, 'Alternative patterns of communication in mathematics classes: Funnelling or focusing?', in M.G. Bartolini-Bussi, A. Sierpinska & H. Steinbring (eds.), *Language and Communication in the Mathematics Classroom*, National Council of Teachers of Mathematics, Reston, VA.

CAROLYN BOULTER

DISCOURSE AND CONCEPTUAL UNDERSTANDING IN SCIENCE

The study of the relationship between discourse and conceptual understanding in science education begins with Piaget (1924/69) and Vygotsky
(1962) who saw speaking as instrumental in the process of acquiring knowledge. It develops through the cognitive and developmental psychology of
researchers such as Bruner (1983) who focus on the processes of the mind,
and is joined by the sociolinguistic research in science education which
has developed rapidly since the late 1970s.

EARLY DEVELOPMENTS

The development of science education over the last century has been
marked by a number of large scale initiatives and emerging themes whose
timing has been different in different countries (Meyer et al., 1992). At
present, reform of the curriculum is underway in many countries. Young
(1971) predicted this emphasis on the curriculum, which followed from
an era with an emphasis on access to education which is based upon the
setting up of a resourced schooling system open to all. Since early this
century, science education has periodically been based on the principles of
practical discovery. The Nuffield Science reforms of the 1960s in England
(Nuffield, 1997) and its earlier parallels in the USA were enquiry-based
and were aimed at pupils over 11 years. Although these projects initially
focused on separate science subjects, characteristically they became more
interdisciplinary and thematic (Baez, 1976). For younger pupils science
was slow to become established and the 1970s and 1980s saw initiatives to
place science at the centre of the curriculum for all pupils, spurred on by
the process-product reports of the small amount of time spent on science
tasks with younger pupils (e.g. Galton, Simon & Croll, 1980). Gradually
science has come to be seen as an entitlement for all pupils, underpinned
by the belief that a scientifically literate population is a key factor in
international competitiveness in technocratic societies where science is
applied, corporate and profitable (Lemke, 1993).
   The actual nature of scientific literacy is debated. Science in schools
can be seen as fulfilling two conflicting interests (Fensham, 1985): that of
producing specialists in science, and that of producing scientifically literate
citizens. The science seen as appropriate for specialists is subject-based

B. Davies and D. Corson (eds), Encyclopedia of Language and Education,
Volume 3: Oral Discourse and Education, 239–248.
© *1997 Kluwer Academic Publishers. Printed in the Netherlands.*

and, theory-based with practical work used to confirm theory. The social applications and importance of science in life is only mentioned by way of examples. In contrast, science for literate citizens begins with problems being set for pupils to work on, often using socially relevant materials. The pupils are expected to work in a practical way at material that is arranged in themes rather than subjects. The former, academic science education, may pay little regard to the nature and functioning of language in science, whilst the latter, popular, science education is often concerned with collaborative problem solving through talk.

The discussion of the methods of science and the extent to which school science should mirror the perceived methods of scientists has also developed as an on-going theme (Millar & Driver, 1987) in science education. At the times when science education has swung away from the hypothetico-deductive methodology of asking questions and making discoveries, it has moved towards inductivism with its rather naive view that all theory is based on observation of reality. The tensions between the elite and the popularist views of science and between the views that science should be taught as content or process and about the way that process might be conceived have constructed a curriculum subject with many faces across cultures.

In parallel with the realisation of these dilemmas in science education there has been an increased interest in classroom language which has come to be seen as central in the process of learning (Edwards & Mercer, 1987). As the content of science has become more prominent in the curriculum (White, 1994) and the issues concerned with science education have become more focused on the dilemma of whose need is to be met, that of society or the individual, the methodology for investigating language in use has shifted towards a sociolinguistic approach in which individual meanings of the pupils and the teacher and their relationship to each other are revealed.

THE SIGNIFICANT THEMES IN THE RELATIONSHIP OF DISCOURSE TO CONCEPTUAL UNDERSTANDING IN SCIENCE

The nature of science and conceptual change

Science is defined by: the criteria used to separate science from non-science; the status of scientific knowledge in relation to other areas of knowledge; the patterns of change in scientific understanding; scientific methodology; the sense data that arise from that method; and the theories that are related to the data. Fundamental to science is the relationship between the world and the sense data that arise from it. In science education the research into teachers' understandings of the fundamental nature of science (Koulardis & Ogborn, 1989) showed that many teachers of science have Baconian inductivist views. They understand science to be dealing with the simple induction of theories which represent reality directly from the observational data collected in the world. Others have Popperian hypothetico-deductivist views that all observation is theory driven and the scientist deduces a hypothesis which is tested to see if it can be disproved by the data. Both of these views admit only one method for science. However, there is some evidence (Lakin & Wellington, 1994) of a recent shift towards the more contextualist view that science is built in human communities and that many scientific methods are possible. It may be that particular patterns of classroom discourse are associated with particular beliefs about the nature of science (Boulter, 1992).

Amongst researchers of science education there is a major focus on attempting to understand the patterns and mechanism of conceptual change in pupils. Science education has come to be seen by them as the process by which pupils come to accept the consensus view of the scientific community and it is vital to appreciate the process by which this happens. The Kuhnian perception of science is that it is constructed within the contexts of communities, and that major changes in scientific ideas occur through revolutionary paradigm shifts. This has led to the drawing of parallels with what might happen during the process of conceptual change in pupils (Posner et al., 1982). For some researchers, conceptual development, in say, understandings of gravity, mirrors the historical development of the explanatory ideas in science from Aristotle to Einstein. The research into children's ideas in science (Carmichael et al., 1990) which is also known as the Alternative Conceptions Movement has identified how resistant to change are the variety of prior conceptions that pupils bring to science classes.

All this has thrown up the question as to whether conceptual change can best be thought of in terms of discontinuous changes in a collection of belief fragments which have arisen from everyday experience (di Sessa, 1988) or if the developing knowledge in the pupil parallels the theory changes of science (Tytler & White, 1996) and has clear developmental stages. The nature of conceptual change and the status of the alternative notions which pupils use in virtually every topic in science (Pfundt & Duit, 1991) remain matters for debate. However, attempts are being made to identify the implications of pupils' conceptual frameworks for the classroom, notably in the UK by the Children's Learning in Science project and the Science Processes And Concept Exploration projects.

The rise of personal and social constructivism

The Alternative Conceptions Movement is seen as arising within the "constructivist" approach to science teaching and learning. The origins are discussed by Magoon (1977) who sees the roots stretching back to Kant who believed that man comes to know his world by actively constructing it, not by passively receiving it. The constructivist epistemology is that knowledge is personally and socially constructed. This was Piaget's (1976/77) view and also that of Kelly (1955) whose Personal Construct Psychology has been a formative influence. For a recent summary of constructivist views of learning on science education see Bell & Gilbert (1996). Initially, however the focus was on finding out how pupils, as individuals, constructed their understanding of science concepts and there was considerable use of interview technique. New methods of interviewing were developed which involved instances of particular phenomena, in the form of drawings or real objects (Gilbert & Watts, 1983). Pupils were asked to predict the outcome of an event (perhaps the connecting of wires to batteries and light bulbs) witness it and then to give an explanation of any discrepancy with what they expected (White & Gunstone, 1992). More recently the importance of the social aspects of experience in building conceptual understanding has been seen as complementary to individual thinking (Solomon, 1987). The personal construction has rationality and logic to the individual, the social construction must be recognised and shared with others. Personal constructions can use internal imagery whereas social constructions must use the socially acceptable rules and structures of speech and shared representations. The individual construction is kept if it is useful to the individual, the social construction is kept because it is affirmed by the social group.

It is the growing recognition of the significance of the social construction of conceptual understanding in science that has coincided with the development of a suitable methodology for investigating social situations involving talk. Science is now often seen within science education research as intimately constructed, through discourse, within communities of knowers. The following themes in research and discourse in science teaching and learning arise from the synthesis of constructivism and sociolinguistic methodology and can be seen in the major work in progress:

The COMPLEXITY of classroom discourse which has complex interactions with the ways teachers teach, the resources they use and with the particular phenomenon of science being studied;

COMMUNITIES in science and science classrooms having characteristic discourse patterns;

COLLABORATION in classroom settings allowing the authentic practice of science and the development of appropriate discourse;

CRITIQUES of science, its methodology, its boundaries, its status, and its language as a cultural construct.

THE MAJOR MOVEMENTS

Science as meaning making within scientific communities

The work of Lemke (1993) views science not as a mental accomplishment but as a discursive performance in which signs and symbols including language are used to make and communicate meanings in the process of constructing the life of a community. It concerns itself with everything that people do that is socially meaningful, including talking, writing, drawing pictures and diagrams, gesturing, dancing, dressing, sculpturing, building. Its basic assumption is that meaning is made, so that words do not carry meaning. Meanings are made by people using the conventions they know and the circumstances they have experienced. Lemke (1993) develops a set descriptions of activity types, teacher and student strategies of control, and thematic development strategies for the analysis of classroom talk in science from 60 science classrooms involving 20 teachers.

Science as collaborative problem-solving

The use of sociolinguistic methods of analysis, has made possible the description of detailed patterns of participation in classroom discourse. In the traditional role, as the transmitter of information about science, the teacher has almost complete control over what is said, who says it and its evaluation (Edwards & Furlong, 1978). The recent emphasis upon the social construction of knowledge has led to attempts to construct and analyse student and teacher discourse in more collaborative situations and to identify characteristics of the discourse and particular facilitating or debilitating moves (Chan, 1994). Researchers, exemplified by Roth (1995), are increasingly interested in the potential of collaborative classroom situations not only for the talk but also the representational devices used during the conversations. Roth talks about teaching science at the conclusion of his extensive study of open-enquiry classrooms where students could identify problems, design procedures, formulate questions, link their experience to science, and share procedures, products and solutions through discussion:

> If I were asked to give in a nutshell the recommendation for teaching science, I would probably say something like this: Provide a learning environment in which students engage in explorations which are framed within rather large parameters set by specific tools and resources. Let students work within small groups, and then provide activity structures which allow students to share what they have learned with others at small group and whole class levels. Help teachers to view and conduct themselves as co-explorers rather than as disseminators of knowledge (Roth, 1995, p. 270).

Science as culturally exclusive

The awareness of the patterns of participation in science has its roots in the ethnographic studies of the practice of science (Latour & Woolgar, 1979). The analysis of these patterns in the making of science as "persuasion through literary inscription" has led to a questioning of the notion that science is a single, universal, ungendered, ahistorical, and acultural discourse (Roth, 1995). The critique of science by feminists (Keller, 1985) reveals science as culturally positioned in the white, male, middle class western world. Whereas previously reasons have been sought for why women have failed to enter and act successfully in a science which was seen as ungendered, present work tends to focus upon the critiquing of the gendered content and process of science itself which excludes women from participation in the discourse of the science community (Harraway, 1989). The cultural identity of women as an undifferentiated group is also being contested especially by research with ethnic minorities. Questions are being asked about whose voice is not being heard, whose story is not allowed to be told, and about the process of exclusion for many groups. These considerations are affecting the methodology of research (Bishop, 1994) and they are beginning to influence the frameworks within which the data and analysis of the oral discourse of the classroom are approached.

Science as rhetorical persuasion

The assumption that science is logical and that it procedes by statements which are open to refutation is at the root of the hypothetico-deductive paradigm of science. The importance of argumentation and the analysis of patterns of argument in science classrooms is a field of present interest on the part of researchers of science education (Boulter & Gilbert, 1995), and those asking philosophical questions of science discourse. The application of rhetorical theory to discourse provides a means of understanding the persuasive power of science explanations both within and outside the classroom.

Science as myth, metaphor and modelling

Sets of beliefs shared by a culture can be seen as perpetuating myths about the nature and working of science well after the time in which they had relevance (Barthes, 1972). The analysis of these myths about science and their historical roots (Milne & Taylor, 1996) is shedding light on the social reality of the classroom and how the discourse of science operates. The scientific process is often seen as using and building models (Geire, 1988). How pupils come to understand, use and build their own models of scientific phenomena and the explanations that they produce as a result is a crucial field of endeavour linking science processes to discourse patterns. Ogborn et al. (1996) analyse the discourse of science classrooms for explanation, Gilbert & Boulter (1995) for models and modelling.

Science as questioning

Within the sociolinguistic analysis of classroom discourse in science, questioning as a strategy has a particular place as it has within the theorising about the nature of the scientific process within science education (Abrams & Wandersee, 1995). Questioning sequences are a prominent feature of science classroom talk where the teacher has the traditional role as the imparter of knowledge (Dillon, 1988). This traditional pattern of questioning appears to have the purpose of evaluating what the students know, but in practice is allowing the students to try to map the understandings that the teacher wants them to acquire. In classrooms where it is the intention of the teacher to elicit what the pupils think, research (van Zee & Ministrell, 1997) shows that a number of new patterns are emerging including the development of the "reflective toss", in which the teacher catches the meaning of the pupil and throws it back as a question so that the pattern becomes, student statement – teacher question to clarify – additional student statement(s).

DILEMMAS AND DIFFICULTIES

The present research in science education and oral discourse raises a number of dilemmas and difficulties related to the themes of: the range of and characteristics of discourses of different communities of learners; the place of collaborative language in teaching and learning, and the critiques of scientific methodology itself.

The knowledge of the teacher

As the concern with accountability and investment in education increases, there has been pressure to define the value of education. In science education in the UK the assessment of the effectiveness of the curriculum has concentrated upon the content of science not the process of being scientific or its social implications. It seems that there is a tension between the simplistic transmission view of teaching science content, often advocated by the politically expedient, and the complex view of learning through social and individual construction of understanding, arising from research. There is concern that many teachers may lack the basic content knowledge, especially those who were not trained as science experts. Such teachers may lack confidence in developing less formal learning experiences in science with their increased opportunities for collaborative talk. The nature of teacher knowledge and its effect upon the discourses used in science teaching is an area ripe for research.

New subjects and new contents

There are debates within science education about the inclusion of new subjects: environmental education, computer science and information technology, and health education. The relationship of technology to science (Layton, 1992) is also part of this debate about subject boundaries. The Science Technology and Society (STS) movement (The International Organisation for Science and Technology Education (IOSTE), 1994) explores these boundaries from the perspective of the creation of citizens who can make decisions on social issues which arise from the broadening of the boundaries of science. There are similar discussions around what should be included in the science curriculum subjects and there is concern over the 'elephantiasis' of the science curriculum and how to limit it. These different subject communities are likely to have different discourse patterns and the effect on classroom verbal interaction is yet to be explored.

The complexity of the analysis

The complexity of the science classroom is not simple to write about or to communicate the findings to the wide range of audiences who are concerned with science education. In particular some in the science community who have been unaffected by the critiques of science and its methods find the constructivist approach unnecessary. It is clear that it is important to forge the connection of science education with practising scientists and to be able to use their skills in the classroom. It is important that the recent conceptualisation of science education as bringing pupils' understandings in line with the views of scientists, through a social and individual construction of understanding, can be communicated effectively.

The rise of the postmodern/poststructuralist idiom

Science education has been slower to take on board the language of postmodernism and poststructuralism (see review by Alloway & Gilbert than literary and art education. The multiple perspectives, the celebration of variety, the construction of local contextual accounts and the importance of discourse as the medium through which power relationships are shown, have however increasingly been the agenda of science education and talk. The concern with what is omitted from the accepted structures of science and through which science operates is similarly a poststructuralist concern. Increasingly science educators are being called to be reflective about how perceptions of scientists, science teachers and pupils learning science are made through the various discourses of science (Gough, 1994). The task is then to be able to take up multiple and perhaps contradictory positions, mobilising different storylines and accepting that our pupils do the same.

University of Reading
England

REFERENCES

Abrams, E. & Wandersee, J.: 1995, 'How does biological knowldge grow? A study of life scientists' research practices', *Journal of Research in Science Teaching* 32(6), 649–664.
Baez, A.: 1976, *Innovation in Science Education World-wide*, UNESCO, Paris.
Barthes, R.: 1972, *Mythologies*, Hill and Wang, New York.
Bell, B. & Gilbert, J.: 1996, *Teacher Development: A Model from Science Education*, Falmer, London.
Bishop, R.: 1994, 'Initiating empowering research?', *New Zealand Journal of Educational Studies* 29(1), 175–188.
Boulter, C.: 1992, 'Collaborating to investigate questions: A model for primary science', unpublished PhD thesis, University of Reading, England.
Boulter, C. & Gilbert, J.: 1995, 'Argument and science education', in P. Costello & S. Mitchell (eds.), *Competing and Consensual Voices*, Multilingual Matters, London.
Bruner, J.: 1983, *Child's Talk*, Open University Press, London.
Carmichael, P., Driver, R., Holding, B., Phillips, I., Twigger, D. & Watts, M.: 1990, *Research on Student's Conceptions in Science: A Bibliography*, Children's Learning in Science Project, Leeds.
Chan, C.: 1994, 'Analysis of student discourse in collaborative science learning', presented at AERA, New Orleans.
Dillon, J.: 1988, *Questioning and Teaching*, Teachers College Press, New York.
di Sessa, A.: 1988, 'Knowledge in pieces', in G. Forman & P. Pufull (eds.), *Constructivism in the Computer Age*, Lawrence Erlbaum, Hillsdale, NJ.
Edwards, A. & Furlong, V.: 1978, *The Language of Teaching*, Heinemann, London.
Edwards, D. & Mercer, N.: 1987, *Common Knowledge: The Development of Understanding in the Classroom*, Routledge Kegan Paul, London.
Fensham, P.: 1985, 'Science for all: A reflective essay', *Journal of Curriculum Studies* 17(4), 415–435.
Galton, M., Simon, B. & Croll, P.: 1980, *Inside the Primary School*, Routledge Kegan Paul, London.
Giere, R.: 1988, *Explaining Science: A Cognitive Approach*, University of Chicago Press.
Gilbert, J. & Boulter, C.: 1995, 'Texts and contexts: framing modelling in the primary science classroom', in the proceedings of the European Conference on Research in Science Education, Leeds 7th–11th April 1995.
Gilbert, J. & Watts, M.: 1983, 'Concepts, misconceptions and alternative conceptions: Changing perspectives in science education', *Studies in Science Education* 10, 61–98.
Gough, N.: 1994, 'Regarding nature in new times: Reconceptualising studies of science and environment', in the proceedings of the Annual Conference of the Australian Association for Research in Education, Newcastle NSW 27th November–1 December, 1994.
Harraway, D.: 1989, *Primate Visions: Gender, Race and Nature in the World of Modern Science*, Routledge, New York.
The International Organisation for Science and Technology Education (IOSTE): 1994, 'Science and technology education in a demanding society', in V. Trommel (ed.), *7th*

IOSTE Conference, Veldhoven, The Netherlands: National Institute for Curriculum Development (SLO), The Netherlands, 327–335.

Keller, E.F.: 1985, *Reflections on Gender and Science*, Yale University Press, New Haven.

Kelly, G.: 1955, *The Psychology of Personal Constructs*, W.W. Norton, New York.

Koulardis, V. & Ogborn, J.: 1989, 'Philosophy of science: An empirical study of teacher's views', *International Journal of Science Education* 11(2), 172–184.

Lakin, S. & Wellington, J.: 1994, 'Who will teach the "nature of science?": Teachers' views of science and their implications for science education', *International Journal of Science Education* 16(2), 175–191.

Latour, B. & Woolgar, S.: 1979, *Laboratory Life: The Social Construction of Scientific Facts*, Sage, London.

Layton, D.: 1992, *Technology's Challenge to Science Education*, Open University Press, Milton Keynes.

Lemke, J.: 1993, *Talking Science: Langauge, Learning and Values*, Ablex, Norwood, NJ.

Magoon, A.: 1977, 'Constructivist approaches to educational research', *Review of Educational Research* 47(4), 651–691.

Meyer, J., Kamens, D. & Benavot, A. (eds.): 1992, *School Knowledge for the Masses*, Falmer, London.

Millar, R. & Driver, R.: 1987, 'Beyond processes', *Studies in Science Education* 14, 109–118.

Milne, C. & Taylor, P.: 1996, 'School science: A fertile ground for the evolution of myths', presented at the NARST Conference, St Louis 31st March–3rd April, 1996.

Nuffield: 1997, *Nuffield Junior Science*, Collins, London.

Ogborn, J., Kress, G., Martins, I. & Mc Gillicuddy, K.: 1996, *Explaining Science in the Classroom*, Open University Press, Buckingham.

Pfundt, H. & Duit, R.: 1991, *Bibliography: Students Alternative Frameworks and Science Education* (3rd ed.), Institute for Science Education, Keil, Germany.

Piaget, J.: 1924/1969, *Judgement and Reasoning in the Child*, Littlefield Adams Totowa, NJ.

Piaget, J.: 1976/1977, *The Development of Thought: Equilibrium of Cognitive Structures*, Basic Books, New York.

Posner, G., Strike, K., Hewson, P. & Gertzog, W.: 1982, 'Accomodation of a scientific conception: Towards a theory of conceptual change', *Science Education* 66(2), 211–227.

Roth, W.M.: 1995, *Authentic School Science: Knowing and Learning in open-Enquiry Science Laboratories*, Kluwer, Dortecht.

Solomon, J.: 1987, 'Social influences on the construction of pupils understanding of science', *Studies in Science Education* 14, 63–82.

Tytler, R. & White, R.: 1996, 'Conceptual change in science: Towards a theory of content', presented at the AERA Conference, New York, April 1996.

van Zee, E. & Ministrell, J.: 1997, 'Using questioning to guide student thinking', *The Journal of Learning Sciences* 6(2), 227–269.

White, R.: 1994, 'Dimensions of content', in P. Fensham, R. Gunstone & R. White (eds.), *The Content of Science: A Constructivist Approach to its Teaching and Learning*, Falmer, London.

White, R. & Gunstone, R.: 1992, *Probing Understanding*, Falmer, London.

Young, M.: 1971, *Knowledge and Control: New Directions for a Sociology of Education*, Macmillan, London.

Vygotsky, L.: 1962, *Thought and Language*, ed. and tr. E. Kanfmann & G. Vakar, Massachusetts Institute of Technology, Camdridge, Mass.

JAMES MCGONIGAL

USING ORAL DISCOURSE IN LITERARY STUDIES

We like to talk about the books we like, whether as youngsters being introduced through picture books to the power and patterning of language, or as teachers or students enthusing about texts, or finding new insights within them. Modern approaches to reading now mean that oral discourse in literary contexts includes not only talk about texts but also talk within them, whether through imaginative responses to character and conflict or, post Bakhtin, through critical awareness of the intrinsically dialogic nature of literary language.

EARLY DEVELOPMENTS

Oral discourse was present from the beginnings of literature: anthropological researches in the poetry of pre-literate cultures have recovered the oral nature of Homeric epic, long studied as classical written text (Ong, 1982). Analysis and imitation of classical rhetoric, a core element in the mediaeval curriculum, continued through the Renaissance with a growing sense of how such models could be adapted to national literatures. The actual 'invention' of English literature, however, has recently been credited to the Scots, in their 18th century Enlightenment study of Rhetoric and Belles Lettres (Crawford, 1992). Adam Smith, an influential exponent, linked the intended 'improvement' of his students' native speech with increased free trading opportunities between Scotland and England, and presented as stylistic models the near contemporary writing of Addison, Pope and Swift. Thus English literary studies emerged in the turning of a rough oral discourse into the smoother language of economic or intellectual persuasion. Emigre Scots educated in this rhetorical tradition continued to influence literature teaching in North American universities into the 19th century (Court, 1992).

In England itself, 'public' schools retained a classical education for sons of privileged families, but study of English literature became important through the provincial and non-conformist Dissenting Academies. In the late 19th century, liberal lecturers from Oxford and Cambridge organised a public Extension programme for a wider working-class audience, in which literary studies figured largely. Countering Doyle (1989) who views this movement as imposing an upper-class, imperialist discourse, Dixon (1991) demonstrates the organisers' links with libertarian causes,

B. Davies and D. Corson (eds), Encyclopedia of Language and Education,
Volume 3: Oral Discourse and Education, 249–257.
© *1997 Kluwer Academic Publishers. Printed in the Netherlands.*

as well as the dialogic and democratic nature of the classes which often accompanied lectures. The characteristically meditative language of early modern literary criticism, and its focus on the oral forms of drama and poetry, may also derive from this public lecturing situation to audiences lacking immediate access to the text.

Oxford and Cambridge meanwhile subordinated English literature to classical, historical and philological studies. Examinations showed a strong linguistic bias with their exercises in grammar, syntax and etymology, and this focus on the language of literature led contemporary philologists to construct oral discourse as Received Standard, with the sense of its difference from dialect feeding into an elitist view of literary and linguistic values (Burgess, 1996). Hunter (1988) has explored similar ambiguities inherent in Matthew Arnold's idea of English literature as bearer of a high cultural heritage, with an implicit devaluation of the dialectal or bilingual inheritance of most of its learners; and Viswanthan (1989) records the impact of such views on the English language curriculum of imperial India.

By 1921, however, literary studies were becoming strongly enough established to influence the Newbolt Report on English teaching in elementary schools, and for Sampson's English For the English to bring together progressive arguments from both literature and child development into a new set of curricular priorities for oral work, listening skills, literature and composition. Mackaness was an Australian contemporary whose Inspirational Teaching (1928) also sought to balance the vocational needs of the workplace, literary appreciation for cultural cohesion, and the inner growth of the learner (Watson, 1987, pp. 36–41). Oral discourse was crucial here, in the reading aloud of poetry and plays and in the exploration and elaboration of ideas.

It was also central to the most innovative university practice of the 1920s and 1930s: in I.A. Richards' Cambridge workshops in practical criticism, attended by mature students soon to become influential university teachers in their turn, notably F.R. Leavis. This discursive exploration of meaning in literary texts led ultimately to a redefinition of the cultural tradition of English literature, through the journal Scrutiny and in Leavis' critical practice which, in its turn, inspired a variety of seminal books on school English teaching in the early 1960s, particularly Holbrook's English For Maturity (1961) and Whitehead's The Disappearing Dais (1966). To his literary influence should be added that of psychologists and philosophers such as Vygotsky and Cassirer, whose explorations of symbolisation in thought and in spoken language were beginning to intrigue a new generation of teachers.

MAJOR CONTRIBUTIONS

Literature teaching came into existence, therefore, within a matrix of competing factors: political and economic, curricular and linguistic. Thus in 1966 social forces could both support the Anglo-American seminar in Dartmouth, New Hampshire, bringing together major figures in language and education, while also ensuring that political support for their deliberations would be shortlived (Dixon, 1975, pp. viii–xviii).

Yet ideas articulated there have remained influential, notably the formulations of Moffett (1968) on 'the universe of discourse', and John Dixon on a 'personal growth' model of English teaching, based centrally on literature and creative or reflective responses to it. Britton (1970) provided a firmer rationale for oral approaches to literature teaching, underpinned by Vygotsky's work on language and thought, influencing many through his classroom research activities, but also, crucially, through his membership of the Bullock Committee set up to enquire on standards of literacy in England. Their *A Language for Life* (Bullock Report, 1975) made official recommendations for developing and assessing classroom talk. His 'Note of Extension' to that Report typically affirms the energies of oral and dialectal forms of expressive and poetic language within cultural groups, balancing these against the cross-curricular and cross-cultural dimensions of standard transactional language.

Dixon's emphasis on oral, expressive (often dramatic) work to enable great texts to become real experiences for young readers was given a clearer pedagogical framework by Barnes' work on communication and learning in small groups (1973), and, after Bullock, by official recognition of the potential of active language use across the curriculum. In English, there was increasing awareness of expressive dimensions of children's writing, and of the effect of prior discussion of audience and purpose in moving such work consciously towards the literary.

Other educational systems developed similar insights in different ways. Squire (1971) was an early North American advocate of a 'response-oriented curriculum' in English In some northern and Canadian states, groupwork developed a sharper focus on co-operative learning through clarifying the roles of participants, and by altering groups according to task: the use of mixed ability 'home groups', differentiated 'expert groups' and the 'jigsaw classroom' enables quite subtle and dialogic exploration of literary texts to be carried out, even by young readers, with a real audience for their deliberations (Johnson et al., 1991).

In Australia, influenced by the 'social semiotic' of Hallidayan linguistics, the teaching of literary and other genres worked towards increasing pupils' awareness of how the writer's generic purpose (to describe, or narrate, or argue etc.) shapes the form and features of texts. Teacher modelling and oral exploration of typical texts are clearly involved in such an approach: however, the metatextual focus can appear to sit somewhat uneasily alongside the expressive emphasis of Britton and Dixon, as also does the metacognitive thrust of the Canadian work of Scardamalia and Bereiter (1981) on the protocols of writing. Watson (1987 and elsewhere) has been influential in keeping such differences in perspective.

Assessment of oral approaches has increasingly become an issue, not always negatively. In the 1980s, a major reform of the Scottish high school examination system was able to incorporate many recommendations of the Bullock Report. Retaining literary texts as a unifying focus for English, this new system now also assessed the group or individual talk activities which textual study encourages. Broad but explicit grade-related performance criteria were developed for such contexts, and shared with learners; and teacher development was supported by exemplary material using oral methods or videos of pupil performance, so that strategies and judgements could be opened up for discussion. Such aspects as accent, dialect, standard and non-standard English and Scots language have all emerged more explicitly, particularly where local literary texts are used.

Generally, the 1980s saw a gradual interpenetration of oral and literary discourse. Classroom discussion of literature developed within a wider range of contexts, as literary theories of reader response (as well as advances in audio and video technology) offered a new rationale for personal talk around and within texts. Protherough (1983) exemplifies this approach in high school English teaching. The Rosens (1985, 1988) demonstrated the value of oral story telling in multilingual classrooms, recovering the ancient energies of accent and traditional form for literary study. In early education, the longtidudinal work of the University of Bristol study 'Language at Home and at School' (Wells, 1987) emphasised the role of shared talk around narrative and illustrations in advancing children's thinking. Book language links powerfully with school language; character and action with exploring cause and effect; and the permanence of print with the ability to revisit, discuss and reshape our first impressions. All reveal the vital interconnections between literary and oral discourse in ensuring success in early reading through shared experience of the symbol-making potential of story.

WORK IN PROGRESS

Clearly, talk can help students of different ages understand and respond to literature at the stage of reception, where meaning is shared and clarified by groups of readers; or of reformulation, where informal explanations and retellings help them to reinterpret textual messages; or before formal or creative written response, where planning and presentation are aided by oral expression; or again in final reflection, where personal learning is made more coherent by being articulated.

The recommendations of the Cox committee, set up in England in 1988 to consider the structure and assessment of a new national curriculum in English, incorporated such recent thinking about classroom practice, despite government opposition. Thus the attainment targets at various levels could specify talk activities arising from literary contexts, and there was exemplification of some 29 practical ways of exploring the 'class novel' (Cox, 1991, pp. 208–215), almost all depending upon talk: hot-seating, thought-tracking, story-boarding, plot-mapping, imaginary interviews with characters, and so forth. Each presumes oral activity aiming to recreate or co-create the literary experience as a necessary precursor to formal essay writing on it, as English teachers and their students strive to articulate anew the impact or intention of texts and the shared experience of readers.

Shakespeare, a crucial figure in the English curriculum for cultural and ideological as well as for literary reasons, was reinstated as a set author at key stages in the national curriculum. Keeping his plays alive for new generations will come not through imposition, however, but through engagement in the sorts of oral activity developed by the Shakespeare and Schools Project (1986–93) in the School of Education of the University of Cambridge (Gibson, 1994). Here the texts are treated not as icons but as scripts to be interpreted, researched and inferred from, in group explorations that issue in performances of choral speaking, improvisations, missing scenes, parodies, trials, intercutting and many other practical ideas for ensuring that Shakespeare continues to speak authentically to new generations of students.

Poetry can all too easily lose touch with its oral roots, particularly if taught with detailed attention to nuances of imagery and tone. Dias (1988) of McGill University has instead researched its teaching and learning as 'process response', using the potential of small-group discussion and also Responding-Aloud-Protocols to reveal different student patterns of reading the same text. This has deep implications for classroom practice, not least because of the international comparisons emerging from co-researchers or teachers in Britain, Australia, Canada and the United States.

This project may be seen as developing the practical criticism of poetry in the light of post-structuralist work on reader-response. Iser and Rosenblatt have provided an influential rationale for classroom teaching of literature in ways that can pay as much attention to the readers experience as to the chosen text, and to articulating the shared understanding of communities of readers. Corcoran and Evans (1987) and Evans (1992) emphasise the active oral engagement and international impact of reader response, with some focus on its effect of 'unsettling the set text' in examinations, where imaginative responses may appear as alternatives to formal essays.

The impact of dialogic insights from the school of Bakhtin continues. Griffiths (1992) explores this approach to reading novels as the primary genres of speech incorporated in self-aware form into the secondary genres of literature, but still recognisable to readers from their oral experience, and perhaps best taught through reference to that. Thus Bialostosky (1994), teaching poems as Bakhtinian speech genres, moves through the life discourse of 'apology' to the art of its poetic equivalent in William Carlos Williams and, ultimately, Milton.

Recent international work on the institutionalisation of English, as well as curriculum developments in Britain, present oral discourse as potentially both liberating and limiting: the former through dialogue and the development of ideas, but the latter through the social attitudes to accent and dialect which it evokes. Its inclusion as an assessable element in English has encouraged developments in performance and diagnostic criteria; and its more audible classroom presence has brought a greater awareness of the relationship between Standard and non-Standard Englishes, and their presence in local literatures. The Language in the National Curriculum Project (1989–92) influenced by Hallidayan perspectives, and the National Oracy Project (1986–93) were large-scale initiatives involving extensive classroom research on oral discourse in England and Wales. Both aroused government displeasure at their 'liberal', celebratory and non-prescriptive approaches to extending awareness of spoken language in schools, in a marvellous variety of forms, registers and contexts. The 'common bonds' of oral storytelling are particularly explored in the Oracy Project (Howe & Johnson, 1992).

Moving from narrative to argument, the Teaching and Learning of Argument Project (1991–94) in the University of Hull has considered both spoken and written modes of handling literary studies, with a focus on the teacher as 'discourse leader' modelling the process of presenting viewpoints on textual issues (Costello & Mitchell, 1995). Important also is the project's reclamation of rhetoric as a unifying focus for literary, educational and philosophical discourse, with implications for the ways in which we teach children to talk persuasively or confidently about the content and style of the texts they are reading (Andrews, 1992). Such talk is central to recent work on the taped responses of dyslexic students to literary questions on texts which they have heard and discussed but not 'read' in the usual sense (McGonigal, 1995).

PROBLEMS AND DIFFICULTIES

Using oral discourse in the teaching of literature can obviously create problems in articulating tasks, in organising the classroom and in assessing the outcomes: Mercer (1991) offers useful guidance on these for elementary and high school teachers. As English teachers increasingly use video versions of classic texts, the inter-relationship between literary and oral discourse has become even more complex. Most media talk is scripted to seem spontaneously spoken, and many students find it easier to absorb the medium than to analyse its mediation of literary texts; yet media studies have also introduced many English teachers to theoretical approaches to literary and oral as well as film texts.

There is now real ideological tension between one view of English teaching as transmitting an unquestioned canon of literature and another view that sees cultural analysis as its radical aim. The university training of younger teachers of English can increasingly distance them from the traditional curriculum in language and literature, especially in regard to attitudes to accent, perceived standards of correctness, and set texts. Elsewhere in the world, the role of Standard English and certainly of 'received pronunciation' may be problematic because of colonial associations and its relationship to the differently developing local English, with its own tunes and turns of phrase. Internationally, modern communications including satellite broadcasting and electronic mail are reshaping both spoken and written language to new communicative purposes, and this will have major, but still largely imponderable, implications for teaching and learning. Desktop publishing makes it more possible than ever before to see children becoming authors of their own literature, but computer spelling and grammar checkers meanwhile seem to undermine traditional aspects of authority and craft.

FUTURE DIRECTIONS

Future directions for research and practice must therefore include the language opportunities and constraints of this interface between voice, screen and distant or unknown readerships. Computers will increasingly respond to spoken commands, and the dictation skills involved in structuring and reshaping such stretches of composed discourse, part oral and part literary, will need to be analysed and taught. Already, the cyberspeak of the internet is developing its own typographical ways of mimicking stress or intonation. Already, it is being used by senior pupils in isolated schools in rural Scotland to 'discuss' their literature projects with distant peers, to exchange notes and ideas on texts in supportive networks.

At the same time, there is a growing and possibly complementary interest in the place of local and dialect writing, where the oral impinges most clearly on the literary and a sense of identity is reasserted within the linguistic complexities of modern cultures. This is noticeable within the European Community, with funding given to support minority or regional languages, and their place in the education system.

Literary theory, which seeks to redefine ideas about text and reading, almost inevitably leads to exploration of the origins of cultural definitions embedded in the subject of English, and of the complex of attitudes towards spoken language within a literate society. Aspects of dialogue and power both within texts and around their classroom teaching will be analysed. Gendered and psychoanalytic readings of children's literature will continue to surprise or dismay the classroom teacher but, in whichever theoretical light, the exploration of this literature will go on. Rhetoric may help frame a spectrum of studies that will include politics and persuasion at one end and oral patterns of language in early stories at the other. Taped oral narrative will also be analysed in post structuralist ways. Possibly most useful as a source will be Bakhtin's social sense of the dialogic nature of language, which Holquist (1990) has outlined, and the potential of diverse textual voices to speak new meanings to readers, listeners and teachers.

University of Glasgow
Scotland

REFERENCES

Andrews, R.: 1992, *Rebirth of Rhetoric: Essays in Language, Culture and Education*, Routledge, London.
Barnes, D.: 1973, *Language in the Classroom*, Open University Press, Milton Keynes.
Bialostosky, D.: 1994, 'From discourse in life to discourse in art', in A. Freedman & P. Medway (eds.), *Learning and Teaching Genre*, Heineman, Boynton, Cook, Portsmouth, NH, 105–115.
Britton, J.: 1970, *Language and Learning*, Allen Lane, London.
Bullock Report: 1975, *A Language For Life*, HMSO, London.
Burgess, T.: 1996, 'A different angle: English teaching and its narratives', *Changing English* 3(1), 57–77.
Corcoran, B. & Evans, E.: 1987, *Readers, Texts, Teachers*, Open University Press, Milton Keynes.
Costello, P. & Mitchell, S. (eds.): 1995, *Competing and Consensual Voices: The Theory and Practice of Argument*, Multilingual Matters, Clevedon.
Court, F.: 1992, *Institutionalising English Literature*, Stanford University Press, Stanford.
Cox, B.: 1991, *Cox on Cox: An English Curriculum for the 1990s*, Hodder & Stoughton, London.
Crawford, R.: 1992, *Devolving English Literature*, Oxford University Press, Oxford.
Dias, P. & Hayhoe, M.: 1988, *Developing Response to Poetry*, Open University Press, Milton Keynes and Philadelphia.
Dixon, J.: 1975, *Growth through English: Set in the perspective of the seventies*, National Association for the Teaching of English, Huddersfield.
Dixon, J.: 1991, *A Schooling in 'English'*, Open University Press, Buckingham.
Doyle, B.: 1989, *English and Englishness*, Routledge, London.
Evans, E.: 1992, *Young Readers, New Readings*, Hull University Press, Hull.
Gibson, R.: 1994, 'Teaching Shakespeare in schools', in S. Brindley (ed.), *Teaching English*, Routledge, London, 140–148.
Griffiths, P.: 1992, *English at the Core: Dialogue and Power in English Teaching*, Open University Press, Buckingham.
Holbrook, D.: 1961, *English For Maturity*, Cambridge University Press, Cambridge.
Holquist, M.: 1990, *Dialogism: Bakhtin and his World*, Routledge, London and New York.

Howe, A. & Johnson, J.: 1992, *Common Bonds: Storytelling in the Classroom*, Hodder & Stoughton, Sevenoaks.

Hunter, I.: 1988, *Culture and Government: the emergence of literary education*, Macmillan, Basingstoke.

Johnson, D. et al: 1991, *Co-operation in the Classroom*, Interaction Book Company, Edina MN.

Mackaness, G.: 1928, *Inspirational Teaching*, Dent, London.

McGonigal, J.: 1995, 'Raised and erased voices', in P. Costello & S. Mitchell (eds.), *Competing and Consensual Voices, Multilingual Matters*, Clevedon, 99–111.

Mercer, N. (ed.): 1991, *Talk and Learning 5–16*, Open University Press, Milton Keynes.

Moffett, J.: 1968, *Teaching the Universe of Discourse*, Houghton Mifflin, Boston, Mass.

Ong, W.: 1982, *Orality and Literacy*, Methuen, London and New York.

Protherough, R.: 1983, *Developing Response to Fiction*, Open University Press, Milton Keynes.

Rosen, B.: 1988, *And None of it Was Nonsense: The Power of Storytelling in School*, Mary Glasgow Publications, London.

Rosen, H.: 1985, *Stories and Meanings*, National Association for the Teaching of English, London.

Sampson, G.: 1921, *English for the English*, Cambridge University Press, Cambridge.

Scardamalia, M. & Bereiter, C. et al.: 1981, *Writing for Results: A Sourcebook of Consequential Composing Activities*, OISE Press, Ontario.

Squire, J.R.: 1971, 'Towards a response-oriented curriculum in literature', in H.B. Maloney (ed.), *New English, New Imperatives*, Urbana, Ill., NCTE, 89–99.

Viswanthan, G.: 1992, *Masks of Conquest*, Columbia University Press, New York.

Watson, K.: 1987, *English Teaching in Perspective*, Open University Press and St. Clair Press, Milton Keynes and Epping, NSW.

Wells, G.: 1987, *The Meaning Makers*, Hodder and Stoughton, London.

Whitehead, F.: 1966, *The Disappearing Dais*, Chatto and Windus, London.

SUBJECT INDEX

259

NAME INDEX

TABLE OF CONTENTS

VOLUME 1: LANGUAGE POLICY AND POLITICAL ISSUES IN EDUCATION

TABLE OF CONTENTS

Section 4: Practical and Empirical Issues

TABLE OF CONTENTS

VOLUME 2: LITERACY

TABLE OF CONTENTS

Section 3: Focus on the Social Context of Literacy

Section 4: Focus on Selected Regions

TABLE OF CONTENTS

VOLUME 4: SECOND LANGUAGE EDUCATION

TABLE OF CONTENTS

TABLE OF CONTENTS

VOLUME 5: BILINGUAL EDUCATION

TABLE OF CONTENTS

VOLUME 6: KNOWLEDGE ABOUT LANGUAGE

TABLE OF CONTENTS

TABLE OF CONTENTS

VOLUME 7: LANGUAGE TESTING AND ASSESSMENT

TABLE OF CONTENTS

TABLE OF CONTENTS

VOLUME 8: RESEARCH METHODS IN LANGUAGE AND EDUCATION

TABLE OF CONTENTS

Encyclopedia of Language and Education

Set ISBN Hb 0-7923-4596-7; Pb 0-7923-4936-9

1. R. Wodak and D. Corson (eds.): *Language Policy and Political Issues in Education.*
   1997
   ISBN Hb 0-7923-4713-7
   ISBN Pb 0-7923-4928-8

2. V. Edwards and D. Corson (eds.): *Literacy.* 1997
   ISBN Hb 0-7923-4595-0
   ISBN Pb 0-7923-4929-6

3. B. Davies and D. Corson (eds.): *Oral Discourse and Education.* 1997
   ISBN Hb 0-7923-4639-4
   ISBN Pb 0-7923-4930-X

4. G.R. Tucker and D. Corson (eds.): *Second Language Education.* 1997
   ISBN Hb 0-7923-4640-8
   ISBN Pb 0-7923-4931-8

5. J. Cummins and D. Corson (eds.): *Bilingual Education.* 1997
   ISBN Hb 0-7923-4806-0
   ISBN Pb 0-7923-4932-6

6. L. van Lier and D. Corson (eds.): *Knowledge about Language.* 1997
   ISBN Hb 0-7923-4641-6
   ISBN Pb 0-7923-4933-4

7. C. Clapham and D. Corson (eds.): *Language Testing and Assessment.* 1997
   ISBN Hb 0-7923-4702-1
   ISBN Pb 0-7923-4934-2

8. N.H. Hornberger and D. Corson (eds.): *Research Methods in Language and Education.* 1997
   ISBN Hb 0-7923-4642-4
   ISBN Pb 0-7923-4935-0

KLUWER ACADEMIC PUBLISHERS – DORDRECHT / BOSTON / LONDON